Civil War
CAMPAIGNS
in the
HEARTLAND

STEVEN E. WOODWORTH
SERIES EDITOR

The Confederate Heartland

Illinois

Indiana

Ohio

Cincinnati

West Virginia

Missouri

Louisville

Lexington

Frankfort

Perryville
Cumberland
River

Kentucky

Virginia

Cairo

Nashville

Knoxville

North Carolina

Forts Henry
and Donelson

Tennessee

Franklin-
Spring Hill

Stones River

Arkansas

Shiloh

Chattanooga

Memphis

Corinth

Iuka

Tennessee
River

Chickamauga

South Carolina

Resaca-Adairsville

Dallas-Pickett's Mill

Kennesaw Mountain-Peachtree Creek

Atlanta

Ezra Church

Jonesboro

Mississippi
River

Tallahatchie
River

Fort Pemberton

Alabama

Yazoo
River

Chickasaw
Bayou

Meridian

Jackson

Montgomery

Savannah

Vicksburg

Grand
Gulf

Champion's
Hill

Georgia

Port Gibson

Mississippi

Mobile

Louisiana

Florida

New Orleans

Gulf of Mexico

Charles D. Grear

The

CHICKAMAUGA

Campaign

Edited by Steven E. Woodworth

Southern Illinois University Press
Carbondale and Edwardsville

13 12 11 10   4 3 2 1

Library of Congress Cataloging-in-Publication Data
The Chickamauga campaign / edited by Steven E. Woodworth.
    p. cm. — (Civil War campaigns in the heartland)
Includes bibliographical references and index.
ISBN-13: 978-0-8093-2980-9 (cloth : alk. paper)
ISBN-10: 0-8093-2980-8 (cloth : alk. paper)
ISBN-13: 978-0-8093-8556-0 (ebook)
ISBN-10: 0-8093-8556-2 (ebook)
1. Chickamauga, Battle of, Ga., 1863. 2. Tennessee—History—
Civil War, 1861–1865—Campaigns. 3. United States—History—
Civil War, 1861–1865—Campaigns. I. Woodworth, Steven E.
E475.81.C49 2010
973.7′35—dc22   2009032714

CONTENTS

ACKNOWLEDGMENTS

As the editor of this series, I take pleasure in expressing my gratitude for the kind assistance of several people who in various ways have aided in the production of this volume and helped to make this series possible. The idea for the series was the brainchild of professors Jason M. Frawley, Charles Grear, and David Slay. In addition, Grear is not only an assistant professor of history at Prairie View A & M University but also a splendid producer of historical maps. Working with him on the maps for this volume was made easy by his thorough knowledge of the subject, which gave him a very clear concept of what was needed in each map. All of the contributors to this volume were prompt and cooperative, a truly notable occurrence and one for which I am indeed grateful. Once again, I am indebted to Southern Illinois University Press acquisitions editor Sylvia Frank Rodrigue for shepherding the project through from beginning to end. We historians don't always herd very well, but Sylvia had the patience and firmness to see it through.

Chickamauga Movements
August 16-30, 1863

McMinnville

Crittenden

Wartrace

Shelbyville

Rosecrans

Manchester

Crittenden

Crittenden

Walden's Ridge

Crittenden

Tennessee

Tullahoma

Thomas

Crittenden

Crittenden

Forrest

Decherd

Winchester

Stanley   McCook

Thomas

Crittenden

Thomas

D. H. Hill

Jasper

Bridgeport

Shellmound

Chattanooga

Polk

Thomas

Lee and Gordon's
Mills

Ringgold

McCook

Stevenson

Racoon Mountain

Stevens Gap

Missionary Mountain

To Dalton

Alabama

Bragg

Bellefonte

Stanley

Pigeon

La Fayette

Wheeler

Sand Mountain

Georgia

Lookout Mountain

Winston's Gap

Union Positions

Confederate Positions

Union Movements

0 mile 5   10   15

Tennessee River

Alpine

Charles D. Grear

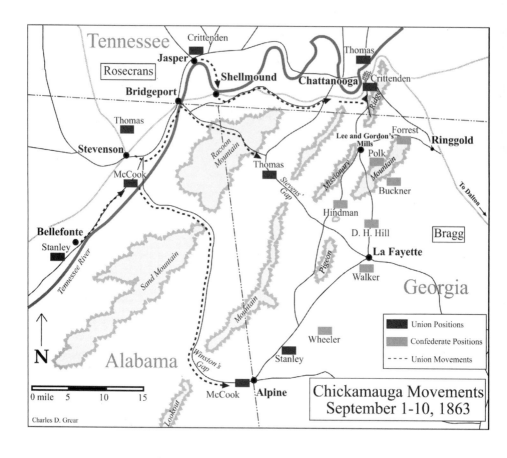

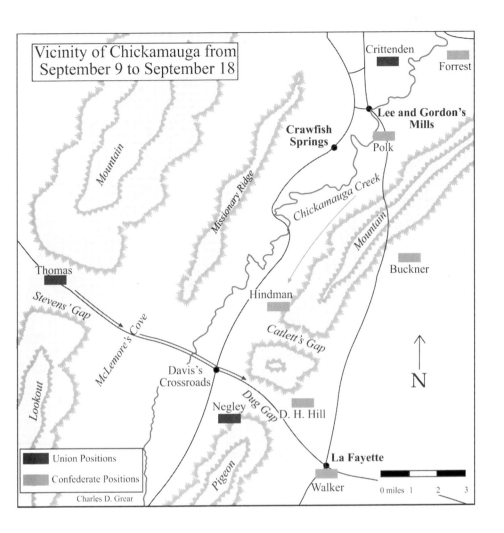

Vicinity of Chickamauga from September 9 to September 18

Crittenden

Forrest

Lee and Gordon's Mills

Crawfish Springs

Polk

Mountain

Missionary Ridge

Chickamauga Creek

Mountain

Buckner

Thomas

Stevens' Gap

McLemore's Cove

Hindman

Catlett's Gap

N

Lookout

Davis's Crossroads

Dug Gap

Negley

D. H. Hill

La Fayette

Union Positions

Confederate Positions

Pigeon

Walker

0 miles 1 2 3

Charles D. Grear

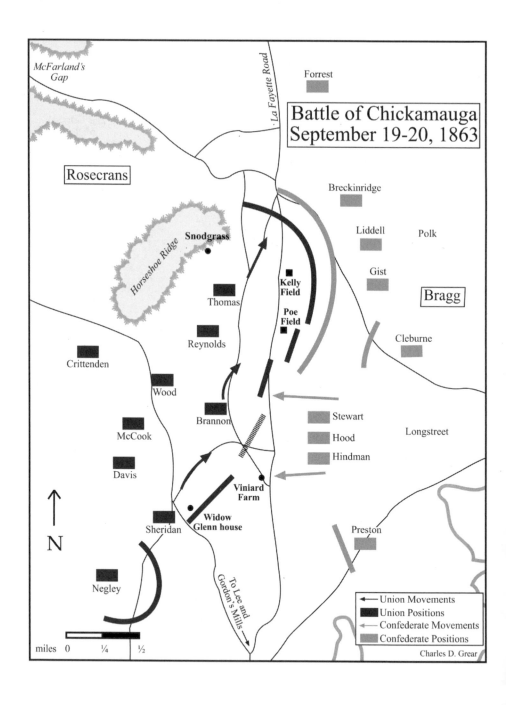

Battle of Chickamauga
September 19-20, 1863

The Chickamauga Campaign

INTRODUCTION

The Battle of Chickamauga was the largest and bloodiest battle in the Civil War's decisive western theater. It was the first major victory won . by the Confederacy's hard-luck Army of Tennessee, and yet the battle was barren of results for its winners. The campaign represented the culmination of long-debated concepts of concentrating Confederate strength against the Union's Army of the Cumberland in quest of a decisive victory, but when it was over, Union momentum in the western theater had been checked for a mere two months, and the way had been cleared for the accession to top command by the general who would ultimately defeat the Confederacy. In short, the Chickamauga campaign was meant to be a turning point, but history stubbornly refused to turn.

The course of events that the Confederates hoped to change by their supreme effort at Chickamauga had begun in February 1862 when Union troops under Ulysses S. Grant, with the able assistance of a naval squadron under Flag Officer Andrew H. Foote, captured Confederate Forts Henry and Donelson, opening the Tennessee and Cumberland Rivers to Union incursion deep into the Confederate heartland. The massive loss of territory and resources this entailed put the Confederacy at a severe disadvantage in the most important section of the continent before the war was a year old. Since that time, the Confederates had made two major efforts to reverse the tide of the war. A large concentration of troops under Albert Sidney Johnston, the man who many had considered to be the South's greatest general, culminated in the April 1862 battle of Shiloh, with Confederate defeat and Johnston's death. That fall, a grand simultaneous offensive by the three Confederate commands between the Appalachians and the Mississippi had seen Edmund Kirby Smith's East Tennessee forces, Braxton Bragg's Army of Tennessee, and Earl Van Dorn's Confederate army in Mississippi all advancing into Union-held territory. Working at cross-purposes and bickering among the top generals, along with what to Confederates was the surprising unwillingness of most Kentuckians to fight for secession and slavery, doomed the operation to failure, despite a distinctly lackluster performance by Union general Don Carlos Buell, who had opposed Bragg and Kirby Smith.

In between the Confederacy's spasmodic major efforts to redeem the heartland, Union forces, especially Grant's own Army of the Tennessee, had steadily exploited the advantage gained in his initial victories, pressing deeper into the Confederate heartland and seizing strategic assets that determined control of thousands of square miles and vast resources. Most notably, Grant had, in the summer of 1863, completed the Union seizure of the Mississippi with the capture of another large Confederate garrison at Vicksburg. The slower-moving Union army in the central portion of the heartland, now commanded by William S. Rosecrans in place of the discredited Buell, had also advanced, albeit less spectacularly. In the midsummer 1863 Tullahoma campaign, Rosecrans maneuvered Bragg almost all the way out of the state of Tennessee, forcing him to fall back to Chattanooga, half a dozen miles from the Georgia line. In these operations, Bragg was severely handicapped by the dissension and uncooperativeness of some of his top generals, including Leonidas Polk and Simon B. Buckner, whose opposition to Bragg had stopped just short of open mutiny.

These operations set the stage for the Chickamauga campaign itself, which began with Rosecrans launching another well-conceived program of maneuver on August 16, 1863, aimed at advancing his army across the Cumberland Plateau, the Tennessee River, and several additional mountain ridges to enter Georgia and perhaps destroy Bragg's Army of Tennessee, opening the way to further Union advances.

Yet while Rosecrans had taken his time after the Tullahoma campaign preparing for his next carefully crafted scheme of maneuvers, the Confederate high command was planning its third and greatest major effort to recover all that had been lost in the heartland since the fall of Forts Henry and Donelson. Prominent voices in Confederate politics and the high command had long been calling for a massive concentration of Rebel forces against Rosecrans's army. Now with that army threatening Chattanooga and with it the Confederacy's main east-west rail link, Jefferson Davis finally took the unprecedented step of transferring troops to Bragg from Robert E. Lee's previously sacrosanct Army of Northern Virginia. Reinforcements also came from what remained of the Confederate forces in Mississippi and from East Tennessee. The total increment to Bragg's force would be enough, once all the troops were on hand, to give him a significant numerical superiority over Rosecrans, the first such advantage a Confederate army had enjoyed since Albert Sidney Johnston's great gambit at Shiloh. Even as Rosecrans's army marched out of its camps on August 16 to begin the campaign, the Confederate reinforcements were already on their way, setting the stage for the Chickamauga campaign—and its subsequent culmination in the Chattanooga campaign—to be a decisive struggle for the possession of momentum and key territory in the nation's heartland.

The first essay in this volume, by Ethan S. Rafuse, examines two of Rosecrans's three corps commanders, major generals Alexander M. McCook and Thomas L. Crittenden. Since Rafuse follows these generals' performance in both the Tullahoma and the Chickamauga campaigns, his chapter is somewhat longer than the others and serves the additional purpose of providing a more detailed lead-in to the further discussion of the Chickamauga campaign.

My own essay, chapter 2, deals with the McLemore's Cove incident, which was perhaps the Confederacy's best opportunity during the campaign, at least from the point of view of Braxton Bragg and his subordinate, Thomas C. Hindman. I was particularly interested in considering whether there was anything in Hindman's previous career as a soldier that might have hinted at his seemingly inexplicable failure in McLemore's Cove.

The third chapter, an essay by Alexander Mendoza, deals with the other Rebel general whose signal failure at McLemore's Cove helped make that incident one of the most tantalizing missed opportunities of the war, Daniel Harvey Hill. Mendoza examines Hill's performance throughout the Chickamauga campaign, including his startling miscue on the morning of the battle's second day and his subsequent punishment by the Confederate high command.

Lee White's essay, chapter 4, is the first of a pair dealing with specific Confederate divisions and their commanders, two of the more promising officers in the Army of Tennessee. White examines Alexander P. Stewart and his division, especially the division's impressive assault on the evening of the first day of the battle of Chickamauga.

John R. Lundberg's essay, chapter 5, examines the night attack by Pat Cleburne's division still later that same evening. Lundberg shows that the attack, forced on an unwilling Cleburne, was costly not only in casualties but also in its effect of putting key elements of the Confederate right wing badly out of position for the vital operations of the next day.

William G. Robertson undoubtedly knows more about the Chickamauga campaign than any other living human being, having studied it intensely for many years. In the sixth chapter of this volume, he argues that Confederate general James Longstreet's performance during the campaign has been much clouded by accretions of legend, creating a lingering false impression of his impact on the course of events. In a carefully researched and reasoned essay, Robertson carefully analyzes the famous general's role in the campaign.

David Powell, in chapter 7, writes about another controversial participant in the campaign, Union major general James S. Negley. The culminating day of the Battle of Chickamauga left Negley under a cloud of censure after a previously solid military record as a citizen-soldier. Powell analyzes Negley's role in the battle and what led to his surprising downfall as a Union general.

In the final chapter, Timothy B. Smith looks at the development of Chickamauga National Military Park and the ways in which the involvement of a veteran of that battle, Henry Van Ness Boynton, not only influenced how Chickamauga was commemorated but also helped shape the way the history of America's great battles and battlefields will be remembered in the future.

IN THE SHADOW OF THE ROCK
THOMAS L. CRITTENDEN, ALEXANDER M.
MCCOOK, AND THE 1863 CAMPAIGNS
FOR MIDDLE AND EAST TENNESSEE

Ethan S. Rafuse

In histories of the great campaign that culminated in the September 1863 Battle of Chickamauga, discussion of the role the Army of the Cumberland's corps commanders played in shaping its course and outcome has understandably been dominated by the performance of Maj. Gen. George H. Thomas. From the time Maj. Gen. William S. Rosecrans assumed command in October 1862 of what eventually became known as the Army of the Cumberland, he relied heavily on Thomas's counsel, which played a significant role in whatever successes Rosecrans achieved in his efforts to organize and manage that army. This was at no time more the case than in the operations and brutal fighting that took place in the late summer of 1863 at Chickamauga. At that battle, on September 19 and 20, Thomas found himself in charge of the critical task of thwarting Confederate efforts to crush the Union left and set the stage for the destruction of the Army of the Cumberland by cutting it off from Chattanooga. Thomas won the immortal nickname, "The Rock of Chickamauga," by taking the magnificent stand that contained the damage inflicted by a dramatic Confederate breakthrough on September 20, which crushed the center of the Union line and sent it and the entire right of the army fleeing to Chattanooga.

Thomas's strong performances throughout Rosecrans's tenure in command of the Army of the Cumberland are familiar to even casual students of the Civil War. Less well known because of the attention Thomas's efforts have received from historians are the roles played by the Army of the Cumberland's other two principal corps commanders, Maj. Gen. Alexander McCook and Maj. Gen. Thomas Crittenden. Indeed, McCook and Crittenden, both of whom ensured a dark cloud would hang over their reputations after abandoning the field of battle at Chickamauga while Thomas made his stand on Snodgrass Hill and Horseshoe Ridge, when not ignored altogether, have usually been offered up as men whose shortcomings help us to better appreciate the greatness of Thomas's character and generalship.

This essay brings McCook and Crittenden out of the large shadow Thomas casts over the history of the Army of the Cumberland by reexamining their performances in the Chickamauga campaign. This is not to make a case either for or against them and certainly not to portray them as misunderstood masters of the military art. However, given the low regard in which McCook and Crittenden have generally been held by historians and the heavy pall the events at Chickamauga cast over them, it is difficult to take a balanced approach to these historical subjects without appearing to be engaged in special pleading on their behalf. Whether or not readers finish this essay believing that has been avoided, at the least they may find information and gain insight that will give them a better understanding of these officers, the history of the Army of the Cumberland in general, and the Chickamauga campaign in particular.

The forces Rosecrans inherited from Maj. Gen. Don Carlos Buell when the Lincoln administration deemed Buell's conduct before, during, and after the October 8, 1862, engagement at Perryville, Kentucky, overly deliberate, had as their first mission securing control of Kentucky and Middle Tennessee. They would then, the administration hoped, establish a permanent Federal presence in East Tennessee and liberate the region's Unionist population. Upon assuming command, Rosecrans immediately recognized that he first needed to impose clear organization on his field forces, which were then officially designated the Fourteenth Corps. Once he finished the process of ensuring his command had secure possession of Nashville, Rosecrans organized his ten divisions into three wings and gave command of them to the three senior officers he inherited from Buell. Rosecrans had no reservations about giving Thomas command of the "Center Wing," which, consisting of four divisions, was the largest. Thomas had compiled an eminently respectable combat record during the first year and a half of the war, and Rosecrans had a long-standing relationship with him that was characterized by mutual professional respect and not a little personal warmth.[1]

Thomas's assignment reflected the fact that he fully possessed the respect and confidence of senior and subordinate officers alike. The same could not be said of the men to whom Rosecrans gave command of his other two wings. Like Thomas, the man who commanded the three-division "Right Wing,"

Maj. Gen. Alexander McDowell McCook, was a veteran of the prewar army from whom much could reasonably have been expected at the outbreak of the Civil War. A member of a formidable Ohio family, McCook graduated from the U.S. Military Academy at West Point in 1852, thirtieth out of forty-three in a class that included such Civil War notables as Henry W. Slocum and George Crook. Commissioned into the infantry, he saw service in campaigns against Native American tribes in the Southwest before being selected in 1858 to teach tactics at his alma mater.[2]

When the Civil War began, seventeen members of the extended McCook clan volunteered their services to the Union and subsequently won renown as the "Fighting McCooks." Early in 1861, Alexander left West Point and, after a brief stint as the mustering officer for Ohio state forces, accepted command of the First Ohio Infantry, which was mustered in only five days prior to his thirtieth birthday. Dispatched shortly thereafter to Washington, McCook's regiment participated in the ill-fated July 1861 First Manassas campaign, after which the highly regarded young officer received promotion to brigadier general and assignment to what was known as the Department of the Cumberland. He arrived at Maj. Gen. Robert Anderson's headquarters in Cincinnati in September and after a minor tiff with the department commander (who shortly thereafter was compelled by poor health to turn over command to Brig. Gen. William T. Sherman), McCook took command of troops posted about fifty miles south of Louisville that would eventually be designated the Second Division.

McCook would lead his division in the Shiloh and Corinth campaigns with sufficient skill to win promotion to major general in July 1862. When Buell reorganized his Army of the Ohio into corps after winning the desultory "race to Louisville" in September, it was practically inevitable that he would select McCook to command one of them. Buell chose McCook although at the time a number of officers openly expressed their desire that McCook take his place at the head of the army—an idea whose popularity the ambitious young general and his friends did little to discourage. McCook's command subsequently saw heavy fighting at Perryville in October, where his conduct in response to a Confederate attack that mauled his corps effectively squelched talk of him as a future army commander and raised serious concerns about his fitness for the command he held. A few months later, on the first day of battle at Stones River, McCook's corps got caught unprepared by a Confederate assault, and the rout very nearly led to a decisive defeat for the Union army. When the battle was over, a third of McCook's command were casualties and its commander's standing in the army had taken yet another hit.[3]

The general impression of McCook on the eve of the Chickamauga campaign was of a man, in the words of historian Peter Cozzens, "in over his head as a corps commander."[4] This sentiment was by no means universal among McCook's contemporaries. After the war one officer declared, "As a member of his personal Staff for more than twelve months, in several campaigns, I learned to greatly esteem him." "McCook was a fighter," insisted another man who rose to the general's defense after the war, "his men realized this and no troops ever fought better than the Twentieth Corps organized and disciplined by him. . . . In no instance can any just criticism be made upon his skill, his ability, or his intense loyalty."[5] In his memoir, one of McCook's division commanders also found much to admire, proclaiming that, "Wherever fighting was hardest there was he to be found. His keen eye enabled him to detect weak points in his line and his quick mind always suggested a remedy in time to avert disaster. . . . [O]ver all, McCook bore himself gallantly and did good service." In his report on the engagement at Stones River, Rosecrans also praised McCook, describing him as a "tried, faithful and loyal soldier," while the author of an 1864 history of the division McCook organized early in the war offered a vigorous defense of his record.[6]

"He is a good fighting man, but coarse, without dignity," was one man's assessment of McCook in May 1862. "He is much set up with his elevation and is overbearing to his officers. We have however confidence in him in battle." By March 1863, however, Perryville and Stones River had done enough damage to McCook's reputation that relatively few in the Army of the Cumberland were still expressing such confidence. Indeed, that month one officer expressed what was undoubtedly a more widely held sentiment when he proclaimed the "young and very fleshy" McCook "a chuckle head." McCook, he added, was a man who "swear[s] like pirates and affect[s] the rough-and-ready style," which combined with his grin to excite "the suspicion that he is either still very green or deficient in the upper story." Several months later, this same officer remarked, "it is astonishing to me that he should be permitted to retain command of a corps for a single hour."[7] A brigade commander in the Army of the Cumberland later concluded that although he had "admirable traits of character," including "a peculiar open frankness of manner and *bonhomie*," McCook seemed "pursued by a strange fatality. He assumed a kind of boastful over-confidence that in war always presages failure, because it takes the place of the careful preparation that secures success." At the end of the war, another contemporary described McCook as "an overgrown school-boy, without dignity," and one of those men "not capacitated by nature or education for the positions they held."[8]

Unlike Thomas or McCook, the man Rosecrans tapped to command the "Left Wing" of the Fourteenth Corps (which in January 1863 would be respectively rechristened the Twenty-first Corps and the Army of the Cumberland), Maj. Gen. Thomas Leonidas Crittenden, was not a West Pointer, although he did see service during the Mexican War.[9] Like McCook, Crittenden benefited from membership in a famous family. His father, Kentucky's longtime U.S. Senator John J. Crittenden, was one of the nation's most famous public officials. His brother George was a general in the Confederate service, although a combination of advanced age, being one of the officers in command of the forces that were defeated at Mill Springs, and accusations of drunkenness had effectively killed his career by 1863. When the Civil War began, Thomas Crittenden held a general's commission in the Kentucky militia and, like his father, made it clear that he believed his place was with the Union. For his efforts organizing loyal Kentucky home guard units, in September 1861 Crittenden received a commission as a brigadier general and shortly thereafter found himself commanding a division under Buell.

Like McCook, Crittenden participated in the counterattack on the second day of battle at Shiloh that drove the Confederates from the field and in the Army of the Ohio's unsuccessful campaign against Chattanooga in June–August 1862. But although he was by then a major general—and McCook's senior by a dozen years—Crittenden was not tapped for corps command when Buell organized the Army of the Ohio into corps. Nonetheless, in part due to Senator Crittenden's support for the controversial Buell and his own efforts to steer clear of intrigues against the general, when it became necessary to reshuffle the army's high command in the aftermath of William "Bull" Nelson's death at the hands of fellow officer Jefferson C. Davis, Buell elevated Crittenden to command of the Second Corps. Unlike McCook's, Crittenden's corps hardly fired a shot in the subsequent Perryville campaign. Also unlike McCook, Crittenden conducted himself well at Stones River and came out of the campaign with his standing in the army enhanced.[10]

Although recent Army of the Cumberland scholars Peter Cozzens and Larry Daniel have had few kind words for Crittenden, he does not seem to have inspired or merited the degree of hostility McCook did from contemporaries. "He is the most modest unassuming, perfect gentleman you can well find," one officer proclaimed in a letter to his wife, "retiring in his manners, kind and courteous, with a high sense of honor." "There was no cooler or more thoroughly self-possessed soldier in the Fourteenth Army Corps," declared a newspaper correspondent after accompanying the Army of the Cumberland through the Stones River campaign. "We always loved our General (Crittenden)," one Twenty-first Corps veteran unapologetically informed a friend shortly after Chickamauga, "at Stone[s] River his corps did splendid fighting."[11] For his part, division commander Richard W. Johnson declared after the war that Crittenden's "gallantry was conspicuous in every engagement. A more earnest, attentive, and faithful corps commander was not to be found in our army." Cavalry commander David Stanley agreed, writing in his memoir: "A braver, more truthful, more noble man never lived." The same brigade commander who lamented McCook's "strange fatality" had nothing but praise for Crittenden. "Greatly beloved by the men," he wrote. "He was always genial, kind, just, and brave to a fault. . . . [I]f it had been in my power I would have made him commander-in-chief of the armies."[12]

Nonetheless, as with McCook, it is clear that Crittenden did not possess the same standing within the army that Thomas did when the campaign season opened in 1863. Aside from his conduct at Stones River, for which he later received a brevet promotion in the regular army, Crittenden had yet to turn in a performance that would lead anyone to expect true greatness from him. "A spare man," one officer wrote of Crittenden in March 1863, "medium height, lank, common sort of face, well whiskered. . . . I doubt not, swears like a trooper . . . is a good drinker." While this same officer saw Crittenden as one of those men who knew "how to blow their own horns exceedingly well," there was also an impression among observers of the Army of the Cumberland that perhaps because Crittenden was the only corps commander in that army who had not attended West Point, he lacked confidence and a willingness to assume responsibility. This made him overly reliant on the counsel of others and less assertive in managing his command than he needed to be if he were to become a truly first-rate corps commander. "Crittenden," one man acidly proclaimed shortly after the war, "was a country lawyer with little legal training and no military ability . . . who never, on the battlefield, had an opinion of his own, or ever assumed responsibility that he could possibly avoid." While there appears to be some truth in this particular statement, the evidence strongly suggests its author went too far, particularly when he concluded that, like McCook, Crittenden was "of that class of men who 'intended to do well'" but was doomed by personal shortcomings to be "doers only of positive evil or negative good, which is just as bad."[13] His actions at Stones River demonstrated that Crittenden could, in fact, be an effective corps commander. Nonetheless, it seems justifiable to conclude that, with corps commanders like Crittenden and McCook, Rosecrans would have needed to bring considerable care to the task of managing his army in 1863.

Another problem that plagued Rosecrans throughout 1863 was impatience on the part of his superiors in Washington with his methodical approach to managing his army. By the first week of August, their badgering became so obnoxious that Rosecrans decided he could take no more. He called his subordinates to his headquarters at Winchester, Tennessee, and, after reading to them a message from Washington demanding an immediate advance, laid out his analysis of the operational difficulties they currently faced—which none dissented from—and then read to them his reply to the message demanding he be relieved from command if its "peremptory" orders for an advance were not revoked. Thomas assured Rosecrans that he and the others in the group would stand by him regardless of the consequences that might flow from his sending the telegram. If McCook or Crittenden disagreed with Thomas, there is no evidence. Indeed, the only member of the group that did not share Thomas's view was Rosecrans's chief of staff, Brig. Gen. James Garfield, but Garfield dared not express his dissent openly, although he made sure his sentiments reached Washington through private letters to well-placed friends.[14]

Rosecrans's salvo—and the fact that by their silence McCook and Crittenden implicated themselves in it—won him and them no friends in Washington. It did, however, have the effect of inducing his superiors to back off long enough for Rosecrans's army to complete its preparations. Finally, on August 16, Rosecrans began his advance against Chattanooga. Crittenden received the task of advancing his three divisions over three separate roads across the Cumberland Plateau and into the Sequatchie Valley, from where they were to dispatch four infantry brigades over Walden's Ridge and into the valley of the Tennessee River to link up with two cavalry brigades. These units, Rosecrans hoped, would deceive Gen. Braxton Bragg, commander of the Confederate Army of Tennessee, into thinking the Federals intended to cross the Tennessee at and above Chattanooga in cooperation with Maj. Gen. Ambrose Burnside's Army of the Ohio, which also began its march from Kentucky toward Knoxville on the sixteenth.[15]

While Crittenden's men began their advance from McMinnville, Manchester, and Hillsboro, Thomas's and McCook's seven divisions advanced from the vicinity of Winchester to points south and west of Chattanooga from which they could cross the Tennessee River below the town. Rosecrans had already laid the foundation for this move by ordering McCook to push Maj. Gen. Philip Sheridan's division forward to occupy Stevenson and Bridgeport during the last week of July. By August 20, thanks in part to the effectiveness of Crittenden's operations, Rosecrans had reached Stevenson and found a relatively undefended Tennessee River. Indeed, that evening McCook and Rosecrans were in such high spirits over the progress their commands had made to that point that during a trip down to the banks of the Tennessee they engaged in what one staff officer described as "a lively conversation with the Rebel Pickets across the River" and tolerated a policy instituted by pickets on both sides that allowed "the most amicable intercourse" between them. Although the mood at army headquarters, one of McCook's brigade commanders later recalled, darkened a bit over the next few days, that same officer nonetheless remembered personally feeling nothing but satisfaction with the ease of the operation that brought the Army of the Cumberland to the banks of the Tennessee. "Everything," he declared, "seemed to progress smoothly, as if a master mind were directing all."[16]

At Rosecrans's instructions, McCook sent Sheridan's division to Bridgeport to prepare and secure a crossing of the river at that point, while Brig. Gen. Jefferson Davis was given the task of laying a pontoon bridge at Caperton's Ferry a few miles below Stevenson. During the morning of August 29, Davis sent a brigade across the river on boats to seize a position from which they could cover construction of the bridge, which did its job effectively and made possible completion of the bridge by the early afternoon. On the thirtieth, with Rosecrans and McCook on hand for at least part of the day, Davis pushed the rest of his division across the river and reunited his command at the foot of Sand Mountain before pushing forward to occupy the heights that night. Brig. Gen. Richard Johnson's division followed Davis's across the river the next day, while McCook managed the movements of his command from Stevenson. By September 1, Rosecrans had four divisions of infantry and one of cavalry across the river, with McCook's last division expected to cross the next day. That same day, McCook had orders sent to Davis to "move your division forward to Winston's early to-morrow. . . . Johnson will move up to your present position, where corps headquarters will also be moved tomorrow night."[17]Sheridan experienced considerably more frustration at Bridgeport. During the morning of September 2, his men successfully completed a bridge over the Tennessee and began crossing. However, that afternoon its trestles collapsed and, although it would not prevent him from getting his entire division across the river by September 3, it did delay his moving south to catch up with the rest of McCook's command.[18] By the end of that day, though, Davis had advanced down Sand Mountain into Lookout Valley, and Johnson's division, accompanied by McCook, was nearly at the summit of Sand Mountain. (Davis's men had the added satisfaction during their march over Sand Mountain of receiving extremely enthusiastic greetings from the much-persecuted Unionist residents of this part of Alabama and Georgia. This undoubtedly contributed to widespread straggling in Davis's command that compelled McCook to issue orders directing its commander to take "immediate and stringent measures . . . to remedy this very dangerous evil.") As this was going on, Thomas's corps was able to get cross the river at Shellmound, Battle Creek, and Bridgeport.[19]

Meanwhile, on August 31 Rosecrans directed Crittenden to bring all of his command, minus two brigades of infantry and some mounted forces, down the Sequatchie Valley and cross the Tennessee. By the end of the next day, Crittenden had two divisions at Jasper with the third a short march away. On September 2, army headquarters sent orders to Thomas to "make such dispositions of your command" on the other side of the Tennessee as were necessary to enable Crittenden to implement orders to cross two brigades quickly at Battle Creek and Shellmound that day.[20] The process of developing the plan for the next phase of the campaign began the evening of September 2 when Rosecrans called his corps commanders to Bridgeport to discuss the situation. It culminated at 2:30 A.M. on September 3 with the issuance of orders containing Rosecrans's plan to exploit his successful crossing of the Tennessee. McCook and his men would continue their march east to Valley Head and seize Winston's Gap in Lookout Mountain. From this point, McCook would support a push by Maj. Gen. David Stanley's cavalry toward Rome, Georgia, and be in position to advance to Alpine, Georgia, from where it could set the stage for Bragg's destruction by cutting his supply line—or at least pose such a menace to it that the Confederate commander would have no choice but to retreat and give up a huge swath of Georgia real estate. Crittenden's command would push forward from the crossings at Shellmound, Battle Creek, and Bridgeport to Whiteside, where the railroad from Stevenson passed between Sand Mountain and Raccoon Mountain en route to Chattanooga. From there Crittenden would "push forward as near to Chattanooga as practicable" to induce Bragg to give up the town or hold him in place while McCook worked his mischief. For his part, Thomas would move over Sand Mountain to Trenton in Lookout Valley and push advanced elements forward to Stevens' Gap in Lookout Mountain.[21]

None of Rosecrans's units experienced much difficulty over the next few days. When night fell on September 8, Thomas's vanguard had reached Stevens' Gap, while McCook had been in control of Winston's Gap since the evening of the fourth (although Sheridan still had yet to catch up with Johnson's and Davis's division), and Crittenden's command was at Whiteside. Bragg responded to Rosecrans's skillfully executed maneuvers by retreating and pulled back from Chattanooga on September 8.[22]

In response to Bragg's decision to abandon Chattanooga, Rosecrans continued pushing his command forward. From Trenton, he sent orders to Maj. Gen.

Gordon Granger directing him to leave Nashville, take direction of all forces north of the Tennessee, and have his Reserve Corps ready to move toward the rest of the army "at once."[23] McCook had already been sent instructions late on September 7 to advance from Winston's Gap to Alpine in the Broomtown Valley "to cover the movements of General Stanley, who has been ordered to cut the enemy's railroad communication between Chattanooga and Atlanta . . . and cover his return." Meanwhile, from his position around Whiteside, Crittenden received instructions to push forward reconnaissance "to gain the summit of Lookout, south of Chattanooga," Rosecrans informed Halleck on September 8, "holding his corps ready to enter the place, if practicable."[24]

After confirming news of the enemy's retreat from Chattanooga on September 9, Rosecrans had a message sent to McCook notifying him of the enemy's actions and directing him "to move as rapidly as possible on Alpine and Summerville." Instead of just supporting Stanley's cavalry, headquarters directed McCook that his movements were now "for the purpose of intercepting the enemy in his retreat; move on to strike him in flank, if possible." The Confederates, Rosecrans surmised, could not be more than two days' march south of Chattanooga. Thus, with the assistance of Thomas's command, which had been directed to move "as rapidly as possible to La Fayette," McCook was informed that Rosecrans had "strong hopes that you may inflict most serious injury upon them." Early on the morning of the ninth, in line with his vow to Washington that the enemy's "retreating column will not escape unmolested," Rosecrans directed Crittenden to leave only a "light brigade" to occupy Chattanooga and "throw your whole command forward . . . [to] pursue the enemy with the utmost vigor. Attack his rear whenever you can do so with a fair opportunity to inflict injury. . . . Should the enemy make a stand in such force as to make it imprudent to attack him, take up a favorable position for defense and advise the general commanding."[25]

Due to the great physical distance between him and Rosecrans, McCook did not receive his orders from headquarters until late in the afternoon of the ninth. He immediately assured headquarters that he would move at three the next morning "in pursuit of the enemy, and will attack him if I have a reasonable hope of success," and forwarded a report that the Confederates intended to concentrate their forces for battle at Rome. Johnson's division and two brigades from Davis's would, he pledged, be at Alpine by the evening of the tenth and Sheridan would take their place at Winston's Gap. For his part, Crittenden was able to claim "peaceable possession" of Chattanooga shortly after noon on the ninth. He was compelled, however, to wait until nightfall for enough of his command to reach him at Ringgold to begin developing plans to take up the pursuit toward Dalton, where Rosecrans incorrectly surmised the Confederates had fled to. On the tenth, both Crittenden and McCook made good on their pledge to carry out Rosecrans's orders, with neither encountering much difficulty as the former's command pushed south from Chattanooga in the direction of Dalton (although Crittenden himself did not exhibit especially great haste in leaving Chattanooga), while McCook personally reached Alpine with his command.[26]

While Crittenden and McCook carried out what proved to be relatively hazard-free movements, on September 10–11 Thomas pushed his lead division from Stevens' Gap into McLemore's Cove and nearly fell victim to a well-conceived Confederate counterattack. Fortunately, Bragg's subordinates failed to execute his plans and allowed Thomas to pull his men back to Stevens' Gap by the morning of the twelfth.[27] These events were among a series of developments that were transforming the campaign and the challenges McCook and Crittenden faced. The phase of the 1863 campaign season in which Rosecrans required no more from his corps commanders than that they follow and implement clear directives from headquarters was ending. Henceforth, unforeseen events and the active, immediate presence of the enemy would create situations that demanded a bit more of McCook and Crittenden and test their ability to think for themselves, make sense of fluid and dangerous developments, and respond appropriately to them.

Rosecrans's growing sense during the second week of September that Bragg's men were no longer in retreat, but gathering themselves around La Fayette for a fight, was reinforced by reports from Crittenden. At midnight on the tenth, army headquarters sent a message to Crittenden responding to reports that Bragg had a strong force at Lee and Gordon's Mill, where the road between Chattanooga and La Fayette crossed Chickamauga Creek, and might be planning "to fight us between this and La Fayette." Crittenden was directed to look into the situation and decide whether he should continue to push toward Dalton.[28] While Maj. Gen. John M. Palmer's and Brig. Gen. Horatio Van Cleve's divisions operated at and a few miles beyond Ringgold, Crittenden, who had been warned by cavalry officer John Wilder that there were strong Confederate forces less than ten miles beyond Ringgold, assigned the task of reconnoitering the area around Lee and Gordon's Mill to Brig. Gen. Thomas Wood's division. After conducting his reconnaissance, Wood wrote directly to Rosecrans's headquarters at 8:30 that night that reports of a large Confederate force at Lee and Gordon's Mill were "not so far from the mark as we were all disposed to believe. . . . [N]ot only was General Bragg here yesterday, but also Generals [Leonidas] Polk and [D. H.] Hill, with a large body of infantry and cavalry."[29]

That same day, evidence reached McCook that the situation had taken a different turn from what Rosecrans had anticipated when directing him to move to Alpine. At 6 A.M. he notified army headquarters that he had reached Alpine with five brigades and saw little to interfere with his plan to move to Summerville later that day. This message took until 10 P.M. to reach army headquarters and prompted Rosecrans's chief of staff to inform McCook that it was "nearly certain that the enemy has concentrated in heavy force in the neighborhood of La Fayette" and suggested, but made clear it was by no means "a peremptory order," that he "close up toward General Thomas."[30] By then McCook had already received an 8 A.M. message from Thomas informing him that Rosecrans had ordered them to open communications and that he did not expect to reach La Fayette before the twelfth. McCook responded by reporting that he had sent a reconnaissance to La Fayette, as his assumption that Thomas would be there had been contradicted by the fact that "all the cavalry we have driven from this vicinity runs in that direction."[31]

As indicated by the message McCook received from headquarters that day, on September 11 Rosecrans was finally, as one man later wrote, "rudely awakened from his oversanguine dream" of destroying Bragg's army through maneuvering—and keenly aware of the fact that his army was dangerously spread out in a way that gave Bragg a wonderful opportunity to strike with his own concentrated army. Even before the full results of Wood's reconnaissance were in, during the afternoon of the eleventh Crittenden received orders to make contact with Thomas, have Palmer and Van Cleve abandon Ringgold, and "move your whole force . . . as quickly as possible, to the Rossville and La Fayette road, to some defensible point . . . where you can maintain yourself, if necessary, against a superior force. Your main object will be to put yourself in such a position that you can fall back on this place [Chattanooga] in case of repulse." Crittenden promptly called his subordinates together at Ringgold and, after consulting with local residents regarding the local road network, issued orders for his men to begin implementing Rosecrans's directive early the next morning.[32]

Van Cleve and Palmer encountered no resistance as they pulled back from Ringgold to reunite with Wood's division and were joined by Col. John Wilder's brigade of mounted infantry during the evening of the twelfth. Wood, who the evening before had seen so many enemy campfires on the other side of Chickamauga Creek that it was clear "the foe was present in considerable force," was no doubt relieved by the arrival of these forces. Wood's relief would have been exponentially greater had he known that early on September 12 Bragg directed Polk to take his corps and, supported by two additional divisions, assault Crittenden's isolated command.[33]

Polk, however, executed his orders with his characteristic disregard for the wishes of his superior officer. This gave Crittenden plenty of time, satisfied by a reconnaissance of his front and reports from subordinates on the thirteenth that the Confederates were "not about to attack me here today," to put his three divisions in defensive positions behind the Chickamauga. Van Cleve's division held the center at the La Fayette Road with Wood to his right at Lee and Gordon's Mill, while men from Palmer's command helped Wilder's mounted force keep watch over Crittenden's left. To Crittenden's right and rear, the 650 men of the Fourth U.S. Cavalry watched the Dry Valley Road and endeavored to open communication with Thomas's command, which was about ten miles away. In line with an exceedingly dangerous misperception of the potential peril his command faced that day, Crittenden assured headquarters that even if the Confederates were to attack, "I think I can whip them." Fortunately, the inability of the Confederate high command to get its act together on September 13 meant that Crittenden's assessment of the situation would not be put to the test.[34]

Meanwhile, Rosecrans was endeavoring to pull Thomas's and McCook's commands together and move them north to link up with Crittenden. While Crittenden pulled back from Ringgold on September 12, about forty miles away McCook's corps continued to hold their position at Alpine. That morning McCook sent a message to Thomas reporting that, based on the reports he was receiving, he now had "no doubt that the rebel army is concentrated at or near La Fayette" and surmised it was Bragg's intention "to oppose his whole force to our fractions as they debouch from the mountain. All citizens here, both Union and secession, say that he will fight, and with the advantages he has I think so also." He added, "I am not desirous of fighting Bragg's whole army," and proclaimed that if the rebels were concentrated at La Fayette, "I am in a false position, for I could not reach you."[35] Fortunately, the day before McCook had taken the precaution of ordering his trains back to Winston's Gap. That order proved to have been wisely made, for during the night of September 12 orders drafted at army headquarters at 10:30 A.M. that morning reached McCook telling him to move two divisions to Thomas's support. By 8:15 A.M. on the thirteenth, with another message having arrived from Thomas reiterating Rosecrans's orders, McCook had his men pulling back from Alpine to Lookout Mountain and sent a message to Thomas informing him of his plan to march directly from "Alpine to the head of McLemore's Cove."[36]

Unfortunately, a march that McCook initially anticipated taking only a day—two at the most—to cover the distance between him and Thomas took much longer. There was no criticizing the promptness with which McCook began his march on September 13. Problems arose during the course of the day, however, when local residents reported the road he expected to take to McLemore's Cove did not exist. In addition, just as McCook personally reached the top of Lookout Mountain, a message Thomas forwarded from army headquarters led McCook to believe that the Confederates were in possession of McLemore's Cove.[37] Reinforcing this perception, and serving as the final straw in undermining McCook's initial plan of march, was another message from Thomas advising him that he wanted the link-up between the two corps to occur at Stevens' Gap. These developments and the commanders' ignorance of the existence of a road linking Dougherty's Gap with Stevens' Gap that ran along Lookout Mountain and provided a means of avoiding contact with any Confederates who might be in the cove, led McCook to reluctantly conclude that he had "but one route to pursue . . . to descend the mountain at Winston's and push down Lookout Valley" from Valley Head toward Stevens' Gap. After crossing the mountain and detaching a brigade from each of his three divisions to protect the corps's trains, McCook turned his command north with Sheridan's division in the lead, followed by Johnson, and Davis's command bringing up the rear.[38]

As if the problems of September 13 were not enough to drive McCook to exasperation, shortly after 5 P.M. on the fourteenth, as his command completed a respectable march that brought it down off Lookout Mountain and covered a good amount of the distance between Valley Head and Stevens' Gap, McCook received a decidedly unwelcome message army headquarters had sent six hours earlier. "The general commanding regrets," it read, "that you are moving back through Winston's Gap. . . . He directs you to turn back at once to the head of McLemore's Cove." A frustrated McCook immediately fired back an angry reply. After laying out his command's accomplishments that day and reporting that he anticipated Sheridan would be in contact with Thomas early the next day, McCook explained that he had taken the route he did based on information received from Thomas "stating that the route by Winston's was in his judgment the only practicable route for me to take. . . . He ordered me to Stevens' Gap, and by his approval I am on this route." He then informed headquarters that he would suspend his movement to Stevens' Gap to await word from them confirming the earlier order, although he added he would "be pained to take my troops over the route again; they certainly will feel as if I were trifling with them."[39]

Meanwhile, Crittenden received orders early on September 14 directing him to pull Palmer's and Van Cleve's divisions back to Missionary Ridge to reduce the distance between them and Thomas, while leaving Wood's on the Chickamauga at Lee and Gordon's Mill. Crittenden managed to do this before noon and spent the rest of the day looking for signs of the enemy's intentions. Then, at 7:40 P.M. Crittenden received orders to move Van Cleve and Palmer back to the Chickamauga. He promptly complied, moving Van Cleve's command into position at Crawfish Spring, located just upstream from Wood's position at Lee and Gordon's Mill, and pushed Palmer's forward to a position a bit further upstream to form the corps' right. Crittenden then spent the rest of the fifteenth and sixteenth keeping track of the cavalry brigade that was responsible for watching the area above Wood's position, issuing rations and ammunition to his men, and awaiting the arrival of the rest of the army. Finally, on the seventeenth, Thomas's command arrived on his right, which enabled Crittenden to better concentrate his own command by moving Palmer closer to Van Cleve.[40]

That same day, McCook finally reached Thomas, but not without a few more headaches. Early on September 15, Rosecrans's chief of staff sent McCook a message telling him to halt his movements until a courier arrived carrying a dispatch that contained Rosecrans's instructions. After sending this, however, another message left army headquarters acknowledging receipt of McCook's message from the evening before at 5:30 A.M. and telling him Rosecrans "says that it is all right; come ahead."[41] McCook responded by sending orders to Sheridan at 9:30 A.M. to "move your division immediately forward . . . and through Stevens' Gap to join General Thomas' forces." Johnson's division, however, remained in bivouac the entire day, while during the afternoon orders were sent to Davis to "reascend Lookout Mountain and proceed to Stevens' Gap by the most direct route to be found on the mountain." Yet not until the sixteenth did Sheridan finally reach Stevens' Gap and cross over it into McLemore's Cove, while the need to issue rations to his men prevented Davis from moving his infantry back up the mountain until the morning of the sixteenth. Nonetheless, after a tough twenty-five-mile march, Davis also managed to reach Stevens' Gap as the sun set that day, with Johnson's division a short march behind him on Lookout Mountain. Soon thereafter, Davis received orders from McCook, who after dispatching a staff officer at daybreak to "meet Johnson and Davis and hurry them up" had spent much of the day looking over the Fourteenth Corps' positions and discussing matters with Thomas, "to move with my command in the morning down the mountain and report to him, which I did about 10 A.M."[42]

It initially appeared during the morning of September 17 that the three divisions of the Twentieth Corps had reached McLemore's Cove not a moment too soon, for a report reached McCook that a strong enemy force was then moving toward their positions. McCook immediately put his men in line of battle and kept them there for a few hours before further investigation revealed that there was in fact no threat. In compliance with orders sent from headquarters the previous day to "mass your force from Pond Spring to Gower's [Ford]" on the Chickamauga, McCook then directed Davis to move north to Pond Spring and close up on Thomas's right.[43] However, they quickly found that the position of Thomas's command made this unfeasible, and McCook, while reporting this fact during the afternoon, also informed army headquarters that it would be impossible to "mass my troops between Pond Spring and Gower's and at the same time protect Catlett's, Dug, and Blue Bird Gaps" in Pigeon Mountain. After receiving a reply from headquarters modifying his directions, McCook spent the rest of the afternoon moving his commands into position. He posted Davis's division in front of Dug Gap in Pigeon Mountain, Sheridan's at the foot of Stevens' Gap, and Johnson's, which arrived in the evening after a twenty-five mile march, at Pond Spring.[44]

Fortunately, due to the time it took an exhausted and frustrated Bragg to regroup after the failure of his efforts during the second week of September to get his subordinates to carry out his plans, the delay in McCook's arrival at McLemore's Cove in itself proved not to be fatal for the Army of the Cumberland. By the morning of September 18, Rosecrans had Crittenden's, Thomas's, and McCook's commands back together again behind the Chickamauga. Nonetheless, Bragg remained determined to strike a decisive blow. Consequently, on the eighteenth he ordered strong forces across the Chickamauga above Lee and Gordon's Mill. These, he hoped, would seize a position from which they could attack the Federal left flank, cut Rosecrans's army off from Chattanooga, and possibly destroy it. Bragg's move necessarily made the performance of the man commanding the corps on the Federal left critical for Rosecrans, who planned to continue the process, begun on the seventeenth, of moving his "whole line northeastwardly down the Chickamauga, with a view to covering the La Fayette Road toward Chattanooga."[45]

Aside from some brisk picket firing during the morning, September 17 passed rather quietly on Crittenden's front, with the main development of that day being the arrival of Thomas's command on his right. At the time, Crittenden's forces were deployed with Wood's division holding the left at Lee and Gordon's Mill, Van Cleve's in the center near Crawfish Spring (which was by the Gordon-Lee mansion where Rosecrans made his headquarters), and Palmer's on the right. During the afternoon, orders arrived from headquarters directing Crittenden to "put General Van Cleve's and General Palmer's commands in readiness to march" so they would be out of the way of Thomas's commands and prepared to move in anticipation of orders for "taking up position farther down Chickamauga Creek."[46]

However, after conferring with Thomas, Crittenden sent a message back to headquarters reporting that he and Thomas had determined that moving both of Crittenden's divisions would be impractical. Consequently, in a message sent from headquarters at 3 P.M. directing him to move his headquarters to Crawfish Spring near Rosecrans, Crittenden was told only to adjust Palmer's position, which he moved leftward. Meanwhile, responsibility for covering the area beyond Wood's left rested with mounted forces commanded by Col. Robert Minty, which Crittenden had sent across the Chickamauga on the fifteenth to operate in the Pea Vine Valley and keep an eye out in the direction of Ringgold. To partially fill the considerable space between Minty and Wood, on the seventeenth headquarters directed Wilder to move his brigade over to Alexander's Bridge on the Chickamauga, which was about midway between Wood and Minty. Quite a bit further north from Wood's position was Granger's corps, which had been occupying Rossville Gap since the thirteenth.[47]

To distract Crittenden as he pushed a strong force across what he believed to be the relatively unguarded Chickamauga below Lee and Gordon's Mill, Bragg ordered part of his army to conduct a strong demonstration at the mill. While this was going on, one Confederate column would cross the Chickamauga at Reed's Bridge and then turn south to facilitate crossings by other forces at Alexander's Bridge and Thedford's Ford. Once crossings at these places had been made, the Confederates would push south to cut the road connecting Lee and Gordon's Mill with Rossville and Chattanooga and place themselves in a position from which they could crush the Federal left flank. Just getting to Reed's Bridge took much longer, however, than Bragg's plan intended due to the superb job Minty and his horsemen did delaying the march of the Confederate column assigned the task of seizing that crossing of the Chickamauga. South of Minty, Wilder also actively engaged the Confederates endeavoring to cross at Alexander's Bridge. Eventually, however, the strength of the forces Bragg threw at their positions pushed Wilder and Minty back, and by 4:00 P.M. the Confederates were making their way across the Chickamauga.[48]

While Minty and Wilder were engaged, Crittenden, the man in command of the largest body of nearby Federal infantry, seems not to have felt much anxiety over the situation below Lee and Gordon's Mill. Indeed, in the absence of directions from Rosecrans to do otherwise, he seems to have decided in the morning of the eighteenth to simply sit tight and await events. Since Rosecrans's headquarters and his own were both at Crawfish Spring that day, this was certainly an understandable stance for him to take. Then, as Minty was contesting the Confederate advance to Reed's Bridge and a report from Wood that the Confederates had advanced skirmishers toward his position at Lee and Gordon's Mill was making its way to Crittenden, shortly after 10:30 A.M. Rosecrans began responding to reports of Confederate activity. To Crittenden, he sent instructions to pull Van Cleve's division back from its position near Crawfish Spring and move it around Wood's position at Lee and Gordon's Mill to extend the Federal left toward Wilder and Minty. Palmer's division would slide to the left to fill the position to Wood's right that Van Cleve evacuated, while Thomas's corps moved up to fill the section of the line previous held by Palmer's men.[49]

As these maneuvers were underway, shortly before 4 P.M. Crittenden received a report from Wilder that he and Minty were in retreat and that to prevent the advancing Confederates from threatening his rear they were falling back toward Wood. Less than an hour later, Wood sent a message to Crawfish Spring informing Rosecrans and Crittenden that Wilder and Minty had not yet pulled back all the way to "the Chattanooga and Rossville road" and the Confederates on the east side of the Chickamauga "apparently outnumber our troops 4 to 1." Given the increasing evidence that Bragg was making a major effort to envelop the Federal left, Crittenden received instructions that evening to also move Palmer's division to the north and extend the corps' position beyond Van Cleve's left. Palmer's division would not move until well after nightfall, however, because of a need to await the arrival of Maj. Gen. James Negley's division of Thomas's corps to take its place in line. Fortunately, thanks to Wilder's and Minty's efforts, the Confederates on the east side of the Chickamauga were able to push no further south on the eighteenth than the Viniard farm.[50]

While the situation was less menacing in McCook's front, this did not mean September 18 was a day free of anxiety for the young commander of the Twentieth Corps. McCook began the day by riding his lines and reporting to headquarters that all was quiet on the Union right. During the late morning, orders arrived from army headquarters informing McCook that Thomas had been told to move his corps in the direction of Crawfish Spring and directing him to "move your command down the Chickamauga and close it up compactly on General Thomas' right. . . . [C]lose in upon it in its new position . . . and watch the enemy's movements in the direction of the gaps of Pigeon Mountain."[51] Shortly after dispatching his chief of staff to his division commanders with orders implementing Rosecrans's wishes, however, a new message from headquarters reached McCook directing him only to be ready to move. A confused McCook immediately wrote back asking, "Which order will I obey?" Around 4 P.M., headquarters replied to McCook's query with two messages. In the first, Chief of Staff Garfield explained Rosecrans wanted him to "move to Thomas' position and then you're yourself in readiness to move farther if necessary. Do so as soon as practicable." In the second, Rosecrans put the directions more bluntly, writing only: "Move up."[52]

After receiving these messages, McCook ordered his divisions to begin moving north. Leaving a brigade from Davis's division behind to hold Stevens' Gap, he proceeded to move the rest of his command north along the Chickamauga. By 8:30, McCook's men had made sufficient progress in their march to enable him to assure headquarters, "My corps will be concentrated at Pond Spring to-night. . . . My men are confident." As these confident men bivouacked in the vicinity of Pond Spring and Gower's Ford, shortly after midnight a message from headquarters reached McCook's headquarters at Pond Springs directing him, he later wrote, "to move down to Crawfish Spring with the Twentieth Corps as soon as General Thomas' troops were out of the way." Rosecrans, McCook learned, had changed his mind about just how far north his corps, and indeed the entire Army of the Cumberland, needed to be on September 19.[53]

Rosecrans had spent September 18 following the course of events from his headquarters at the Gordon-Lee mansion and throughout most of the day seemed content to continue moving his army north along the west bank of the Chickamauga with Thomas following Crittenden and McCook following Thomas. Then, around 4 P.M., Rosecrans decided this would not be sufficient to deal with the problems to the north. Consequently, he decided that, in addition to Crittenden moving Palmer around Wood and Van Cleve, Thomas would take three of his divisions out of line, march around behind the Twenty-first Corps, and then take up a position from which it would assume responsibility for the army's left. The last of Thomas's divisions, Negley's, would remain in the place in line it took over from Palmer. McCook would continue moving down the Chickamauga until he reached Negley at Crawfish Spring.[54]

During the first phase of the operation that carried their commands to and across the Tennessee River McCook and Crittenden were the beneficiaries of a well-conceived plan that had the great merit of giving them relatively explicit directions as to what Rosecrans expected of them and how they were to achieve their commander's goals. It also had the effect of shaping events so that neither did Crittenden and McCook come into contact with the enemy nor did the enemy exercise his ability to throw a wrench into Rosecrans's plan. Once contact with the enemy became imminent and Bragg began to stamp his imprint on the situation during the second and third week of September, though, more was required from Crittenden and McCook.

Inevitably, as circumstances changed they compelled deviations from a clear plan, and problems developed. Although acting largely in compliance with the wishes of his commanding officer, after pushing south from Chattanooga, Crittenden initially put his divisions in positions where they provided a ripe target for a Confederate attack. For his part, although also attributable in large part to problems that had their source elsewhere, McCook's delay in reaching Thomas could have been mitigated had he gained more familiarity with the road network south of Stevens' Gap. Fortunately, thanks to far more extensive and much less excusable fumbling on the other side of the field by Bragg's subordinates, these problems did not have the serious consequences they might have had. Whether Federal luck would hold was an open question as the two armies spent the anxious night of September 18 anticipating the battle that was certain to come on the following day.

As temperatures plummeted into the thirties during the night, Thomas's three divisions successfully made their march and by midmorning had settled into a defensive line at the Kelly farm. Meanwhile, Crittenden finished adjusting his position behind the Chickamauga with Palmer's division going into position to Van Cleve's left around 4 A.M., the right of his corps being held by Wood at Lee and Gordon's Mill, and his line between those points running along the critical La Fayette Road that connected the Army of the Cumberland with Chattanooga. Understandably nervous about that section of his line, Crittenden decided early in the morning to ride over to the left of his line to see what was going on. He found Wilder's command there, with two regiments from Van Cleve's division supporting his position and little of consequence occurring. After looking over the situation, talking with Wilder, and directing Palmer to send out one of his brigades on a reconnaissance, Crittenden decided shortly after 7:30 A.M. to send a message to headquarters informing Rosecrans that "four or five cannon have just fired in the direction of Reed's Mill. . . . General Palmer in position on the left of my Corps, and [Col. William] Grose's Brigade just under orders to make a reconnaissance in direction of Reed's Mill. . . . I can hear Gen Thomas' Arty [artillery] passing on my rear, and it has been passing since 2 A.M." Shortly thereafter, having received an 8:10 A.M. message from headquarters telling him that Rosecrans was "anxious to know what are the developments on the left," Crittenden decided to make his way to headquarters and personally brief the army commander on the situation.[55]

Meanwhile, McCook had his command up early on the nineteenth, having sent messages to Davis and Sheridan at 3:30 A.M. advising them that "Johnson has orders to move at early dawn this morning on the road from here to Crawfish Spring," and directing Davis to "move your division upon the same road immediately in the rear of General Johnson," while telling Sheridan to "move your division immediately in the rear of General Davis." Shortly thereafter, McCook rode over to Crawfish Spring just ahead of Johnson's division and reported to Rosecrans, who directed him simply to continue massing his corps "at that place and await further orders."[56]

The Battle of Chickamauga began in earnest at midmorning when elements from Thomas's command ran into Confederates attempting to carry out Bragg's plan to roll up the Union left. Rosecrans's response was to send orders shortly after 10 A.M. to McCook, whose men had arrived at Crawfish Spring, directing him to have Johnson take his division north and report to Thomas. McCook was also instructed to assume direction of the right wing of the army, including the division at Crawfish Spring that Thomas had left behind when he moved north. Almost immediately thereafter, another order arrived from Rosecrans directing McCook to send Davis's division to army headquarters at the Widow Glenn house. McCook complied promptly with both orders. Upon reporting to Thomas, Johnson was immediately thrown into the battle and drove back the Confederates in a fierce fight along the Brotherton Road near the Winfrey farm in the early afternoon.[57]

Also participating in that fight were elements from Crittenden's command. The sound of Thomas's men opening the battle reached Crittenden shortly after he returned to the left of his line after meeting with Rosecrans. Shortly before 10 A.M., Palmer received a message Thomas had dispatched one hour earlier stating: "The rebels are reported in quite heavy force between you and Alexander's Mill. If you will advance on them in front while I attack them in flank, I think we can use them up." Palmer immediately advised Thomas that Crittenden had dispatched Grose's brigade on a reconnaissance earlier that morning and indicated he was willing to do what Thomas suggested "as soon as he returns."[58] Shortly thereafter, Palmer learned Grose had encountered a strong force of Confederates and wanted to know whether he should engage them. Palmer directed Grose not to do so but to instead fall back and rejoin the rest of the division. Before Grose was back, however, Crittenden, exercising what Rosecrans later proclaimed "great good sense," decided around 11 A.M. on his own initiative to order Palmer's division to Thomas's assistance.[59]

Shortly after informing Rosecrans of what he had done, Crittenden received a 10:45 A.M. note from Thomas stating, "If another division can be spared, it would be well to send it up without any delay."[60] Hearing heavy firing coming from the direction of Thomas's command, Crittenden directed two staff officers to find Palmer and find out what was going on. They returned shortly thereafter to say they had been unable to reach Palmer, due to having come under fire from enemy infantry. Crittenden immediately sent two officers back to Rosecrans to report on the situation and ask permission to send Van Cleve's men to Palmer's assistance. While awaiting Rosecrans's response, Crittenden took the precaution of directing Van Cleve to leave a brigade with Wood at Lee and Gordon's Mill and bring the rest of his division north. This enabled Crittenden to act immediately upon learning Rosecrans had approved his request and personally lead Van Cleve's men toward the battle. Van Cleve's men arrived on the scene just in time. At Crittenden's direction, Van Cleve's brigades went into position to the right of Palmer (who had picked up Grose's command en route) and then, together with Johnson's division of McCook's command, they crushed a strong Confederate division during the early afternoon. In doing so, they enabled Thomas to continue thwarting Bragg's efforts to break what had become a tactical stalemate and cut the Federal route to Chattanooga.[61]

Crittenden, however, was far from done for the day. Shortly before 1 P.M., a message reached him from Palmer reporting at 12:35 that his division was "just going in" to the fight in Thomas's section of the field and that it promised to be a heavy one.[62] Being close to the scene, Crittenden was already aware of this, and shortly thereafter he deemed it necessary to draft a message to Wood informing him that Van Cleve's and Palmer's divisions were heavily engaged and that Wood needed to keep an eye on his left. Crittenden followed this up by dispatching his chief of staff to Rosecrans to report Van Cleve's men had been committed to the fight and ask permission to shift Wood's division north to support them. Rosecrans quickly approved Crittenden's plan. Around 2 P.M., Crittenden also learned army headquarters had instructed McCook to move his forces up from Crawfish Spring to assume responsibility for the area around Lee and Gordon's Mill. Rosecrans also advised Crittenden that he was especially concerned about the situation on his corps' right and that Sheridan's division from McCook would be sent to his assistance if it proved necessary to ensuring the security of this section of his line.[63]

While Crittenden was actively engaged supporting Thomas and managing his corps during the morning of September 19, McCook remained in the vicinity of Crawfish Spring. Rosecrans had relocated his headquarters north from the Lee-Gordon mansion to the Widow Glenn house shortly after 10 A.M., leaving McCook in charge of the units on the Union right and directing him to send Davis's division to the Widow Glenn house. This left McCook with only Sheridan's and Negley's divisions and a cavalry division to hold the line south of Wood's command at Lee and Gordon's Mill.[64]

After inspecting the ground on his right, McCook received a message from headquarters directing him to pull the cavalry forces south of him "in upon our right, and send a detachment to look out for our rear." Then, between 1 and 2 P.M., McCook sent two messages to headquarters reporting there appeared to be no enemy in Negley's front, Johnson's and Davis's divisions had departed, and "Sheridan's division is watering here at Crawfish Spring. I am posting it in line, so as to effectively cover Wood's right." Once Sheridan had formed his command in line, McCook told headquarters, he planned to withdraw Negley's division from the Chickamauga and move it to a position "on my right and rear, a little retired."[65] Then, however, McCook learned to his surprise that Wood had left Lee and Gordon's Mill, and he promptly directed Sheridan to move his whole division over "to hold the ford at Gordon's Mills." In the message informing headquarters of his decision, McCook advised his superiors that "as I think this point needs great attention, and I do not know how far I am without support on my left . . . I will retain Negley here until further orders." Shortly thereafter, a message arrived from headquarters instructing McCook to begin moving Negley and Sheridan northward, while leaving a brigade at Lee and Gordon's Mill to hold that point. Within an hour after Rosecrans sent this message, however, McCook found his command reduced to just Sheridan's division and the cavalry when "further orders" arrived from headquarters shortly after 3 P.M. directing him to send Negley back to Thomas.[66]

When Crittenden received the note from headquarters authorizing him to call for Sheridan's division to be sent to his assistance, there had been a considerable pause in the fighting in Thomas's section of the field, a development that undoubtedly inspired Rosecrans's concern that, stymied by Thomas, Bragg might be preparing to try his luck elsewhere on the field, and thus Rosecrans's note of warning to Crittenden. Consequently, Crittenden decided to return again to Rosecrans's headquarters for instructions.[67] Meanwhile, Davis's division had reached the Widow Glenn house and as the sound of renewed fighting in the form of what Davis later described as "rapid and increased fire of musketry" reached army headquarters, Rosecrans ordered Davis to move his division forward and take up a position from which it might "make an attack with a view, if possible, of turning the enemy's left flank." Davis promptly pushed his division forward, but with no one to guide him, ended up moving so far to the right that he ended up about a half mile south of the right flank of a brigade from Van Cleve's division that was at the Brotherton field.[68]

Then, while Crittenden was on his mission to army headquarters, Davis pushed his two brigades across the La Fayette Road in search of the Confederates. Their advance was brought to a halt about one hundred yards east of the road by Confederates belonging to Maj. Gen. John Bell Hood's command, and a brutal engagement ensued.[69] As this was going on, Crittenden told his chief of staff to find Wood and suggest that he take advantage of "an opportunity, by leaving the road before he reached our position and moving to his right, to strike the enemy on the flank." Then, however, Crittenden notified Rosecrans of his suggestion to Wood. Rosecrans promptly disapproved it, much to the chagrin of Crittenden, who afterward lamented that "had General Wood been in the position I suggested, he would have been on the flank of the enemy, and, I think, would have punished him severely. . . . I should regret that I had not sent an order instead of a mere suggestion." Meanwhile, Davis made his way back to Crittenden's command post and told the staff he needed assistance. At the time, Crittenden was en route from Rosecrans's headquarters, having been given command over all the Federal forces in that part of the battlefield. Crittenden rode over to a battery that belonged to Davis's command, where he had been told he would find Davis and Wood.[70]

With his plan for using Wood's two brigades to roll up Hood's flank vetoed by Rosecrans, Crittenden decided he wanted to instead use them to fill the gap in the line between Davis and Van Cleve. Davis, however, found Wood before Crittenden did and convinced him that his men must be used to bolster his own "sorely pressed" line. As this was going on, Hood's men, not needing to concern themselves with their southern flank, kept up the pressure. Shortly after Wood began moving his men into position, Davis's lines east of the La Fayette Road began falling apart. Aided by the arrival of Col. Sidney Barnes's brigade, the unit Van Cleve had left back at Lee and Gordon's Mill when ordered north by Crittenden that morning, Davis managed to rally on a low ridge east of the La Fayette Road. Efforts to hold this position and keep the Confederates from the La Fayette Road were undermined, however, by the gap of approximately three-quarters of a mile that separated the forces fighting for the Viniard field from the other two brigades of Van Cleve's command. Inevitably, the Confederates found the exposed condition of Crittenden's left and began pushing into the gap to envelop the Federals.[71]

As the Federal position east of the La Fayette Road collapsed, Crittenden rushed forward to rally his men, at great personal risk. A somewhat astonished Colonel Wilder looked on, thinking "he would certainly be killed or captured, being in an open field between the two lines." As his men crossed the road, Crittenden rode among them "more exposed," one officer wrote afterward, "than I have ever seen a general officer in my experience" as he endeavored to rally them in a ditch just to the west. The ditch, however, provided insufficient cover to satisfy the men, and when Crittenden's chief of staff suggested he let the men fall back to a tree line about one hundred yards to the west, he agreed.[72]

Fortunately for Crittenden and his men, that tree line was where Wilder's brigade was posted behind a line of fence rails. As Hood's men moved forward in pursuit of what one brigade commander later conceded were "panic-stricken" Federals, Wilder's men opened a blistering fire that halted the Confederates and forced them to fall back to the cover of the ditch they had just driven Crittenden's men out of. Wilder then pushed forward some artillery to a position from which the gunners could "rake the ditch with canister." Meanwhile, Crittenden managed to rally enough of his men for a counterattack that eventually drove off the Confederates and reclaimed possession of Viniard field for the Federals. At this point, two brigades from Sheridan's division, which McCook had ordered north at 3:15 in compliance with directions from army headquarters, arrived on the field from Lee and Gordon's Mill. Sheridan immediately saw that Crittenden and his men were "hard pressed and nearly exhausted" and threw his men into the battle, tipping the scales once and for all in favor of the Federals on that part of the field. By then Crittenden was exhausted and showed little interest in exercising control over Sheridan's efforts, which one brigade commander, later recalling Crittenden's passivity during this phase of the fight for the Viniard field, said struck him as "unfortunate under the circumstances." After what he later described as "an ugly fight," Sheridan proposed to Crittenden that they should follow it up by launching a strong attack. Unfortunately, Sheridan lamented, "investigation showed that his troops, having been engaged all day, were not in condition, so the suggestion could not be carried out."[73]

While Crittenden managed the fight for Viniard field, back at Brotherton field the part of Van Cleve's division that had not been sent to Crittenden's assistance was having a rough time. Just as they had in their fight to the south, the Confederates were able to take advantage of the gap between the Federals fighting for Viniard field and those at Brotherton field. Hitting the uncovered right flank of Van Cleve's position enabled two Confederate divisions to achieve a potentially major penetration of Rosecrans's line. Fortunately, Bragg did not have the force on that section of the field necessary to exploit this success. This enabled Rosecrans, by pushing Negley's division forward to the Brotherton field, to close the gap in his line before nightfall.[74]

Historians Steven Woodworth and Peter Cozzens have declared that Crittenden had "his finest day as a corps commander" on September 19. Crittenden certainly would not have disputed this assertion. Shortly after the battle, he proclaimed he "would rather be tried for his conduct in the battle of Chicamauga [sic], than for any other event in his military career, that at Shiloh & Murfreesboro his troops were in position, and his duty only required him to keep them there—but that at Chicamauga he had displayed, in his judgment, the capacity and qualities of a general."[75] The commander of the Twenty-first Corps had indeed managed his command well during the morning and early afternoon, with his efforts contributing substantially to Thomas's ability to fight off Bragg's assaults. Then, in the course of the fight for the Viniard field, he developed a plan for the use of Wood's division that might have set the stage for a more decisive Federal victory on that part of the field and significantly altered the course of the battle. Unfortunately, Rosecrans overruled Crittenden's suggestion and, lamentably, the criticism of Crittenden as an officer who was too quick to defer to the judgment of others appears to be supported by this incident. While he later expressed frustration with what Rosecrans did, there is no evidence Crittenden made any significant effort to press the case for his course of action with his superior. And so the fight on the southern end of the field produced only a stalemate—a result that, if not all that might have been accomplished, nonetheless fully served Federal operational and tactical needs that day.

As he had the day before, McCook had little to do with the fighting on September 19, other than to dispatch troops north in a timely fashion, something that was well within his capabilities, to help Rosecrans achieve his objective of protecting his access to Chattanooga. "The result of the battle," Assistant Secretary of War Charles A. Dana, who had been accompanying the Army of the Cumberland for a little over a week, informed Washington that night, "is that the enemy is defeated in attempt to turn and crush our left flank. . . . His attempt was furious and obstinate, his repulse was bloody and maintained till the end."[76] This was an assessment that McCook and Crittenden would have no doubt fully endorsed. Neither would have predicted that the next day would bring ruin for both of them and their army commander.

As dropping temperatures added to the misery of the men who had fallen on September 19, Rosecrans called his subordinates to headquarters to discuss the situation. After McCook and Crittenden laid out as best they could the positions and condition of their commands, Thomas told the group that he was convinced (correctly, it turned out) that the Confederates were planning to renew their attacks against his position in the morning. To prevent Bragg from gaining a position from which the Confederates could block the main road to Chattanooga, Thomas insisted he needed reinforcements. Rosecrans and his subordinates continued the conversation until around 10 P.M., when Rosecrans's chief of staff went to work putting the army commander's plan for the following day into writing. Thomas would continue to hold the northern part of the field, with authority over the four divisions of his own corps, plus the divisions from McCook's and Crittenden's commands that had fought under him on the nineteenth. McCook would have two divisions under his direction, Sheridan's and Davis's, which Rosecrans directed McCook to form on Thomas's right and extend the Union line from there to the Widow Glenn house. Crittenden would command two divisions, Van Cleve's and Wood's, which Rosecrans told him to post "on the eastern slope of Missionary Ridge" so they could serve as the army's reserve. Before letting his subordinates depart, Rosecrans fed them and persuaded McCook to entertain them with a ballad before the council of war broke up and the generals returned to their commands to tend to business.[77]

When daylight broke on September 20, Rosecrans was preparing to inspect his lines when McCook appeared at headquarters to report on the disposition of his two divisions. Rosecrans responded by expressing concern about how McCook had posted Davis's command, but was convinced by McCook to leave the matter to the corps commander's discretion before leaving to conduct his inspection. Rosecrans also heard from Crittenden early that morning, who shortly after 7 A.M. reported to headquarters that he had Van Cleve's and Wood's divisions in position and that "both officers and men are in fine spirits."[78]

McCook and Crittenden encountered someone with a less cheery view of things when they made their way to the headquarters of Sheridan's division, which along with Wilder's brigade had responsibility for the Union right. Sheridan had left the evening meeting at Rosecrans's headquarters in a foul mood, and while at his headquarters Crittenden and McCook undoubtedly caught an earful, for Sheridan was not shy about speaking his mind, and he was deeply troubled. His mood certainly was not improved by Rosecrans's decision to quickly accede to Thomas's 6 A.M. request that Negley's division leave its position at the Brotherton farm to reinforce Thomas's left, with orders being sent to McCook at 6:35 A.M. "to fill the space left vacant by his removal, if practicable."[79]

Whatever anxiety this may have prompted in McCook's mind (manifest in his failure to move to comply with Rosecrans's directive as quickly as the commanding general wanted) was no doubt relieved a bit by the fact that Wilder's brigade had reported to him earlier and taken up a strong position south of Sheridan. Sheridan, however, saw only what he deemed an ill-executed general "drifting" of the army to the left. This was something Sheridan accepted as necessary due to the importance of securing Thomas's left flank, but as the man whose division held the other end of the line, Sheridan did not believe it was being done in a proper manner. As a consequence of Rosecrans's moving around the various components of the army, Sheridan later complained, "columns naturally stretch out into attenuated lines, organizations become separated, and intervals occur, all of which we experienced; and properly I doubt if it could have been executed without serious danger. . . . [I]t is possible that justification may be found for the maneuvers by which the army thus drifted to the left. We were in a bad strait, unquestionably."[80]

Rosecrans got a chance to hear Sheridan's view of matters, but it seems to have been to little effect. Returning to headquarters from his early morning inspection, Rosecrans once again found McCook there. The two men resumed their earlier discussion, one man later recalled, "on a hill a little in rear of the right of the line," during which the army commander once again stated he "did not very well like our position on the right." After being chastised by Rosecrans for what he believed had been insufficient promptness earlier in the morning in complying with directions to extend his line to relieve Negley, McCook requested that Rosecrans come with him to Sheridan's headquarters. Rosecrans agreed to do so; however, whatever words were exchanged at the meeting between the three men does not seem to have significantly affected Rosecrans's view of affairs. "Whatever might be the value of Sheridan's position," Rosecrans later recalled, "it was still more important that we should keep our line closed to the left" and that however important it was to be strong on the right, it "would be nothing in comparison with the importance of keeping a compact center."[81]

That Sheridan was right to be concerned that all of the shifting around of divisions might prove costly was not evident during the first few hours of fighting on September 20. Indeed, at midmorning it seemed Bragg was destined to once again be frustrated in his efforts to achieve anything at Chickamauga. Around 9:30 A.M., his forces resumed their attacks against the Union left, and Thomas was able to fight off the Confederate assaults, with Rosecrans doing everything he could to support him. After directing Negley's command to move to Thomas's assistance and exasperated by McCook's failure to extend his line in the manner he wanted, Rosecrans sent a staff officer over to Crittenden to direct him to push Wood's division and Col. Sidney Barnes's brigade from Van Cleve's division forward to the Brotherton field to take Negley's place there. The staff officer, however, found Wood first and "deeming the case urgent, gave him the orders informing him that he should report the fact of his having done so to General Crittenden."[82]

This was soon followed by orders from Rosecrans to Crittenden directing him to move Van Cleve's two remaining brigades forward as well. When Rosecrans made his way back to his headquarters after examining the ground on Thomas's front, however, he encountered Van Cleve posting his men on a hill that was "about 150 or 200 yards further back," Rosecrans later stated, "than the place where I wanted him to be." After advising Van Cleve of this fact, Rosecrans saw Crittenden and his staff in a peach orchard and decided to discuss the situation with him. After riding along the lines with Rosecrans, Crittenden issued orders to Van Cleve to, Rosecrans later stated, "form in close column by division, in the direction indicated, reiterating them for fear General Van Cleve would not understand them fully." Around 10 A.M., Crittenden further refined his directions to Van Cleve to move his two brigades forward.[83]

Shortly after Negley had left to go to Thomas's assistance, McCook rode with Sheridan to the position Negley had vacated. They found Wood's division had moved up to replace Negley and were informed by its commander that he and the division to his left were in contact. McCook then rode south along Wood's line and found some of the breastworks on the right were unoccupied. Thereupon, he turned to Sheridan and instructed him to have one of his brigades fill the gap between Wood and Wilder's command. Shortly after doing so, however, McCook caught sight of a substantial body of Federal troops moving toward him. It turned out to be Davis's two brigades, which McCook learned, Rosecrans had personally ordered forward to plug the gap to the right of Wood's position. McCook and Davis then rode together along the front, with McCook directing Davis to post one brigade in line, with the other in reserve. As he finished this task, McCook learned Col. Bernard Laiboldt's brigade from Sheridan's division was also nearby. It was posted on a ridge south of Rosecrans's headquarters and given the mission of supporting Davis's right and rear.[84]

Although the arrival of two of Negley's brigades helped him thwart the only action by the Confederates that morning that threatened to achieve anything, a two-brigade advance that briefly managed to work around his northern flank, Thomas continued to appeal to Rosecrans for assistance. And Rosecrans continued to oblige him by drawing troops from McCook's and Crittenden's commands. McCook had just finished posting Davis's and Sheridan's men, when shortly after 10:30 A.M. two messages arrived almost simultaneously from headquarters directing him to "make immediate disposition to withdraw the right so as to spare as much force as possible to . . . send two brigades of General Sheridan's division at once and with all possible dispatch to support General Thomas, and send the third brigade as soon as the lines can be drawn in sufficiently."[85]

Even though increasingly anxious at the sight of large clouds of dust rising through the woods east of Wood's and Davis's lines, McCook immediately moved to comply with the orders of his commanding general and forwarded headquarters' directions to Sheridan, although instructions from Rosecrans to report to army headquarters for further directions appear not to have reached McCook. Meanwhile, at 10:45 A.M. army headquarters also issued orders to Crittenden to "send Van Cleve's command to General Thomas' support with all dispatch." Like McCook, Crittenden moved to comply with Rosecrans's orders and, since he had nothing else to do, told the army commander, "as this is the last of my command, I presume I had better go with it." Rosecrans replied, "Certainly, and take them, general, where you see that smoke and hear that heavy firing and do what you can there." Around the same time he prepared and gave these orders to Crittenden, Rosecrans dictated another order, this one to Wood, directing him to move to the assistance of Maj. Gen. Joseph Reynolds's division of Thomas's command in order to fill a gap in the line. Although he could not know that this order carried the seeds of disaster for the Army of the Cumberland and the end of his career as a corps commander, Crittenden appears to have taken no interest in what exactly the orders headquarters was sending one of his division commanders (albeit one whose command was effectively under McCook's control that morning) said.[86]

Rosecrans assigned the task of transmitting his orders for Wood to Lt. Col. Lyne Starling, Crittenden's chief of staff. Starling reached Wood's command shortly after 11 A.M. and found its commander discussing the situation with McCook, who had arrived on the scene about fifteen minutes earlier. Despite the fact that McCook was the senior officer, Starling handed the message from headquarters to Wood, who, according to one of McCook's staff officers, "peered quizzingly at the order, turned to McCook, and read it aloud," before informing Starling that what Rosecrans proposed was based on a fundamental misconception. There was no gap that needed filling, Wood pointed out, to which Starling later testified he replied, if that was the case "then there is no order." As McCook looked on, Wood insisted he would obey Rosecrans's instructions, which would compel him to pull his division out of line in order to move around behind Brig. Gen. John M. Brannan's division to reach Reynolds's position. Starling then departed to tell Rosecrans what had happened, and Wood told McCook, "I'll move out by the right flank and rear to hide my movement from the enemy." "No, Tom," McCook replied, "just march out by the left flank, and I'll order Jeff [Davis] . . . to close your gap." McCook then left the scene hoping he could pull enough men from Davis's division north quick enough to plug the gap Wood's departure was going to create before the Confederates could exploit it. Meanwhile, Wood directed his men to pull out of line and begin the move north.[87]

Upon returning to army headquarters, Starling reported to Rosecrans that "General Wood had a nice little breastwork in his front and ought not to be moved." This, however, made no impression on Crittenden, who apparently had been waiting for his chief of staff's return before heading over with Van Cleve's command to assist Thomas. Indeed, nothing Starling had to say to Rosecrans seemed to make enough of an impression on Crittenden to overcome his preoccupation with getting over to Van Cleve's division. When Rosecrans finally released him, Crittenden took Starling with him. Just as he had gotten Van Cleve's men in motion, however, Crittenden received a message from Maj. John Mendenhall, his corps' chief of artillery, involving difficulties in posting some batteries. Crittenden then left Van Cleve's infantry and rode over to some batteries posted on a hill about two hundred yards behind the Union frontlines to address the problems with the artillery. Shortly thereafter, as he wrestled with them, Crittenden later wrote, "my difficulty was suddenly removed by the enemy."[88]

As Wood was removing his division from its place in line, a massive Confederate assault column unknowingly took advantage of Wood's absence to achieve a deep penetration into the Federal lines. Upon seeing Wood's men depart, Davis was attempting to slide his two battered brigades northward at the double-quick in a futile attempt to fill the gap Wood's three strong brigades had previously occupied. The Confederate assault was made with too much speed and power, however, for them to do any good. It did not take long for Davis to see that, as he later wrote, "Nothing but precipitate flight could save my command from annihilation or capture." Within minutes, his shattered command was indeed in full flight, with thousands of triumphant Confederates in hot pursuit.[89]

Because of the speed and strength of the Confederate assault, before he could fully comprehend what was happening, Crittenden found himself cut off from Van Cleve's division. Once he realized this was the case, Crittenden turned his attention to the batteries in his immediate area and assured his staff, "we will go to the batteries and will yet drive those fellows back and hold them in check." As the Confederates advanced toward the hill on which he and his artillerists were posted, however, Crittenden and the gunners with him soon found themselves unsure of which troops were in the woods to their immediate front, as some of them were carrying flags that appeared similar to one carried by the Army of the Cumberland's regular brigade. As soon as the Confederates cleared the woods and their uniforms eliminated all questions as to their allegiance, Crittenden directed the gunners to open fire. After several anxious moments hoping in vain that adequate support for his guns "would come from somewhere or be driven on me," Crittenden decided to ride back toward Missionary Ridge to look for Rosecrans, Mc-Cook, or anyone else who might have infantry available. As he and his staff were making their way to a ridge just west of the Dry Valley Road, where they were joined by Van Cleve, Crittenden learned his gunners had just been compelled to leave the hill by advancing enemy infantry. Shortly thereafter, as Crittenden waited on the ridge "in hopes of receiving orders or hearing from General Rosecrans," the sound of a shell flying overhead punctuated a report from Mendenhall that "the enemy had turned the guns on the hill we had shortly left and were firing on the transportation, artillery, & c., moving down the Dry Valley road." "My whole object is to do my duty as an officer," Crittenden then remarked to his staff. "I believe I have done all I can. Can any of you make a suggestion?"[90]

Unable to find Rosecrans or McCook, frustrated in his efforts to rally any more than a hundred men, and advised by his staff that "there could be no doubt, if Generals McCook and Rosecrans were killed or taken, his proper position was in Chattanooga, to reorganize the scattered troops," it did not take Crittenden long to decide to make his way to either Rossville or Chattanooga.[91] After riding north for about a mile, Crittenden encountered Col. John G. Parkhurst, the provost marshal for Thomas's corps, who had part of the Ninth Michigan, along with another regiment, formed across the Dry Valley Road. Parkhurst, who reported he had rallied enough stragglers to add the equivalent of at least another small regiment to their line, informed Crittenden that Rosecrans had gone to Chattanooga and asked him to take command of the troops he had rallied. According to Parkhurst, Crittenden replied, "This is no command for me." When Parkhurst objected that "the force I . . . had collected and should succeed in collecting was too much of a command for me," Crittenden again declined to take command. "You have done marvelously well," he informed Parkhurst, "and you had better keep command." Just then, a sergeant come up to Crittenden and told him that a significant Confederate force was approaching Parkhurst's left flank. Crittenden advised Parkhurst that he had better change his position and, as the colonel proceeded to do so, left for Chattanooga. Shortly thereafter, though, one of Crittenden's aides returned to direct Parkhurst to take his force and "move it with the trains on the road in as much order as possible to Chattanooga, which would be our next point for making a stand." Around this time, Crittenden learned from two members of Rosecrans's staff that the army commander had definitely gone to Chattanooga, which confirmed his decision to go there also.[92]

Meanwhile, as Davis's routed command fell back through the Brotherton Woods and into the Dyer field on its eastern edge, McCook rode ahead of it searching for Sheridan's command. Upon reaching a ridge on the field's western edge, he found Laiboldt's brigade posted in what its commander described as "a very favorable position on the slope of a hill." Rather than have Laiboldt take advantage of this position and fight defensively, McCook decided to throw the brigade forward in a counterattack, while orders went out to Sheridan's other two brigades to halt their march north and assist in the defense of Dyer field and to Wilder to "close up to the left and fill the gap made by the withdrawal of Sheridan." Over the objections of their commander, McCook ordered Laiboldt's brigade to immediately attack and not take the time to deploy from column into line before doing so. As Laiboldt's men advanced with bayonets fixed, McCook encountered Rosecrans, advised him of what he had done, and assured the army commander that he thought Laiboldt's men would "soon set the matter to rights." McCook's confidence was badly misplaced. As they approached the Confederates, one observer later wrote, "I saw the poor fellows struggling to deploy into line in order to use their arms against the enemy. But the enemy was too close at hand to permit Laiboldt to deploy. A volley was poured into Laiboldt's compact, almost solid mass of men at only a few steps distant." Their efforts further compromised by the disruption of their ranks by Davis's men and facing far superior numbers, Laiboldt's men quickly found themselves in serious trouble. "The loss of men was very great," and within a few minutes, wrote one of Davis's brigade commanders, "The organization was broken, and the brigade melted away and went to the rear."[93]

Although a futile endeavor in light of the strength of the Confederate forces in Dyer field, Laiboldt's charge did buy enough time to enable Sheridan to push the brigade from his command led by Brig. Gen. William Lytle to the ridge where Laiboldt had launched his attack. This time, the Federals fought from the high ground and put up a better fight. Nonetheless, although not resolved as quickly as Laiboldt's attempt to stem the Confederate tide, the result was the same. In a bitter battle for control of the ridge, Lytle was killed and his men driven off it. Shortly thereafter, Sheridan's command and the two brigades from Davis's command still under McCook's command retreated toward Chattanooga, as did Wilder, who was responding to a demand by Assistant Secretary of War Dana that Wilder's brigade provide him with an escort to Chattanooga. Succumbing to panic, McCook also departed for Chattanooga, en route pointing a revolver in the face of a civilian and threatening him with summary execution if the poor fellow mismanaged the task of guiding him to safety. Thus, Thomas was left behind to rally the Union left and conduct the magnificent stand on Horseshoe Ridge that enabled his command to leave the field that evening less ignominiously.[94]

Fate had smiled on the Army of the Cumberland for so long in 1863 that in retrospect it seems inevitable that at some point the pendulum would swing badly against it, and on September 20 it did. Principal responsibility for the catastrophic event that decided the battle, of course, clearly rests with Rosecrans. On the surface, Rosecrans faced a fairly clear and straightforward problem at Chickamauga—preventing the enemy from turning his left flank and cutting him off from Chattanooga. However, Crittenden would later proclaim that while Rosecrans was "of the first order of military mind . . . in his impulsiveness lay a military defect, which was to issue too many orders while his men were fighting."[95] Although Crittenden wrote this in an essay on Stones River, events at Chickamauga clearly colored his views, for during that battle Rosecrans had in fact compromised his efforts by injecting a degree of complexity into the management of his army that greatly increased the odds of a serious misstep.

The Union high command began September 20 well enough. Rosecrans's arrangements for how he wanted his army positioned that morning and the roles he assigned to each of his subordinates were sound, simple, and brought clarity to what the events of the previous day had made a somewhat muddled situation. His assigning of two divisions to McCook on the right, two to Crittenden in reserve, and the rest to Thomas on the critical left should have been sufficient to once again thwart the efforts of the dysfunctional Confederate high command to win a decisive victory. All that was needed once the battle began was cautious good sense in how Rosecrans and his subordinates managed their commands. Initially, they provided this, and the Army of the Cumberland appeared at midmorning to be once again on the road to a day of tactical success.

Then, out of a complex shuffling around of divisions in the late morning came what Wood, according to one source, proclaimed the "fatal order" of the day and the sequence of events that made it so.[96] It took Rosecrans's confusion to make these "fatal" to the Army of the Cumberland at Chickamauga; however, Crittenden and McCook were by no means faultless. Both had opportunities to shape the construction and implementation of the fatal order in a way that might have blocked it—or at least mitigated its consequences. Unfortunately, they failed to act properly when presented with these opportunities, or even to recognize they existed. Even though he was on the scene when Rosecrans conceived, drafted, and transmitted the fatal order to Wood, it is clear that Crittenden did not devote sufficient attention to what Wood was being asked to do. Had he done so, he could not have missed the fact that a problem was being created where none existed. Crittenden's failure to take sufficient care in the matter and failure to intercede to prevent a serious error in judgment suggest a serious lack of situational awareness on his part. It can also be seen as a consequence of Rosecrans's whittling away at Crittenden's authority over the various components of his corps throughout the course of the morning. The effect was that by the time the order was issued, Crittenden appears to have been so focused on what was left under his direction, Van Cleve's division, that he mentally surrendered responsibility over anything that involved Wood.

As bad as Crittenden's failures in this episode were, McCook's were worse. McCook was with Wood when he received and responded to what was obviously a problematic order. For some reason, however, McCook evidently saw no compelling need to assert his authority as senior officer on the scene to stop or even delay Wood from undertaking what even a cursory understanding of the situation at that critical point on the Federal line would have told him was an exceedingly dangerous move. His passivity at this critical juncture in the battle and his thinking that Davis could move up and take over the part of the line Wood was vacating further suggest either a poor sense of situational awareness or just gross irresponsibility on McCook's part. He had to be aware that Davis's two brigades had brought into the battle at most only 1,500 men, and they had been badly roughed up the day before. To think these already stretched brigades could cover the void left by Wood's departure was simply preposterous.

Neither Crittenden nor McCook did much to compensate for their errors in dealing with the "fatal order" in their subsequent handling of matters. In Crittenden's case, this was largely a consequence of the situation he found himself in, isolated from his subordinate commands and having only some scattered artillery and infantry to work with as he endeavored to hold off the rebel hordes. Given these circumstances, it is hard to see what more he could have done. The same could not be said of McCook. The aggressive spirit manifest in his decision to throw Laiboldt into a counterattack may have been somewhat commendable, but acting on it in that particular situation clearly was a mistake. Laiboldt's attack was hastily conceived, clumsily executed, and accomplished little. Moreover, while Laiboldt's counterattack had little effect in slowing down the Confederate assault, other elements from Sheridan's command subsequently made a somewhat respectable fight for the same ridge from which McCook ordered Laiboldt's men forward. It is conceivable that had McCook exercised some restraint and conducted the fight from the ridge defensively with Laiboldt's and Lytle's commands, enough time might have been bought for them, Sheridan's third brigade, and Wilder's command to materially impede, if not halt, the Confederates' momentum east of the Brotherton Woods.

Given the less-than-heroic circumstances under which they left the field, McCook and Crittenden could not have been surprised that their conduct at Chickamauga almost immediately became the subject of intense scrutiny. "The generals of division and of brigade feel deeply they can no longer serve under such superiors," Dana venomously (and falsely, according to one man who also spent time with the Army of the Cumberland after Chickamauga) reported to Washington on September 27. "The feeling against McCook," Dana stated, "is deepened by the recollection of his faults at Perryville and Murfreesborough, and of the great waste of life which they caused; while toward Crittenden it is relieved somewhat by consideration for his excellent heart, general good sense, and charming social qualities. Against these, however, is balanced the fact that, which I can testify to from my own observation, that he is constantly wanting in attention to the duties of his command."[97]

Nonetheless, the speed with which Washington rendered its verdict on Crittenden's and McCook's performances was remarkable. No doubt this was in part due to the fact that McCook and Crittenden had done themselves no favor in earlier supporting Rosecrans in his resistance to pressure from Washington to prematurely advance. The fact that Rosecrans's course was vindicated by his operational success prior to Chickamauga did little to redeem him or them in the eyes of Washington strategists. (Indeed, with the War Department being run by the petty and vindictive Edwin Stanton, the Army of the Cumberland's successes may have made Washington more enthusiastic about bringing down Rosecrans and those who supported him than would otherwise have been the case.) Thus, during the first week in October orders issued by the War Department on September 28 reached Chattanooga that announced McCook's and Crittenden's commands were to be consolidated into a single corps, christened the Fourth Army Corps, and placed under Granger's command.[98] Even before the orders arrived, McCook and Crittenden were, as one man who spent an evening with them put it, "in a bitter and depressed frame of mind," and defending their conduct to anyone they thought would listen. When word that the orders had arrived relieving them from command and directing them to report to Indianapolis to await a court of inquiry, both men understandably took the news—and the implied censure of their conduct—very hard. Their fury was evident in the orders both men issued their corps upon relinquishing command. McCook made it clear to his associates that he was not going to take his dismissal lying down and was, as one of his relatives put it, "determined to have the matter thoroughly ventilated."[99]

Both McCook and Crittenden got their chance for vindication in February 1864 when the War Department convened the promised courts of inquiry in Louisville. After a few weeks taking testimony, the proceedings ended with both men largely exonerated. In McCook's case, the court commended him for doing "his whole duty faithfully . . . with activity and energy" on the nineteenth. Yet, after overlooking some significant evidence to the contrary to determine that McCook was in no way responsible for the army's turn of fortune on September 20, the court did find that "in leaving the field to go to Chattanooga, General McCook committed a mistake." However, it declared that McCook's personal conduct in the battle precluded the possibility of his decision having been motivated "by considerations of personal safety" and that it was natural for him to conclude that since Rosecrans had gone to Chattanooga, he should go there also. Nonetheless, the court proclaimed McCook's acting on this conclusion a clear "error in judgment."[100]

The court's findings in Crittenden's case went even further—indeed, as in McCook's case, probably a bit too far—in absolving its subject. Quickly disposing of what it clearly concluded was an open-and-shut case in Crittenden's favor, the court found in his conduct on the nineteenth "not only . . . no cause for censure, but, on the contrary, that his whole conduct was most creditable." As with McCook, the court absolved Crittenden of all responsibility for the following day's disaster. It then commended him for doing "everything he could, by example and personal exertion, to rally and hold his troops" and concluded, unlike with McCook, there was no cause for complaint in Crittenden's decision to make his way to Chattanooga during the afternoon of the twentieth.[101]

By the time these findings were issued, however, there was no chance McCook and Crittenden would ever see service with the Army of the Cumberland again. In McCook's case, this was clearly justified. Chickamauga was but the latest in a series of episodes that taken together offered a fairly compelling case that McCook did not possess the personal or intellectual qualities necessary to lead a corps effectively on a Civil War battlefield, even though he had proven himself capable of handling a corps administratively and when given relatively simple operational tasks. That these tasks were well within his capabilities would be evidenced by the fact that despite his failures as a field commander during the Civil War, McCook would have a respectable career in the postbellum army that ended with his retirement as a major general and included an especially distinguished stint as commandant of the Army Infantry and Cavalry School at Fort Leavenworth, the forerunner to the modern Command and General Staff College.[102]

Crittenden, on the other hand, deserved better. His career prior to Chickamauga had been quite credible, containing none of the black marks that darkened McCook's record—and at least one quite commendable performance.

This fact, and the effectiveness with which he handled his command for much of September 19, suggest that whatever lapses in judgment Crittenden committed at Chickamauga should be seen as aberrations in what was otherwise a respectable career, rather than viewed as reflective of general unfitness to command a corps. Yet, even though his actions at Chickamauga were largely vindicated and he would see brief service as a division commander in Virginia in 1864 (making him an aberration to a larger trend in which Federal officers seeking redemption tended to be shuffled from the East to the West, rather than vice versa), Crittenden would never enjoy the regard from his contemporaries—and historians—that his solid service with the Army of the Cumberland merited. Like McCook, Crittenden would enjoy a respectable postwar career in the regular army and retire as a brevet brigadier general, an especially notable accomplishment given his lack of a West Point pedigree.[103] Nonetheless, the course of events in 1863 had ensured that, regardless of what happened afterward, neither Crittenden nor McCook would ever escape the great shadow cast by George Thomas over the history of the Army of the Cumberland and the Chickamauga campaign.

Notes

1. General Orders No. 168, October 24, 1862, in U.S. War Department, *The War of the Rebellion: A Compilation of the Official Records of the Union and Confederate Armies*, 70 vols. in 128 parts (Washington, D.C.: Government Printing Office, 1880–1901), ser. 1, vol. 16, pt. 2: 641–42 (hereafter cited as *OR*; all references are to series 1 unless otherwise noted); Thomas B. Van Horne, *Army of the Cumberland* (1875; repr., New York: Smithmark, 1996), 162–65; Larry J. Daniel, *Days of Glory: The Army of the Cumberland, 1861–1865* (Baton Rouge: Louisiana State University Press, 2004), 190–93; William H. Lamars, *The Edge of Glory: A Biography of General William S. Rosecrans, U.S.A.* (New York: Harcourt, Brace & World, 1961), 13, 182–83; Christopher J. Einolf, *George Thomas: Virginian for the Union* (Norman: University of Oklahoma Press, 2007), 141–43.

2. Despite the conspicuous role McCook played in the Civil War, no satisfactory full treatment of his life and career exists. The most extensive source on McCook's life prior to 1864, written in a decidedly hagiographic tone, is the lengthy profile in William Sumner Dodge, *History of the Old Second Division, Army of the Cumberland* (Chicago: Church and Goodman, 1864), 238–74. In addition to this source, the information on McCook's background and career prior to the 1863 campaign contained in this and the next few paragraphs has been gleaned from the critical treatments in Daniel, *Days of Glory*, 15, 18–20, 81–83, 127, 206–15; Whitelaw Reid, *Ohio in the War: Her Statesmen, Her Generals, and Soldiers*, 2 vols. (Cincinnati: Moore, Wilstach, and Baldwin, 1867), 1:806–9; and E. C. Bearss, "McCook, Alexander McDowell," in *American National Biography*, edited by John A. Garraty and Mark Carnes, 24 vols. (New York: Oxford University Press, 1999), 14:897–98. Further information on the entire McCook clan can be found in Charles Whalen and Barbara Whalen, *The Fighting McCooks: America's Famous Fighting Family* (Bethesda, Md.: Westmoreland, 2006).

3. William P. Carlin, *The Memoirs of Brigadier General William Passmore Carlin*, edited by Robert I. Girardi and Nathaniel Cheairs Hughes (Lincoln: University of Nebraska Press, 1999), 66–67; Kenneth W. Noe, *Perryville: This Grand Havoc of Battle* (Lexington: University Press of Kentucky, 2001), 92–95, 234, 243–76, 303, 316–21, 326; Peter Cozzens, *No Better Place to Die: The Battle of Stones River* (Urbana: University of Illinois Press, 1990), 83–134, 172–74; Daniel, *Days of Glory*, 209–11, 224.

4. General Orders No. 9, January 9, 1863, *OR*, vol. 20, pt. 2:311; Peter Cozzens, *This Terrible Sound: The Battle of Chickamauga* (Urbana: University of Illinois Press, 1992), 10; Daniel, *Days of Glory*, 18, 190.

5. Frank J. Jones, "Personal Recollections of Some of the Generals in Our Army during the Civil War," in *Sketches of War History, 1861–1865: A Compilation of Miscellaneous Papers Read before the Ohio Commandery of the Loyal Legion*, 9 vols. (Wilmington, N.C.: Broadfoot, 1993), 9:71; Geo. B. Jenness, "Gen. A. M'D. McCook: A Soldier's Pen in Defense of a Gallant Officer," *National Tribune*, March 18, 1886.

6. Richard W. Johnson, *A Soldier's Reminiscences in Peace and War* (Philadelphia: J. B. Lippincott, 1886), 309–10; Rosecrans to Thomas, January 3, 1863, *OR*, vol. 20, pt. 1: 198; Dodge, *Old Second Division*, 239–71.

7. Alfred Lacey Hough, *Soldier in the West: The Civil War Letters of Alfred Lacey Hough*, edited by Robert G. Athearn (Philadelphia: University of Pennsylvania Press, 1957), 63; John Beatty, *Memoirs of a Volunteer, 1861–1863*, edited by Harvey S. Ford (New York: W. W. Norton, 1946), 176–77, 218.

8. William B. Hazen, *A Narrative of Military Service* (Boston: Ticknor and Co., 1885), 152–53; William F. G. Shanks, *Personal Recollections of Distinguished Generals* (New York: Harper & Brothers, 1866), 249.

9. General Orders No. 9, January 9, 1863, *OR*, vol. 20, pt. 2:311. Crittenden has attracted even less attention from historians than McCook. The information in the following paragraphs on Crittenden's life prior to 1863 has been gleaned from Larry J. Daniel's work, which offers a very critical portrayal (*Days of Glory*, 6, 41, 81–83, 130, 137), as well as the biographical sketches in these reference works: Thomas Speed, Alfred Pirtle, R. M. Kelly, and Union Soldiers and Sailors Monument Association, *The Union Regiments of Kentucky* (Louisville: Courier-Journal, 1897), 53–55; Ezra Warner, *Generals in Blue: Lives of the Union Commanders* (Baton Rouge: Louisiana State University Press, 1964), 100–101; Lowell H. Harrison, "Crittenden, Thomas Leonidas," in Garraty and Carnes, *American National Biography*, 5:742, and Nathan R. Meyer, "Crittenden, Thomas Leonidas (1819–1893)," in *Encyclopedia of the Civil War*, edited by David S. Heidler and Jeanne T. Heidler, 5 vols. (Santa Barbara, Calif.: ABC-CLIO, 2000), 1:523–24.

10. Cozzens, *No Better Place to Die*, 128, 172–73, 180, 191–93; David S. Stanley, *An American General: The Memoirs of David Sloan Stanley*, edited by Samuel W. Fordyce IV (Santa Barbara, Calif.: Narrative Press, 2003), 134.

11. Shanklin to his wife, March 22, 1862, in *"Dearest Lizzie": The Civil War as Seen through the Eyes of Lieutenant Colonel James Maynard Shanklin . . . Recounted in Letters to His Wife*, edited by Kenneth P. McCutchan (Evansville, Ind.: Friends of Willard Library Press, 1988), 127; William D. Bickham, *Rosecrans' Campaign with the Fourteenth Corps or the Army of the Cumberland: A Narrative of Personal Observations* (Cincinnati: Moore, Wilstach, Keys, & Co., 1863), 41; C. Lender to Friend Ben, October 17, 1863, Chickamauga and Chattanooga National Military Park Library, Fort Oglethorpe, Ga.

12. Johnson, *Soldier's Reminiscences*, 319–20; Stanley, *American General*, 150–51; Hazen, *Narrative of Military Service*, 152–53.

13. Beatty, *Memoirs of a Volunteer*, 176; Shanks, *Personal Recollections of Distinguished Generals*, 249, 266.

14. Halleck to Rosecrans, August 4, 5, 1863, OR, vol. 23, pt. 2, 592; Rosecrans to Halleck, August 6, 1863, ibid., 594; Cozzens, *This Terrible Sound*, 24–26.

15. John T. Wilder, "Preliminary Movements of the Army of the Cumberland before the Battle of Chickamauga," in *Sketches of War History, 1861–1865: A Compilation of the Miscellaneous Papers Compiled for the Ohio Commandery of the Loyal Legion, February 1885–February 1909* (Wilmington, N.C.: Broadfoot, 1993), 263; Rosecrans to Adjutant-General U.S. Army, October 1863, OR, vol. 30, pt. 1: 50–51.

16. Philip H. Sheridan, *Personal Memoirs of P. H. Sheridan*, 2 vols. (New York: Charles L. Webster, 1888), 1:271; Rosecrans to Adjutant-General U.S. Army, OR, vol. 30, pt. 1: 50; Jones to his parents, August 21, 1863, Frank Johnston Jones Papers, Cincinnati Historical Society, Cincinnati, Ohio; Carlin, *Memoirs*, 95.

17. Heg to his wife, August 30, 1863, in *The Civil War Letters of Colonel Hans Christian Heg*, edited by Theodore C. Blegen (Northfield, Minn.: Norwegian-American Historical Association, 1936), 239; McCook to Garfield, October 2, 1863, OR, vol. 30, pt. 1: 485; Rosecrans to Halleck, September 1, 1863, ibid., pt. 3: 279; Thruston to Davis, September 1, 1863, ibid., 285.

18. Sheridan to Rosecrans, September 2, 1863, OR, vol. 30, pt. 3: 303, 304; Rosecrans to Halleck, September 2, 1863, ibid., 296.

19. McCook to Garfield, October 2, 1863, OR, vol. 30, pt. 1: 485; Sheridan to Thruston, September 30, 1863, ibid., 579; Thomas to Garfield, September 30, 1863, ibid., 245–46; Rosecrans to Adjutant-General U.S. Army, October 1863, ibid., 52; Carlin, *Memoirs*, 94–95; Heg to his wife, September 4, 6, 1863, *Civil War Letters*, 241, 242–43; Thruston to Davis, September 6, 1863, Twentieth Army Corps, Letters Sent, October 1862–September 1863, Records of U.S. Army Continental Commands: 1821–1920, Entry 6464, RG 393, National Archives and Records Administration, Washington, D.C.

20. Crittenden to Garfield, October 1, 1863, OR, vol. 30, pt. 1: 601; "Itinerary of the Twenty-first Army Corps," ibid., 671; Crittenden to Garfield, August 31, September 1, 1863, ibid., pt. 3: 257, 287; Garfield to Thomas, September 2, 1863, ibid., 298; Garfield to Crittenden, September 2, 1863, ibid., 305.

21. Garfield to Crittenden, September 2, 1863, OR, vol. 30, pt. 3: 305; Garfield to Thomas, McCook, Crittenden, Stanley, and Hazen, September 3, 1863, ibid., 322–23; Rosecrans to Adjutant-General U.S. Army, October 1863, OR, vol. 30, pt. 1: 52.

22. Thomas to Garfield, September 30, 1862, OR, vol. 30, pt. 1: 246; McCook to Garfield, October 2, 1863, ibid., 485; Rosecrans to Adjutant-General U.S. Army, October 1863, ibid., 52; Steven E. Woodworth, *Six Armies in Tennessee: The Chickamauga and Chattanooga Campaigns* (Lincoln: University of Nebraska Press, 1998), 63–67.

23. The Reserve Corps had been part of the Army of the Cumberland since June. Granger shared McCook's and Thomas's West Point pedigree, but shared little history with the Army of the Cumberland prior to June 1863, having begun his war service in Missouri. Granger subsequently provided solid service as a cavalry commander in Missouri and the Corinth Campaign before receiving command of an "Army of Kentucky" in January 1863. It was to a large extent this "army" that Rosecrans re-

christened the Army of the Cumberland's "Reserve Corps" in June 1863. Van Horne, *Army of the Cumberland*, 221; Carl H. Moneyhon, "Granger, Gordon," in Garraty and Carnes, *American National Biography*, 9:401–2; John H. Eicher and David J. Eicher, *Civil War High Commands* (Stanford, Calif.: Stanford University Press, 2001), 263.

24. Garfield to McCook, September 7, 1863, *OR*, vol. 30, pt. 3: 412; Garfield to Stanley, September 7, 1863, ibid., 432; Rosecrans to Halleck, September 8, 1863, ibid., 442.

25. Rosecrans to Granger, September 9, 1863, *OR*, vol. 30, pt. 3: 499; Garfield to McCook, September 9, 1863, ibid., 488–89; Garfield to Thomas, September 9, 1863, ibid., 483; Rosecrans to Halleck, September 9, 1863, ibid., 479; Garfield to Crittenden, September 9, 1863, ibid., 492, 493.

26. McCook to Garfield, September 9, 1863, *OR*, vol. 30, pt. 3: 489; Crittenden to Garfield, September 9, 1863, ibid., 494; Crittenden to Goddard, October 1, 1863, ibid., pt. 1: 602–3; McCook to Garfield, October 2, 1863, ibid., 485–86.

27. Woodworth, *Six Armies*, 67–73; Cozzens, *This Terrible Sound*, 65–75.

28. Garfield to Crittenden, September 10, 1863, *OR*, vol. 30, pt .3: 517; Crittenden to Goddard, October 1863, ibid., pt. 1: 603.

29. Wilder, "Preliminary Movements," 265; Palmer to Oldershaw, September 30, 1863, *OR*, vol. 30, pt. 1: 711; Van Cleve to Starling, September 30, 1863, ibid., pt. 3: 802; Crittenden to Garfield, September 11, 1863, ibid., 545; Wood to Garfield, September 11, 1863, ibid., 547–48.

30. McCook to Garfield, September 11, 1863, *OR*, vol. 30, pt. 3: 540; Garfield to McCook, September 11, 1863, ibid., 541.

31. Thomas to McCook, September 11, 1863, *OR*, vol. 30, pt. 3: 538; McCook to Thomas, September 11, 1863, ibid., 539.

32. William J. Richards, "Rosecrans and the Chickamauga Campaign," in *War Papers Read before the Indiana Commandery, Military Order of the Loyal Legion of the United States* (1898; repr., Wilmington, N.C.: Broadfoot Publishing Company, 1992), 472; William S. Rosecrans, "From Tullahoma to Chattanooga," in *Battles and Leaders of the Civil War,* edited by Peter Cozzens (Urbana: University of Illinois Press, 2002), 5: 417; Garfield to Crittenden, September 11, 1863, *OR*, vol. 30, pt. 3: 545–46; Crittenden to Garfield, October 1, 1863, ibid., pt. 1: 604.

33. Palmer to Oldershaw, September 30, 1863, *OR*, vol. 30, pt. 1: 711–12; Van Cleve to Starling, September 30, 1863, ibid., 802; Crittenden to Garfield, October 1, 1863, ibid., 604; Wood to Oldershaw, September 29, 1863, ibid., 630; Woodworth, *Six Armies*, 74–75.

34. Cozzens, *This Terrible Sound*, 81–85; Crittenden to Garfield, October 1, 1863, *OR*, vol. 30, pt. 1: 604–5; Rosecrans to Adjutant General of the U.S. Army, October 1863, ibid., 54; Crittenden to Garfield, September 13, 1863, Twenty-first Army Corps, Letters Sent, December 1861–October 1863, Records of U.S. Army Continental Commands: 1821–1920, Entry 6538, RG 393, National Archives and Records Administration, Washington, D.C.

35. McCook to Thomas, September 12, 1863, *OR*, vol. 30, pt. 3: 569–70.

36. Garfield to McCook, September 12, 1863, *OR*, vol. 30, pt. 3: 570; McCook to Garfield, October 2, 1863, ibid., pt. 1: 486; Thomas to McCook. September 13, 1863, ibid., pt. 3: 602; McCook to Thomas, September 13, 1863, ibid., 598.

37. McCook to Garfield, September 13, 14, 1863, *OR*, vol. 30, pt. 3: 603, 628; McCook to Garfield, October 2, 1863, ibid., pt. 1: 486.

38. McCook to Garfield, September 14, 1863, *OR*, vol. 30, pt. 3: 629; McCook to Garfield, September 14, 1863, ibid., 628; McCook to Garfield, October 2, 1863, ibid., pt. 1: 486; Cozzens, *This Terrible Sound*, 88.

39. Garfield to McCook, September 14, 1863, *OR*, vol. 30, pt. 3: 628–29; McCook to Garfield, September 14, 1863, ibid., 629–30.

40. Rosecrans to Adjutant-General U.S. Army, October 1863, *OR*, vol. 30, pt. 1: 54; Crittenden to Garfield, October 1, 1863, ibid., 605.

41. Garfield to McCook, September 15, 1863, *OR*, vol. 30, pt 3: 648; Bond to Mc-Cook, September 15, 1863, ibid.

42. Thruston to Sheridan, September 15, 1863, *OR*, vol. 30, pt. 3: 650; Davis to Thruston, September 28, 1863, ibid., pt. 1: 498; McCook to Garfield, September 16, 1863, ibid., pt. 3: 674, 675; Flynt to Reynolds, September 16, 1863, ibid., 674.

43. Davis to Thruston, September 28, 1863, *OR*, vol. 30, pt. 1: 498; Goddard to McCook, September 16, 1863, ibid., pt. 3: 676.

44. McCook to Garfield, September 17, 1863, *OR*, vol. 30, pt. 3: 705, 706, 708; McCook to Thomas, September 17, 1863, ibid., 705.

45. Cozzens, *This Terrible Sound*, 89–92; Rosecrans to Adjutant-General U.S. Army, October 1863, *OR*, vol. 30, pt. 1: 55.

46. Crittenden to Garfield, September 17, 1863, *OR*, vol. 30, pt. 3: 708; Garfield to Crittenden, September 17, 1864, ibid., 709.

47. Oldershaw to Garfield, September 17, 1863, *OR*, vol. 30, pt. 3: 709; Garfield to Crittenden, September 17, 1863, ibid.; Crittenden to Goddard, October 1, 1863, ibid., pt. 1: 605; Minty to Sinclair, December 26, 1863, ibid., 922; Goddard to Wood, September 17, 1863, ibid., pt. 3: 711; Granger to Goddard, September 30, 1863, ibid., pt. 1: 853.

48. Woodworth, *Six Armies*, 80–82; Minty to Sinclair, December 26, 1863, *OR*, vol. 30, pt. 1: 922–23; Wilder to Goddard, September 18, 1863, ibid., 116; Wilder to Rosecrans, September 18, 1863, ibid., pt. 3: 724–25.

49. Garfield to Crittenden, September 18, 1863, *OR*, vol. 30, pt. 1: 110; Crittenden to Goddard, October 1, 1863, ibid., 605.

50. Crittenden to Goddard, October 1, 1863, *OR*, vol. 30, pt. 1: 605; Wood to Crittenden or Rosecrans, September 18, 1863, ibid., pt. 3: 728; Palmer to Oldershaw, September 30, 1863, ibid., pt. 1: 712; Wilder to Rosecrans, November 10, 1863, ibid., 447.

51. McCook to Garfield, September 18, 1863, *OR*, vol. 30, pt. 1: 107; Garfield to McCook, September 18, 1863, ibid., 108.

52. McCook to Garfield, September 18, 1863, *OR*, vol. 30, pt. 1: 114; Garfield to McCook, September 18, 1863, ibid., 115; Rosecrans to McCook, September 18, 1863, ibid.

53. Johnson, *Soldier's Reminiscences*, 226; McCook to Garfield, September 18, 1863, *OR*, vol. 30, pt. 3: 727; Thruston to Mitchell, September 18, 1863, ibid., pt. 1: 117–18; McCook to Garfield, October 2, 1863, ibid., 487.

54. Rosecrans to Adjutant-General U.S. Army, October 1863, *OR*, vol. 30, pt. 1: 55–56; Woodworth, *Six Armies*, 84–85; Cozzens, *This Terrible Sound*, 115.

55. Thomas to Garfield, September 30, 1863, *OR*, vol. 30, pt. 1: 248–49; Garfield to Crittenden, September 19, 1863, ibid., 123; Crittenden to Garfield, September 19, 1863, ibid., 123; Crittenden to Goddard, October 1, 1863, ibid., 606.

56. Bates testimony to McCook Court of Inquiry, February 1, 1864, *OR*, vol. 30, pt 1: 933; McClurg to Davis, September 19, 1863, ibid., 123; McClurg to Sheridan, September 19, 1863, ibid, pt. 3: 740; McCook to Garfield, October 2, 1863, ibid., pt. 1: 487.

57. McCook to Garfield, October 2, 1863, *OR*, vol. 30, pt 1: 487; Johnson to Thruston, September 28, 1863, ibid., 534–35.

58. Crittenden to Goddard, October 1, 1863, *OR*, vol. 30, pt. 1: 606; Thomas to Palmer, September 19, 1863, ibid., 124; Palmer to Thomas, September 19, 1863, ibid., 125.

59. Palmer to Oldershaw, September 30, 1863, *OR*, vol. 30, pt. 1: 712–13; Grose to Norton, September 27, 1863, ibid., 780; Starling testimony to Crittenden Court of Inquiry, February 9, 1864, ibid., 982; Rosecrans to Adjutant General U.S. Army, October 1863, ibid., 56; Crittenden to Goddard, October 1, 1863, ibid., 606–7.

60. Thomas to Crittenden, September 19, 1863, *OR*, vol. 30, pt. 1: 126.

61. Crittenden to Goddard, October 1, 1863, *OR*, vol. 30, pt. 1: 607; Beatty to Otis, September 28, 1863, ibid., 808; Van Cleve to Starling, September 30, 1863, ibid., 803.

62. Palmer to Crittenden, September 19, 1863, *OR*, vol. 30, pt. 3: 741.

63. Starling testimony to Crittenden Court of Inquiry, February 9, 1864, *OR*, vol. 30, pt. 1: 984; Crittenden to Goddard, October 1, 1863, ibid., 607–8.

64. Goddard to Negley, September 19, 1863, *OR*, vol. 30, pt. 1: 126; McCook to Garfield, October 2, 1863, ibid., 487.

65. Ducat to Rosecrans, September 19, 1863, *OR*, vol. 30, pt. 1: 127; Garfield to McCook, September, 19, 1863, ibid., 128; McCook to Garfield, September 19, 1863, ibid., 128.

66. Sheridan to Thruston, September 30, 1863, *OR*, vol. 30, pt .1: 579; McCook to Garfield, September 19, October 2, 1863, ibid., 129, 487; Garfield to McCook, September 19, 1863, ibid., 67; Ducat to Rosecrans, September 19, 1863, ibid., 131; Negley to Flynt, September 26, 1863, ibid., 329.

67. Crittenden to Goddard, October 1, 1863, *OR*, vol. 30, pt 1: 608.

68. Davis to Thruston, September 28, 1863, OR, vol. 30, pt. 1: 498; Cozzens, *This Terrible Sound*, 198.

69. Starling testimony to Crittenden Court of Inquiry, February 9, 1864, *OR*, vol. 30, pt. 1: 984; Carlin, *Memoirs*, 99; Woodworth, *Six Armies*, 92–93.

70. Davis to Thruston, September 28, 1863, *OR*, vol. 30, pt. 1: 498–99; Starling testimony to Crittenden Court of Inquiry, February 9, 1864, ibid., 984; Crittenden to Goddard, October 1, 1863, ibid., 608.

71. Wood to Oldershaw, September 29, 1863, OR, vol. 30, pt. 1: 631; Davis to Thruston, September 28, 1863, ibid., 499; Van Cleve to Starling, September 30, 1863, ibid., 803; Crittenden to Goddard, October 1, 1863, ibid., 608; Woodworth, *Six Armies*, 93–95.

72. Starling testimony to Crittenden Court of Inquiry, February 9, 1864, *OR*, vol. 30, pt. 1: 984; Wilder to Crittenden Court of Inquiry, February 12, 1864, ibid., 987.

73. Carlin, *Memoirs*, 100; Wilder to Rosecrans, November 10, 1863, *OR*, vol. 30, pt. 1: 447–48; Crittenden to Goddard, October 1, 1863, ibid., 608–9; Garfield to McCook, September 19, 1863, ibid., 67; Thruston to Sheridan, September 19, 1863, ibid., 132, 133; Sheridan to Thruston, September 30, 1863, ibid., 579; Cozzens, *This Terrible Sound*, 226, 228–29; Sheridan, *Personal Memoirs*, 1: 278.

74. Van Cleve to Starling, September 30, 1863, *OR*, vol. 30, pt. 1: 803; Negley to Flynt, September 26, 1863, ibid., 329; Garfield to Thomas, September 19, 1863, ibid., 68; Rosecrans to Adjutant General U.S. Army, October 1863, ibid., 56–57.

75. Woodworth, *Six Armies*, 93; Cozzens, *This Terrible Sound*, 200; Van Cleve to his wife, October 18, 1863, Horatio Van Cleve Papers, Minnesota Historical Society, St. Paul, Minn.

76. Lamars, *Edge of Glory*, 334–35; Charles A. Dana, *Recollections of the Civil War* (1898; repr., Lincoln: University of Nebraska Press, 1996), 107; Dana to Stanton, September 19, 1863, *OR*, vol. 30, pt. 1: 191.

77. Dana, *Recollections*, 113; Garfield to Crittenden, September 19, 1863, *OR*, vol. 30, pt. 1: 609; Garfield to Granger, September 19, 1863, ibid., 69; Garfield to Thomas, September 19, 1863, ibid.

78. Rosecrans testimony to McCook Court of Inquiry, February 4, 1864, *OR*, vol. 30, pt. 1: 940; Crittenden to Garfield, September 20, 1863, ibid., pt. 3: 752.

79. Cozzens, *This Terrible Sound*, 298–99; Thomas to Rosecrans, September 20, 1863, *OR*, vol. 30, pt. 1: 137–38; Garfield to Negley, September 20, 1863, ibid., 69; Garfield to McCook, September 20, 1863, ibid., 70.

80. Wilder, "Preliminary Movements," 268; McCook to Garfield, October 2, 1863, *OR*, vol. 30, pt. 1: 488; Sheridan, *Personal Memoirs*, 1: 279–80.

81. Rosecrans testimony to McCook Court of Inquiry, February 4, 1864, *OR*, vol. 30, pt. 1: 940; McCook statement to McCook Court of Inquiry, February 18, 1864, ibid., 967; Morton testimony to McCook Court of Inquiry, February 13, 1864, ibid., 950; Cozzens, *This Terrible Sound*, 313–14.

82. Cozzens, *This Terrible Sound*, 320–47; Garfield to Negley, September 20, 1863, *OR*, vol. 30, pt. 1: 69; Rosecrans to Crittenden Court of Inquiry, February 4, 1864, ibid., 979.

83. Oldershaw testimony to Crittenden Court of Inquiry, February 12, 1864, *OR*, vol. 30, pt. 1: 987; Rosecrans to Crittenden Court of Inquiry, February 4, 1864, ibid., 979–80; Rosecrans to Adjutant-General U.S. Army, October 1863, ibid., 58; Van Cleve to Starling, September 30, 1863, ibid., 803; Crittenden to Goddard, October 1, 1863, ibid., 609.

84. McCook to Garfield, October 2, 1863, *OR*, vol. 30, pt. 1: 489; Thruston testimony to McCook Court of Inquiry, February 6, 1864, ibid., 944–45; Davis to Thruston, September 18, 1863, ibid., 500; Davis testimony to McCook Court of Inquiry, February 15, 1864, ibid., 952; Sheridan to Thruston, September 30, 1863, ibid., 580.

85. Garfield to McCook, September 20, 1863, *OR*, vol. 30, pt 1: 70.

86. McClurg testimony to McCook Court of Inquiry, February 17, 1864, *OR*, vol. 30, pt. 1: 958; Garfield to Crittenden, September 19, 1863, ibid., 71; Rosecrans testimony to Crittenden Court of Inquiry, February 4, 1864, ibid., 979; Thruston testimony to McCook Court of Inquiry, February 6, 1864, ibid., 944–45; Crittenden to Goddard, October 1, 1863, ibid., 609–10; Bond to Wood, September 20, 1863, ibid., 635; Starling testimony to Crittenden Court of Inquiry, February 9, 1864, ibid., 983–84.

87. Wood to Oldershaw, September 29, 1863, *OR*, vol. 30, pt. 1: 635; Starling testimony to Crittenden Court of Inquiry, February 9, 1864, ibid., 983–84; Rosecrans testimony to McCook Court of Inquiry, February 5, 1864, ibid., 943; Editor's note to Richards, "Rosecrans and the Chickamauga Campaign," in *War Papers Read before the Indiana Commandery*, 475.

88. Starling testimony to Crittenden Court of Inquiry, February 9, 1864, *OR*, vol. 30, pt. 1: 984; McCook testimony to Crittenden Court of Inquiry, February 3, 1864, ibid., 977; Crittenden to Goddard, October 1, 1863, ibid., 609–10.

89. Cozzens, *This Terrible Sound*, 368–75; Woodworth, *Six Armies*, 116–17; Davis to Thruston, September 28, 1863, *OR*, vol. 30, pt. 1: 500.

90. Crittenden to Goddard, October 1, 1863, *OR*, vol. 30, pt. 1: 610–11; Starling testimony to Crittenden Court of Inquiry, February 9, 1864, ibid., 984; Oldershaw testimony to Crittenden Court of Inquiry, February 12, 1864, ibid., 989; McCook testimony to Crittenden Court of Inquiry, February 3, 1864, ibid., 977–78.

91. Starling testimony to Crittenden Court of Inquiry, February 9, 1864, *OR*, vol. 30, pt. 1: 984.

92. McCook testimony to Crittenden Court of Inquiry, *OR*, vol. 30, pt. 1: 977–78; Parkhurst to Flynt, September 17, 1863, ibid., 264–65.

93. McCook to Garfield, October 2, 1863, *OR*, vol. 30, pt. 1: 490; Laiboldt to Lee, September 29, 1863, ibid., 590; Rosecrans testimony to McCook Court of Inquiry, February 4, 1864, ibid., 941; Thruston testimony to McCook Court of Inquiry, February 16, 1864, ibid., 955; Sheridan, *Personal Memoirs*, 1: 282–83; Carlin, *Memoirs*, 102.

94. Sheridan to Thruston, September 30, 1863, *OR*, vol. 30, pt. 1: 580–81; McCook to Garfield, October 2, 1863, ibid., 490; McCook statement to Court of Inquiry, February 18, 1864, ibid., 969–71; Wilder, "Preliminary Movements," 270; Cozzens, *This Terrible Sound*, 391–92; Woodworth, *Six Armies*, 118–30.

95. Thomas L. Crittenden, "The Union Left at Stones River," in *Battles and Leaders of the Civil War*, edited by Robert U. Johnson and Clarence C. Buel, 4 vols. (New York: Century, 1887), 3:633.

96. Cozzens, *This Terrible Sound*, 363.

97. Dana to Stanton, September 27, 1863, *OR*, vol. 30, pt. 1: 201–2; Henry Villard, *Memoirs of Henry Villard, Journalist and Financier, 1835–1900*, 2 vols. (New York: Houghton Mifflin, 1904), 2: 188–89.

98. General Orders No. 322, September 28, 1863, *OR*, vol. 30, pt. 3: 911; General Orders No. 228, October 9, 1863, ibid., pt. 1: 1051.

99. Villard, *Memoirs*, 2:187–88; McCook to Officers and Soldiers of the Twentieth Army Corps, October 6, 1863, *OR*, vol. 30, pt. 4: 126; Crittenden to the Officers and Soldiers of the Twenty-first Army Corps, October 10, 1863, ibid., 253; Anson G. McCook to George W. McCook, October 8, 1863, McCook Family Papers, Manuscript Division, Library of Congress, Washington, D.C.

100. Finding and Opinion in Major-General McCook's Case, February 23, 1864, *OR*, vol. 30, pt. 1: 961–62.

101. Finding and Opinion in Major-General Crittenden's Case, February 23, 1864, *OR*, vol. 30, pt. 1: 996–97.

102. "Gen. A. McD. McCook Dead," *New York Times*, June 13, 1903; Timothy K. Nenninger, *The Leavenworth Schools and the Old Army: Education, Professionalism, and the Officer Corps of the United States Army, 1881–1918* (Westport, Conn.: Greenwood, 1978), 28–37.

103. Harrison, "Crittenden, Thomas Leonidas," 732; "Gen. Crittenden Dead," *New York Times*, October 24, 1893.

2

"IN THEIR DREAMS"

BRAXTON BRAGG, THOMAS C. HINDMAN, AND
THE ABORTIVE ATTACK IN MCLEMORE'S COVE

Steven E. Woodworth

During September 10 and 11, 1863, the Confederate Army of Tennessee had the opportunity to attack an isolated segment of William S. Rosecrans's Union Army of the Cumberland, striking it in front and flank with overwhelming force and cutting off its retreat. The potential existed to cripple Rosecrans's army, leaving its three sundered corps unable to support each other against the centrally positioned Confederate force. Yet the Confederate troops stood idle until it was too late, allowing the exposed Union detachment to withdraw to safety. To compound the incomprehensibility of their failure to act, the Confederate commander who was chiefly responsible had a reputation for extreme aggressiveness. All in all, the great military nonevent in McLemore's Cove during the second week of September was one of the more remarkable incidents of the war.

Rosecrans had launched his campaign on August 16, advancing from his army's camps around Winchester, Tennessee, southwestward toward Chattanooga and Braxton Bragg's Army of Tennessee. Bragg had hoped to hold the line of the Tennessee River, but Rosecrans skillfully maneuvered so as to conceal his intended crossing points and had most of his army on the south bank before Bragg's scouts detected the crossing. The Cumberland Plateau simply presented too many gaps for the Confederates to watch, and the Union Army of the Ohio, under the command of Ambrose Burnside, which was moving simultaneously from Kentucky against Knoxville, Tennessee, compounded the strategic problem for Bragg.

Early on the morning of August 29, Union troops began crossing the Tennessee at Caperton's Ferry, Alabama, about fifty miles west of Chattanooga. The first brigade crossed in boats to cover the construction of a pontoon bridge, and before the day was out all of Brigadier General Jefferson C. Davis's division was across, with more troops to follow. Simultaneously, one brigade of the division of Brigadier General John M. Brannan crossed the river at the mouth of Battle Creek, fifteen miles upstream from Caperton's Ferry and thus closer to Chattanooga, but they encountered no opposition as they swam the river, pushing their bundles of clothing and equipment on logs or other pieces of wood in front of them. Two days later the rest of the division followed. In the meantime, Major General Joseph J. Reynolds's division crossed the river in flatboats at Shellmound, several miles upstream from Battle Creek. At almost the same time, Major General Philip H. Sheridan's division began crossing the river by constructing a trestle bridge on the ruins of an earlier span at Bridgeport, Alabama, between Battle Creek and Caperton's Ferry. Delayed by the collapse of their make-shift bridge, Sheridan's men erected it yet again and were across the river by September 3. By the next day, Rosecrans's entire army was on the south bank. Within the space of five days the Army of the Cumberland had spanned the Tennessee at four different points to the west and west-southwest of Chattanooga.[1]

On August 31, Confederate cavalry brought word to Bragg that Union troops were across the Tennessee in force at Caperton's Ferry. Subsequent reports revealed that the Federals were crossing at several points in very great numbers and moving south but keeping to the west side of Lookout Mountain.[2]

That was a problem for Bragg. Lookout Mountain is actually a narrow and elongated plateau extending for nearly one hundred miles from near Gadsden, Alabama, to Chattanooga, Tennessee, cutting through the northwest corner of Georgia for thirty miles in between the two. At its highest point, overlooking Chattanooga at its northeastern tip, Lookout towers 2,392 feet above sea level and some 1,700 feet above the Tennessee River, which flows past its foot. Throughout its length, it posed a major barrier to the movement of wagons, cannons, and caissons, especially because its gently rolling summit is ringed with a more or less sheer, fifty-foot cliff called the Palisades. Horse-drawn vehicles could with difficulty negotiate the steep roads that clawed their way up the forested sides of the mountain, but they had no hope of getting up over the Palisades save at the few places where natural breaks in the cliff wall allowed a more gradual ascent to the summit plateau. The first such gap southwest of Chattanooga was Stevens' Gap, twenty-four miles from the town. The next was Winston's Gap, another eighteen miles to the southwest. Since armies could not travel without their supply wagons and their artillery, their transit of Lookout was limited to those gaps.

This might have seemed an advantage to the defender, Bragg, but in the first phase of the campaign it had quite the opposite effect, largely because

Rosecrans held the initiative. Bragg did not have troops enough to hold every possible gap, as well as the Tennessee gorge itself at Chattanooga, where the Federals could potentially simply pass around the north end of the mountain. Yet the possible routes of Union advance were too far apart to allow his army to move rapidly from one to the other or for separate detachments at the various gaps to support each other. In short, Bragg could meet Rosecrans in a gap only if he could successfully guess which gap the Union general would choose. If he guessed wrong, the Federals would pour through an unguarded gap, quickly gain his rear, and very possibly trap him, without supplies or escape route, against the mountains and the Tennessee River. As Bragg put it, "A mountain is like the wall of a house full of rat-holes. The rat lies hidden at his hole, ready to pop out when no one is watching." And in this case, the "rat," if it emerged unwatched, could be lethal to Bragg and his army. While he remained west of Lookout Mountain, Rosecrans could move farther and farther south, posing an increasingly dire threat to Bragg's supply line, while Bragg dared not reciprocate with a thrust toward Rosecrans's communications because of the threat of Burnside's army lurking to the northeast.[3]

Confronted with the evidence that Rosecrans was turning his position at Chattanooga, a movement Bragg would be unable to counter because of Lookout Mountain, the Confederate commander had no other option but to withdraw to the south to avoid being trapped and to reposition his army to counter Rosecrans when he finally did emerge from one of Lookout Mountain's "rat-holes." On September 7, Bragg put his troops in motion marching south out of Chattanooga on the La Fayette Road. The town of La Fayette, Georgia, lay about twenty-five miles due south of Chattanooga and was the destination for the leading elements of the Army of Tennessee, where they would form the army's left wing as it faced westward toward the eastern slope of Lookout Mountain. The movement out of Chattanooga and its environs continued on September 8, and when all the units of the army had reached their assigned positions, the army stretched thirteen miles from La Fayette, on the south, to Lee and Gordon's Mill on the north, on the La Fayette Road at the crossing of Chickamauga Creek, roughly halfway between Chattanooga and La Fayette. Bragg's army was deployed along the road, with major units spaced at wide intervals, able to move rapidly north or south along the road so as to be ready to respond to Rosecrans as soon as his plans should become clear.[4]

In fact, Rosecrans, believing Bragg was in headlong retreat toward either Rome, to the south, or Atlanta, to the southeast, had divided his army into three widely separated columns and was preparing to advance via all three of the routes around or over the northern end of Lookout Mountain.

Major General Thomas L. Crittenden's Twenty-first Corps was to advance eastward along the Tennessee River to approach the point of Lookout Mountain, threatening to move around the point, between mountain and river, and enter Chattanooga should the Rebels abandon the town. Major General George H. Thomas's Fourteenth Corps would cross the mountain at Stevens' Gap, eighteen miles to the south, and Major General Alexander McCook's Twentieth Corps was assigned to cross Lookout at the next gap to the south, fully forty-two miles from the Tennessee River and the opposite flank of Rosecrans's army. This widely spread deployment made Rosecrans's army vulnerable, but in truth there was no good way to cross Lookout Mountain with an enemy lurking on the other side. To have attempted to pour his army through a single gap would have slowed the advance intolerably, made it easy to stop if detected, and in part negated Rosecrans's advantage in numbers. So he opted instead to spread his forces. If Bragg remained ignorant or at least inert for a few more days, all would be well and the danger past.[5]

Each of Rosecrans's columns advanced. In the center, Major General James S. Negley's division marched at the head of Thomas's Fourteenth Corps. On the afternoon of September 7, Negley's division ascended the western side of Lookout and bivouacked atop the mountain that night and the next, as Negley advanced cautiously across the plateau. A regiment Negley had sent forward as skirmishers had encountered a few Confederate cavalry videttes on the west slope of the mountain on the evening of September 6, but the Rebel horsemen had withdrawn, and the only sign of hostile activity on the summit was to be found in the obstruction of Stevens' Gap, the break in the eastern rim of the palisades, by numerous felled trees. By the morning of September 9, Negley's men had cleared the road, and the division marched down the eastern slope, arriving at the foot of the mountain at four o'clock that afternoon. During the last hours of daylight, Colonel Timothy R. Stanley's brigade, leading the march, reconnoitered ahead some three and a half miles from the base of the mountain, skirmishing with Confederate cavalry.[6]

The valley into which Negley's division had descended was known locally as McLemore's Cove. It was bounded on the west by Lookout Mountain and on the east by a spur of Lookout Mountain called Pigeon Mountain that diverged from the main ridgeline about seven miles south of Stevens' Gap and the east-west road that spanned McLemore's Cove. The spur then extended another dozen or so miles to the northeast, before trailing off into more gently rolling terrain. Through most of its length, the cove was about six miles wide—narrower at its head, broader at its mouth. Two creeks ran the length of McLemore's Cove, Chattanooga Creek on the western side of the valley and Chickamauga Creek on the eastern side. Their waters were divided by Missionary Ridge, a chain of low hills that ran up the center of McLemore's Cove and extended many miles beyond the mouth of the valley, where it achieved more impressive height.

The only road that spanned the width of the valley—the road on which Negley's division bivouacked on the evening of September 9—ran from the foot of Lookout Mountain, below Stevens' Gap, on the west, to the foot of Pigeon Mountain, on the east, then ascended Pigeon and crossed it via Dug Gap to descend the other side directly into the town of La Fayette, where Bragg had posted the right wing of his army. The only road that ran the length of the valley followed more or less the course of Chickamauga Creek, sticking to the east side of the cove, in the shadow of Pigeon Mountain. It crossed the east-west road about a mile and a half from Dug Gap, at a place the locals called Davis's Crossroads, and thence extended northeastward, down the valley, to connect with the Chattanooga–La Fayette Road at the mouth of the cove near Lee and Gordon's Mill, where Bragg had posted the right wing of his army. Rosecrans had unwittingly sent the central column of his widely scattered army directly into the maw of an enemy who was not fleeing but had turned at bay and was still full of menace.

The Confederate commander did not long remain ignorant of the situation. With Negley's division little more than ten miles from his headquarters and skirmishing briskly with his cavalry, Bragg received reports of its presence that same evening. From the accounts he received, Bragg estimated the Union strength in McLemore's Cove to be between four and eight thousand men, a remarkably accurate assessment, since Negley probably had between five and six thousand men.[7]

The opportunity this presented Bragg was amazing, and his best course of action was clear. While threatening Negley with a frontal assault via Dug Gap, he could bring his right wing up a good road from Lee and Gordon's Mill, scarcely ten miles away, to crash directly onto Negley's unprotected flank. As the Union formation began to crumple under flank attack from overwhelming numbers, the threatened frontal assault would become real, and Negley's hapless division would collapse in a rout. Attacked as they would be from the north and east, the Federals' line of retreat would have to lead to the southwest, where the head of McLemore's Cove would become a cul-de-sac from which no organized body of troops could escape. Even if it could fall back to the road below Stevens' Gap, Negley's division would never be able to withdraw up that steep, rough, and narrow track quickly enough to escape capture by the pursuing Confederates.

Bragg saw the opportunity and determined to make it happen. His headquarters were at Lee and Gordon's Mill that evening, and he spoke personally with Major General Thomas C. Hindman, commanding a division there, explaining that Hindman would be leading the advancing into McLemore's Cove from the north. At 11:45 P.M. Bragg had formal orders drawn up and delivered to Hindman, directing him to march at once to Davis's Crossroads in McLemore's Cove and there be prepared to join Cleburne and launch an attack on Negley's Federals at dawn. At the same time Bragg sent orders to Lieutenant General D. H. Hill, commanding a corps at La Fayette, to send Major General Patrick R. Cleburne's division—the army's best division under its best division commander—marching through Dug Gap and into McLemore's Cove to be ready to join Hindman in the attack on Negley. By the time he issued these orders, Bragg had revised his estimate of Negley's numbers to between four and five thousand men.[8]

Trouble for Bragg began almost at once. On receipt of the order for the movement, Hill sent a reply to say that he could not comply. General Cleburne, he claimed, was sick, and besides, Confederate cavalry had obstructed the road through Dug Gap by felling trees across it, just as they had in their ineffectual efforts to hinder Negley's advance through Stevens' Gap two days before. As far as Hill was concerned, the obstructions would require twenty-four hours to clear and necessitated calling off the entire operation.[9]

Bragg was not ready to give up yet and selected another expedient. Instead of sending Cleburne to reinforce Hindman via Dug Gap, Bragg opted to support the attacking column from the rear by having Major General Simon B. Buckner take the two divisions of his corps, presently encamped near Lee and Gordon's Mill, and march directly in the wake of Hindman's division so as to be on hand to join in the attack against Negley with even more overwhelming strength. Bragg's order went out to Buckner at eight o'clock on the morning of September 10.[10]

Hindman, meanwhile, had begun his march, but after covering about ten miles from his camps, he halted the division near the farmstead of a local inhabitant named Morgan, about three miles short of Davis's Crossroads, where Bragg's orders had directed him to go. Hindman's division was still waiting at Morgan's when Buckner's two additional divisions caught up with it that afternoon.[11]

Almost everything about the life of Thomas Carmichael Hindman, up to this point, seemed to indicate that he would have been the most aggressive of generals. Hindman was born January 28, 1828, in Knoxville, Tennessee. During his childhood, his family relocated first to Jacksonville, Alabama, and then to Ripley, Mississippi. After he had received the rudimentary education that was available in Ripley, his parents sent him off to the Lawrenceville

Classical Institute in Lawrenceville, New Jersey, to complete his education. Upon the outbreak of the Mexican War, Hindman helped raise a company of volunteers and with them became part of the Second Mississippi Volunteer Regiment, serving first as lieutenant and then as captain of his company. Returning to Ripley upon the conclusion of hostilities, Hindman took up the practice of law. He served in the Mississippi legislature from 1854 to 1856 and then after moving to Helena, Arkansas, won election to the U.S. House of Representatives from that district, serving until the outbreak of the Civil War.

While building a public career in law and government, the fiery Hindman also built a reputation for direct and forceful dealing in practically every area of life. He was said to have scaled a convent wall on the way to the acquisition of his wife. He also had a habit of saying and publishing highly insulting denunciations of his political opponents, and his friends had to intervene on occasion to prevent his fighting duels. In 1856, after publishing a statement calling a rival candidate "the mullato would-be Senator," Hindman was badly wounded when his enemies ambushed him on the streets of Helena.[12]

Hindman was a fire-eater during the secession crisis, eagerly urging Arkansas on toward disunion, consulting with the governor about whether to attack the Federal arsenal at Little Rock, and writing the Confederate secretary of war to offer the services of Arkansas troops for the Confederacy even before that state was officially incorporated into the slaveholders' republic. When Arkansas's convention finally passed an ordinance of secession, it was Hindman who first excitedly telegraphed the fact to Jefferson Davis. On the outbreak of war, he raised a regiment, the Second Arkansas Infantry, and was commissioned as its colonel. Hindman hoped for assignment to Virginia, where the prospects for early and dramatic action seemed best, but his orders kept him and his regiment in Arkansas for the time being.[13]

That September new orders promoted Hindman to brigadier general and transferred him to Kentucky and the army of Albert Sidney Johnston. During the winter of 1861–62, he led his brigade aggressively in several small engagements, winning the praise of his immediate commander, Major General William J. Hardee. General Hardee "hail[ed] the brilliant courage shown in the affair as a bright augury of [Hindman's] valor when the actual hour comes for striking a decisive blow." As neither Hardee nor Hindman could know, that hour was to come on September 10, 1863.[14]

Hindman's first experience in a major battle of the Civil War came in the April 6, 1862, battle of Shiloh, where he aggressively pressed his command forward, leading by example and repeatedly personally leading desperate charges on Union positions. His aggressiveness was striking. With a Union battery dominating an open field and stemming the tide of Confederate advance, Hindman ordered a charge. Informed by the commander of the Seventh Arkansas that that regiment was almost out of ammunition, Hindman replied, "You have your bayonets." After the battle, General Hardee had high praise for Hindman., and Braxton Bragg himself noticed him "ardently pressing forward and engaging the enemy at every point" and showing "a heroism rarely equaled," while General P. G. T. Beauregard wrote in his report of the battle that Hindman "was conspicuous for a cool courage, efficiently employed in leading his men ever in the thickest of the fray, until his horse was shot under him and he was unfortunately so severely injured by the fall" as to be put out of action for the remainder of the battle.[15]

Hindman soon recovered from his injuries and in recognition of his fine performance at Shiloh was promoted on April 18, 1862, to the rank of major general. He briefly commanded a division in the Confederate Army of the Mississippi during the Corinth campaign. Shortly before the fall of Corinth, Beauregard on May 26, 1862, ordered Hindman to take over command of the defense of Arkansas "at the earnest solicitation of the people" of that state. In his order Beauregard expressed his high regard for Hindman's services and his regret at parting with so valuable an officer. He also noted that Hindman was fully authorized, under the terms of a recent act of the Confederate Congress, to raise and organize troops in Arkansas. The very next day, Major General Earl Van Dorn, commanding the entire Confederate Trans-Mississippi Department, turned over that command to Hindman— Van Dorn's having personally led most of the department's troops to join Beauregard in Mississippi. With that, Hindman found himself in command of a department of vast geographic extent but almost devoid of troops and with only a scant amount of equipment, most of it unserviceable.[16] With his customary aggressiveness, Hindman plunged at once into the duties of his new command. "I have come here," he assured the soldiers and civilians of his department in an address he issued upon taking command, "to drive out the invader or to perish in the attempt," and he exhorted them all to show similar devotion. To the authorities in Richmond, he wrote, "The only limit to the force I can put in the field will be the amount of money and the quantity of arms, ammunition" that Richmond could provide. He knew where to get the men. With that he launched the most ruthless application of the Confederate conscription act that the war would ever see, amounting at times to wholesale use of the press gang to round up hapless farmers and herd them into the ranks, and when Richmond could not provide the requisite weapons, Hindman set out to acquire them locally from private citizens, buying the firearms when he could, seizing them when necessary. To the amazement of Confederate leaders who believed the trans-Mississippi had been stripped of almost all war-making potential, Hindman had soon raised a relatively substantial army. If only he could get enough arms, he wrote to Richmond, he believed hè could "drive the enemy from this State before August."[17]

As he was rigorous toward his fellow Confederates so Hindman was relentlessly aggressive toward the Federals. In a June report to Richmond, he proudly claimed that he had been "constantly attacking [the Union army] in front and flanks and threatening [it] in rear," forcing the Federals to fall back forty miles from the line they held when Hindman had taken command. This might have been somewhat of an exaggeration, but the young lawyer turned general was clearly eager to take the war to the enemy.[18]

Hindman's ruthlessness in taking every right that Confederate law allowed—as well as some that it did not—in order to build up his force naturally made him a number of enemies. Albert Pike, commanding Confederate forces in the neighboring Indian Territory, complained incessantly of Hindman's appropriation of men and materiel for Arkansas that Pike thought should have been left to him for the defense of the Indian Territory. Others also appealed to Richmond to rein in Hindman. Jefferson Davis was, in any case, little inclined to leave in command of a large department a general who did not have professional military training or long-term experience in the peacetime regular army. In the late summer of 1862, Davis therefore ordered the aged and somewhat decrepit—but nonetheless professional and thoroughly "Old Army"—Major General Theophilus H. Holmes to assume overall command of the Trans-Mississippi Department, retaining Hindman as commander of the department's field army in Arkansas.[19]

Late that fall Hindman correctly perceived that the Union forces opposing him in northwestern Arkansas were in a vulnerable position. One segment of the Union Army of the Frontier, under the immediate command of Brigadier General Francis J. Herron, was in Springfield, Missouri, while the other segment, commanded by Herron's superior, Brigadier General James G. Blunt, had pushed into Arkansas. Hindman decided to strike Blunt's isolated force before Herron could come to its aid. Hindman marched out of Fort Smith with eleven thousand men on December 3, bent on destroying Blunt. The cagey Federal perceived the danger and sent an urgent summons to Herron to march to his support. By December 6 Hindman had discovered Herron's approach and decided to slip around Blunt and attack Herron before he could join the other Union force. The Confederates marched through the night, and by the morning of December 7 were approaching Herron's column, which by hard marching had already reached Fayetteville. With Herron approaching in front and Blunt's force still somewhere to the rear, Hindman, for the first time in the war and, one is tempted to say, perhaps for the first time in his life, took the less aggressive of two courses open to him and chose to place his army in a defensive position near Prairie Grove to await Herron's attack.[20]

Throughout the morning, Herron's superior artillery pounded the Confederate position, silencing most of Hindman's guns. Then in the afternoon Herron followed up with an infantry attack, which Hindman's men handily repulsed. Hindman answered with an assault of his own, equally futile and bloody. Hindman's second assault came to grief when Blunt arrived, piling into the Confederate flank and driving back the Rebel assault. Nightfall found Hindman's army still holding the position it occupied that morning, but the Confederate outlook was not good. The army was battered and demoralized and low on ammunition and food. Worse, Blunt could receive reinforcements while Hindman could hope for none. Under cover of darkness he pulled his troops off the battlefield and retreated to Van Buren, Arkansas. Before the month was out, the Federals had chased him out of that position as well.[21]

The Battle of Prairie Grove all but wrecked Hindman's army. Casualties on the battlefield had come to more than thirteen hundred men, or about 12 percent of the force with which he had advanced from Fort Smith, but the real losses came in the days that followed, as Hindman's demoralized conscripts, who from the outset had been less than enthusiastic about the cause and military service, reacted to a brutal campaign through the Boston Mountains on the edge of winter by deserting in droves. In the weeks and months that followed, Confederate fortunes in Arkansas steadily waned.

And the Confederate debacle at Prairie Grove may have been unnecessary. Even the combined forces of Blunt and Herron numbered scarcely more than nine thousand men, two thousand less than Hindman's command. Throughout the morning of December 7, Hindman had enjoyed almost three-to-one superiority in numbers over Herron, yet he had sat passively and allowed the Federals to make use of the one arm in which they were superior, their artillery. By the time he was prepared to act aggressively, most of the advantage he had gained by rapid maneuver was gone, as Blunt had arrived on the scene.[22]

In response to Bragg's oral and written orders at Lee and Gordon's Mill on the evening of September 9, 1863, Hindman initially showed the aggressiveness and efficiency that had characterized most of his career. He marched his division out of its camps between 1:00 and 2:00 A.M., and by daylight he had covered ten miles and reached Morgan's farm, three miles short of his specified destination at Davis's Crossroads. There he halted because he had not received any communication from Hill, and he was still waiting at Morgan's farm when Buckner joined him around five o'clock on the afternoon of September 10.[23]

It was at about that time that Bragg decided to move his headquarters to La Fayette, hoping to "secure more prompt and decided action" from Hill. Certainly some drastic step was needed in order to get service out of Hill. Bragg found that Cleburne was not sick nor had he been any time lately. The division commander reported himself and his men ready for action and was amazed that Hill should have suggested otherwise. With Bragg on hand to give the order, Confederate troops went to work on the obstructions in Dug Gap and cleared them away between midnight and dawn of September 11. Hill's excuses had been lame at best, a reminder of the fact that Hill was present in the western theater chiefly because Robert E. Lee had found him badly lacking as a general in Virginia. Bragg swallowed his frustration with Hill and ordered the two divisions of Major General William H. T. Walker's corps to move up in support of Cleburne and be ready to follow his division through Dug Gap and into McLemore's Cove as soon as Hindman should get things rolling on the morning of September 11.[24]

Bragg confidently expected that Hindman would indeed attack that morning because he had renewed his orders for such an attack just a few hours before. When Hindman and Buckner's commands had joined late on the afternoon of September 10, Hindman had taken command of the combined force by virtue of his senior rank, but he had conferred with Buckner about what they ought to do next.

Unlike Hindman, who was a relatively recent transfer from the Trans-Mississippi Department, Buckner was a veteran of long service in the Army of Tennessee and had done his share to help it establish its record of losing every major battle it had fought. He was among the coterie of generals who consistently undermined Bragg's authority, thus producing failure for which they in turn blamed Bragg and worked harder than ever to undermine him. During the Tullahoma campaign the preceding June, Buckner had conspired with Leonidas Polk and William J. Hardee with a view to possibly removing Bragg from command and taking over the army themselves in what would have amounted to a mutiny. They stopped short of such a step when Bragg, who knew nothing of their sinister plans, acquiesced in their insistent urging that the army should retreat from Rosecrans's advancing Army of the Cumberland. Ever since he had played a key role in the fall of Fort Donelson during the first winter of the war, Buckner had consistently taken an overly pessimistic view of prospective operations, routinely predicting not only failure but a level of losses that would make the whole effort immoral.[25]

Though subordinate to Hindman, Buckner persuasively pressed on him his view of the planned advance into McLemore's Cove. In Buckner's rather predictable analysis, any such movement would be doomed from the outset, first because it had been ordered by Bragg, whom Buckner despised, and second on general principles. Hindman was in no frame of mind to resist Buckner's urging. Buckner, after all, was a professional soldier and an 1844 graduate of West Point. Besides, Hindman, by halting contrary to orders at Morgan's, had demonstrated that he was following the pattern he had shown at Prairie Grove, losing his aggressiveness when the responsibility of opening a major battle seemed to rest on his shoulders.

Hindman called a conference of all the general officers of the three divisions, and together they demonstrated the truth of the old aphorism that "councils of war don't fight." Their conclusion was that Crittenden's Twentieth Corps, advancing south out of Chattanooga, might somehow evade the force Bragg had posted to halt it and thus march up McLemore's Cove and trap them. Rumors of phantom Union forces hovering about unnerved them, and they concluded that they should not carry out the attack Bragg had ordered unless they were sure that Hill's troops would join them through Dug Gap.[26]

Reflecting Buckner's habitually pessimistic thinking and the conclusion of his recently convened council of timidity, Hindman wrote a message to Bragg suggesting "a change in the plan of operations," namely abandoning the entire operation in McLemore's Cove and turning the whole army to attack Crittenden somewhere north of Lee and Gordon's Mill.[27]

Buckner was so eager to support that course of action that he offered one of his own staff officers to carry it to the army commander. The officer reached Bragg in La Fayette some time after 11:30 P.M., September 10. Bragg weighed the suggestion contained in Hindman's dispatch and considered the intelligence available from the Confederate cavalry operating in front of Dug Gap. Everything served to confirm the vulnerability of the Union force in the cove and the desirability of proceeding according to his original plan. He so informed Buckner's staff officer and gave him a written order to carry back to Hindman. After noting that headquarters were now at La Fayette, Bragg's order stated, "Crittenden's corps is advancing on us from Chattanooga. A large force from the south has advanced within 7 miles of this. Polk is left at Anderson's to cover your rear. General Bragg orders you to attack and force your way through the enemy to this point at the earliest hour that you can see him in the morning. Cleburne will attack in front the moment your guns are heard." Bragg's point was clear: It was essential that Hindman should attack and complete the destruction of the Federals in McLemore's Cove as soon as possible.[28]

While Bragg and the staff officer were on the move to and from La Fayette that evening, some of the Union actors in the drama were also afoot. The division of Brigadier General Absalom Baird, next in Thomas's Fourteenth

Corps column behind Negley, labored hard all day September 10 marching over Lookout Mountain, and at nine or ten o'clock that night, General Baird, along with advance elements of his division, finally went into camp at the eastern foot of the mountain, just below Stevens' Gap, in McLemore's Cove.[29]

Simultaneous with Baird's march over the mountain, Negley had spent September 10 advancing farther east across the cove, finally halting at Davis's Crossroads, almost at the foot of Pigeon Mountain and directly below, but unaware of, Cleburne's position at Dug Gap. Negley might not have known the full gravity of his situation, but he was aware that his men had skirmished with Confederate cavalry all the way across McLemore's Cove and that they were now facing a heavy skirmish line that seemed unwilling to yield any more ground. He had also learned from Unionist civilians of the presence of a large Confederate force—Hindman's—three miles farther down the cove on his left. Indeed, Negley's information was remarkably accurate. He believed he was threatened in front by three divisions of Hill's corps (in fact, it was one division of Hill's and two of Walker's) and on his left by two division's of Buckner's corps (Hindman's division was also present, and of course Hindman was in command). With growing concern for the safety of his division, Negley sent a dispatch urging Baird to move up and support him. Meanwhile, he dispatched a single regiment—all he could spare—to watch Hindman's approach and, somewhat optimistically, in hopes that it might persuade the Rebel commander that Negley was about to attack.[30]

Baird received Negley's dispatch upon his arrival at the eastern foot of Lookout Mountain late that evening with seven regiments and two batteries of his division, numbering about twenty-eight hundred men in all. He too had heard from local civilians of the presence of a large Confederate force down the valley, and he responded to Negley's message with one of his own, suggesting that it might be better for Negley to fall back on his position but offering to march at 3 A.M. to join him if Negley thought that advisable. Back from Negley later that night came a courier with a message urging Baird to move up as soon as possible. So as promised, Baird marched at three o'clock and joined Negley at Davis's Crossroads at about eight.[31]

Baird's arrival may have eased Negley's previously growing state of nervous anxiety, but it did little to change the overall balance of power in McLemore's Cove. The one and a half Union divisions at Davis's Crossroads were threatened by Hindman's three Confederate divisions moving up the valley toward their left and the three additional Confederate divisions under Bragg's immediate command in front of them at Dug Gap. Against the overwhelming Confederate advantages of numbers and position, Baird's addition to Negley's numbers merely increased the number of prisoners Bragg could reasonably expect to take after crushing Union resistance in the cove.

On the morning of September 11, while Baird marched across the cove to join Negley, Bragg took his station with Cleburne's division so as to make sure that no strange mood of General Hill's interfered with Cleburne's prompt advance as soon as Hindman's guns sounded in the cove. Dawn came, and there was silence from the valley west of Pigeon Mountain. Minutes passed, then hours, in what Bragg later reported was "great anxiety." Staff officers waiting with the Confederate commander wrote of Bragg's dismounting and pacing back and forth in impatience, digging his spurs into the ground and smiting the air with his fist. Of more practical utility, he dispatched at various times during the morning "several couriers and two staff officers," all charged with urging Hindman "to move with promptness and vigor."[32]

Meanwhile down in McLemore's Cove, Hindman at 4:20 that morning had received Bragg's urgent message of the previous evening, ordering him to advance and attack the Federals at first light and assuring him that Hill's troops—Cleburne's division—would indeed be joining the fight as soon as Hindman's troops opened it. Incredibly, Hindman later claimed that he had interpreted Bragg's dispatch as indicating "that the general commanding considered my position a perilous one, and therefore expected me not to capture the enemy, but to prevent the capture of my own troops, forcing my way through to La Fayette, and thus saving my command and enabling him to resist the forces that seemed about to envelop him."[33] Such an interpretation of Bragg's dispatch can only indicate an absolutely stunning lack of knowledge and understanding of the operational situation in northwest Georgia at the time.

By 6:30 A.M., Hindman had received word from Hill that the obstructions were clear in Dug Gap and that Hill was prepared to cooperate with Hindman's attack. Hindman later reported that his command had moved out at seven o'clock—about ten minutes before sunrise—but if so, it must have proceeded at a snail's pace. Hindman accounted for the slow pace by explaining that "frequent reconnaissances were necessary, consuming considerable time," in order to determine the enemy's strength, despite Union strength in McLemore's Cove having been determined and reported to him before he left his camps back at Lee and Gordon's Mill. Hindman's scouts did discover Baird's arrival, and the Confederate general grew more apprehensive.[34]

By 11:10 A.M. Hindman's Confederate column had spent far more time halted than marching and had advanced no more than a mile and a half toward Davis's Crossroads. There the Confederates encountered the single regiment Negley had sent out in the forlorn hope of detaining them. The Union commander could hardly have imagined how successful his move would be. Believing, as Negley had hoped, that the few hundred men in front of him were skirmishers for a much larger force, Hindman halted and deployed his eighteen thousand men. Fearing for the safety of his communications with La Fayette, he deployed Buckner's two divisions to the left of the road, then put his own division, now commanded by Brigadier General Patton Anderson, still farther to the left. Then thinking better of that deployment, he shifted Anderson to the right of the line. All this took time in the densely wooded countryside.[35]

Then, according to Hindman's story, he received a dispatch from Bragg, through his chief of staff, reading, "If you find the enemy in such force as to make an attack imprudent, fall back at once on La Fayette by Catlett's Gap, from which obstructions have now been removed. Send your determination at once and act as promptly." No record of this dispatch exists outside of Hindman's report, and veracity was not necessarily his strongest attribute. If Bragg did indeed send the message, it was probably in response to Hindman's repeated indications that he had found in McLemore's Cove a force much larger than previous reconnaissance had indicated. In fact, Hindman enjoyed a three-and-a-half-to-one advantage in numbers over Negley and roughly two-and-a-half-to-one over the combined forces of Negley and Baird. Hindman claimed that he responded to the dispatch with one of his own, stating that he would need more time to decide what to do.[36]

About an hour later, according to Hindman's report, he received another dispatch from Bragg's chief of staff, also unaccounted for in any other record of the battle. This one, Hindman claimed, asserted that the enemy was threatening Dug Gap with twelve to fifteen thousand men and urged communication and rapid decision. Though no other copy of this dispatch has been preserved, it is possible that Bragg and his staff might have estimated the combined force of Negley and Baird at that number. It was an exaggeration by almost a factor of two, but such inadvertent exaggeration of enemy numbers was extremely common in the Civil War. In any case, each of the Confederate columns, Hindman's in the cove and Bragg's at the gap, outnumbered even the exaggerated strength attributed to the Union force in McLemore's Cove.[37]

Hindman, however, assumed that the twelve to fifteen thousand troops in front of Dug Gap were in addition to the troops with which he was contending—in fact a single regiment but in his imagination many thousands of men—who were also in front of Dug Gap. He responded by ordering an immediate retreat. Before his troops could begin the retreat, his scouts brought him word that the Federals themselves were retiring toward Stevens' Gap.

Negley had finally grasped the magnitude of his danger and had ordered his and Baird's divisions to fall back. The Federals conducted their retreat skillfully, and though Hindman followed them and some skirmishing took place, he was not able to do them any significant damage before they escaped back onto Lookout Mountain.[38]

The sound of Hindman's skirmishing with Negley's rearguard brought Bragg, along with Cleburne's division, down from Dug Gap. Bragg and Hindman met at Davis's Crossroads, and, now that all chance of a victory in McLemore's Cove had vanished, Bragg ordered the army to withdraw to La Fayette. During the past three days, Bragg, Hindman, Buckner, and Hill had combined to lose an opportunity such as, in the words of one Confederate officer, "comes to most generals only in their dreams."[39]

The failure of the Confederate Army of Tennessee to trap and destroy one and a half Union divisions in McLemore's Cove between September 9 and 11, 1863, seems, on its face, to be one of the most inexplicable missed opportunities of the Civil War. Examined in detail, the event remains a missed opportunity but is much more explicable. Four reasons stand out.

One reason was the skill and alertness of the Union commanders and their troops. Negley was to be tried and found wanting at the battle of Chickamauga nine days after the conclusion of the stand-off in McLemore's Cove, but his caution and attention to careful reconnaissance during his division's foray into the cove were important factors in detecting and evading the trap Bragg had set for him. If his foes were unable to spring the trap successfully, it was at least partially because he gave them minimum chance to do so. Union leadership in the western armies tended, with a few exceptions, to be consistently competent. If the Confederates were going to wrest a victory from their foes in the nation's heartland, they were going to have to earn every bit of it, and they could afford few if any mistakes.

A second reason for the failure to trap Negley and Baird lay in the Union allegiance of many local residents. Despite that fact that the campaign was being waged in the Deep South state of Georgia, it was nevertheless being fought among a populace that was at least as likely to be Unionist as it was to be Secessionist. Unionist civilians gave timely and remarkably accurate information to both Negley and Baird regarding the location and strength of Hindman's column, and this was an important aid to the Union generals in dodging Bragg's intended ambush. That this was so was not Bragg's doing but a fact of life for the Confederacy and its cause. Erecting an independent slaveholders' republic simply never commanded anything like unanimous support among southern whites, at least until it had been defeated and the specter of racial equality loomed in the form of Reconstruction.

Despite the difficulties posed by the quality of Union troops and their leaders and the opposition of its own citizens, the Confederate army suffered even more significantly from problems of its own manufacture. One key reason for the failure was Thomas C. Hindman's personality and his ability as a general. Hindman was inconsistent, prone to constant, rash aggressiveness most of the time, but, as had appeared at Prairie Grove, he showed a propensity to choke under pressure and become timid when the whole weight of responsibility for a battle rested on him. As he had done in Arkansas, Hindman reacted to that kind of pressure in McLemore's Cove by halting and assuming a passive posture toward the enemy. Bragg had no choice but to try to work with the generals Jefferson Davis gave him, and though Davis could undoubtedly have done better (especially if armed with the modern historian's advantage of hindsight), the fact remains that the Confederacy did not have and could not have obtained as many good generals as it needed.

The final reason, and perhaps the most effective and most avoidable of them all, was the culture that prevailed among the general officers of the Army of Tennessee. Bragg's weakness as a general was his inability to motivate and win the cooperation of difficult generals, but even Robert E. Lee wrote that he doubted he could gain the cordial cooperation of the western generals if he were transferred to that theater. The bitterness, backstabbing, cross-purposes, and mistrust among the Army of Tennessee's generals became the greatest handicap of that long-suffering Confederate host. Davis bore considerable responsibility for the mess. He steadfastly supported his old crony Leonidas Polk, a corps commander in the Army of Tennessee, who was militarily incompetent, smoothly persuasive, and filled with jealousy and resentment of Bragg's authority. His influence within the army's officer corps was the original wellspring of its perennial discontents. Others joined him, sometimes as a cloak for the own failures, sometimes, in the case of several Kentuckians, out of spite for the fact that their home state had chosen the Union and Bragg could not change it, and sometimes under the influence of more senior generals, like Polk and William J. Hardee, who constantly undermined Bragg with criticism.

The result in McLemore's Cove was the distrust that led Hindman, Buckner, and their subordinate generals to dismiss Bragg's accurate assessment of the situation and correct orders and instead draw back from what might well have been the opening phase of a truly decisive victory.

Notes

1. U.S. War Department, *The War of the Rebellion: Official Records of the Union and Confederate Armies*, 70 vols., 128 pts. (Washington, D.C.: Government Printing Office, 1881–1901), vol. 30, pt. 1: 52, 398, 439, 497, 578–79, 602 (hereinafter *OR*; except

as otherwise noted, all references are to Series 1); Peter Cozzens, *This Terrible Sound: The Battle of Chickamauga* (Urbana: University of Illinois Press, 1992), 45.

2. *OR*, vol. 30, pt. 2: 27.

3. Ibid.; Judith Lee Hallock, *Braxton Bragg and Confederate Defeat* (Tuscaloosa: University of Alabama Press, 1991), 54; Thomas Lawrence Connelly, *Autumn of Glory: The Army of Tennessee, 1862–1865* (Baton Rouge: Louisiana State University Press, 1971), 174–75.

4. *OR*, vol. 30, pt. 2: 27.

5. *OR*, vol. 30, pt. 1: 53.

6. Ibid., 326.

7. *OR*, vol. 30, pt. 2: 27–28; Connelly, *Autumn of Glory*, 175.

8. *OR*, vol. 30, pt. 2: 28.

9. Ibid.

10. Ibid.

11. Ibid., 29.

12. Howell Purdue and Elizabeth Purdue, *Pat Cleburne, Confederate General: A Biography* (Tuscaloosa: Portals Press, 1972), 31–32.

13. *OR*, vol. 1: 683–84, 690; vol. 3: 587–88, 592, 690.

14. *OR*, vol. 4: 481; vol. 7: 2–3, 19–21.

15. *OR*, vol. 10, pt. 1: 389–90, 403, 423, 427, 465, 569, 574, 578, 591.

16. *OR*, vol. 10, pt. 2: 510, 547; vol. 13: 829.

17. *OR*, vol. 13: 830, 832–33, 835.

18. Ibid., 836.

19. Ibid., 876, 884–85; *OR*, vol. 52, pt. 2: 596.

20. *OR*, vol. 22, pt. 1: 73, 138–42.

21. Ibid., 101, 138–42.

22. Ibid., 76–77, 138–39.

23. *OR*, vol. 30, pt. 2: 28–29, 292–93.

24. Glenn Tucker, *Chickamauga: Bloody Battle in the West* (Indianapolis: Bobbs-Merrill, 1961), 69; *OR* , vol. 30, pt. 2: 138.

25. Steven E. Woodworth, *Six Armies in Tennessee: The Chickamauga and Chattanooga Campaigns* (Lincoln: University of Nebraska Press, 1998), 41.

26. *OR*, vol. 30, pt. 2: 293–94.

27. Ibid., 294.

28. Ibid., 29, 294–95.

29. Ibid., 270–71.

30. Ibid., 270–71, 326.

31. Ibid., 270–71.

32. Ibid., 29–30; Tucker, *Chickamauga*, 67–68.

33. *OR*, vol. 30, pt. 2: 295.

34. Ibid., 295.

35. Ibid., 295–96.

36. Ibid., 296.

37. Ibid.

38. Ibid., 296–97.

39. Ibid., 30–31, 297; William J. Wood, *Civil War Generalship: The Art of Command* (Westport, Conn.: Greenwood, 1997), 133; William Weir, *Fatal Victories* (New York: Pegasus Books, 1993), 144.

3

THE CENSURE OF D. H. HILL
DANIEL HARVEY HILL AND THE
CHICKAMAUGA CAMPAIGN

Alexander Mendoza

O n July 13, 1863, as Maj. Gen. Daniel Harvey Hill evaluated the effects of the Confederacy's summer campaigns from his headquarters east of Richmond, Virginia, he focused his attention on a group of riders galloping from the direction of the Confederate capital. Dressed in a plain gray suit, President Jefferson Davis led the entourage. Davis dismounted, congratulated Hill on his recent defense of Richmond, and explained the reason for his unexpected visit to the general's camp. "Rosecrans is about to advance upon Bragg," Davis explained. "I have found it necessary to detail Hardee to defend Mississippi and Alabama. His corps is without a commander. I wish you to command it." "I cannot do that," Hill pointed out, "as General Stewart ranks me." "I can cure that by making you a lieutenant general," answered Davis. "Your papers will be ready tomorrow. When can you start?" "In twenty-four hours," replied Hill.[1] The next day, as Hill and his staff prepared for their westward journey, he received formal instructions from the war department, ordering him to report to Gen. Braxton Bragg at Chattanooga, for duty as a corps commander in the Army of Tennessee.[2] Although Hill was highly touted as a courageous soldier who would not hesitate to follow orders, it is likely that if he could have foreseen the ramifications of serving under Bragg, which included his relief from command after the Chickamauga campaign and Davis's refusal to nominate him to the Confederate Senate at the grade to which he had appointed him, he most certainly would have paused before accepting the Confederate president's proposal that July.

Born in South Carolina on July 12, 1821, Hill graduated from West Point in 1842, and later served in the Mexican War, where he earned two brevets for gallantry. Resigning from the army in 1849, Hill taught mathematics at Washington College from 1849 to 1854 and Davidson College from 1854 to

1859. Immediately prior to the war, Hill was superintendent of the North Carolina Military Institute. He joined the Confederate army as colonel of the First North Carolina Infantry and rose to the rank of brigadier general on July 10, 1861. He earned promotion to major general on March 26, 1862, and fought under Gen. Joseph E. Johnston in the Battle of Seven Pines and under Gen. Robert E. Lee in the Seven Days Battles and the Battle of Antietam. Although Hill had earned a reputation for valor under fire, he suffered from chronic spinal pain and dyspepsia, two conditions that did nothing to assuage his vituperative and sarcastic nature. In addition, Hill was a devout Presbyterian, like his brother-in-law, Lt. Gen. Thomas J. "Stonewall" Jackson. His abrasive personality did not endear him to Lee, who disapproved of Hill's sharp tongue. After the Antietam campaign, Lee recommended Hill's transfer from the Army of Northern Virginia to command the District of North Carolina.[3] Hill realized his shortcomings. "I had always a strong perception of right and wrong," he claimed, "and when corrected from petulance or passion, I brooded over it, did not forget, and I am afraid did not forgive it."[4] Nevertheless, when Hill arrived in the Tennessee theater on July 19, he assumed command of a corps consisting of the divisions of Maj. Gen. Patrick Cleburne and Maj. Gen. John J. Breckinridge.[5]

When Hill first met Bragg, his thoughts shifted back to his service in the Mexican War, when he served under his fellow North Carolinian. Although Hill looked forward to serving under his old captain, his hopes were dashed upon meeting with Bragg. "My interview at Chattanooga was not satisfactory," Hill later wrote. "He was silent and reserved and seemed gloomy and despondent. He had grown prematurely old since I saw him last, and showed much nervousness."[6] Bragg, an 1838 graduate of West Point, had endured a discordant relationship with his subordinate officers since taking command of the Confederacy's western army after the fall of Corinth. The failure of Bragg's invasion of Kentucky in the fall of 1862 and his subsequent retreat after the Battle of Stones River, December 31, 1862, to January 2, 1863, led to open dissatisfaction among Bragg's senior officers.[7] Despite the large rift between him and his senior lieutenants, Bragg remained in command of the Army of Tennessee.[8]

Shortly before Hill reached Bragg, the Army of Tennessee had retreated to Chattanooga on July 4, the day Pemberton surrendered at Vicksburg and the day after Lee began his retreat from Gettysburg. Following those losses, the authorities in Richmond again focused on events in Tennessee. In addition to Hill's promotion to corps command in Bragg's army, the war department ordered 9,000 troops under Maj. Gen. Breckinridge and Maj. Gen. William H. T. Walker, stationed in Mississippi, to report to Tennessee. Moreover,

Davis directed Maj. Gen. Thomas Hindman to replace Maj. Gen. Jones M. Withers as commander of a division in Lt. Gen. Leonidas Polk's corps. A month later, Davis further reinforced Bragg by ordering Maj. Gen. Simon Buckner, commanding the Department of East Tennessee, to lead another corps in the Army of Tennessee. Although Davis's decision to reinforce Bragg appeared logical, his choice of replacements suggests a naiveté about the condition of the Tennessee army. Without regard to the persistent discord between Bragg and his corps commanders, the personnel he transferred to Tennessee insured continued conflict and a lack of cooperation.[9]

Upon his arrival in the west, Hill met and was influenced by Bragg's dissatisfied lieutenants. Led by Polk, who still chafed after last fall's failed invasion of Kentucky, the senior officers disliked Bragg for an assortment of reasons, but rallied under the premise that he was incompetent to command the Confederacy's foremost western army.[10] Buckner detested his demotion from independent command in Knoxville and thus held Bragg in contempt. Breckinridge, on the other hand, disliked Bragg because he had criticized his fellow Kentuckians during the 1862 Perryville campaign. Hindman and Walker were loyal supporters of Gen. Johnston and were thus prejudiced against Bragg, the man they believed kept Johnston from obtaining an active field command. Moreover, with the portending addition of Lt. Gen. James Longstreet, a vocal critic of Bragg and a loyal supporter of Johnston, the Army of Tennessee would have all its corps commanders prejudiced against its commander. Yet Hill's gloomy fatalism and uninhibited criticisms of his commanding officer would make him conspicuous among the Army of Tennessee's senior officers. Despite Davis's best intentions, his reorganization and reinforcement of the Army of Tennessee failed to unify its volatile command structure.[11]

Previous to Hill's arrival, Union Maj. Gen. William S. Rosecrans's Army of the Cumberland had skillfully maneuvered Bragg's army out of its base near Tullahoma, Tennessee, and sent it more than eighty miles southward, without fighting a major battle.[12] The loss of middle Tennessee only exacerbated the general discontent in the Confederate high command. As historian Steven E. Woodworth has noted, the ranks of the Army of Tennessee's high command were comprised of "misfits and malcontents" who had been thrust upon Bragg for a number of reasons, ranging from politics to cronyism. Consequently, the Confederacy's foremost western army remained a toxic environment with senior officers working at cross-purposes.[13]

In the midst of the Army of Tennessee's reorganization, in early September, Rosecrans advanced toward the Confederates in Chattanooga using the same flanking movements that had successfully maneuvered Bragg out of middle Tennessee. The strategy worked. On September 8, the Army of Tennessee abandoned Chattanooga and retreated toward La Fayette, Georgia, twenty miles south of the city, near Chickamauga Creek, unsure as to the Federals' intentions. The area near La Fayette where they bivouacked lay about twenty-five miles southeast of the Tennessee River via Shellmound, Tennessee. Four mountain ridges running southwest to northeast shielded Bragg's army from the Federals' area of concentration between Shellmound and Bridgeport, Alabama, along the Nashville and Tennessee Railroad. Sand and Raccoon Mountains stood closest to the river. Lookout Mountain, more than a thousand feet high in places, lay to the east of Sand Mountain. About ten miles farther east of Lookout Mountain stands a spur, Pigeon Mountain. In between the two ranges rests Missionary Ridge. Only a few roads and gaps provided direct access from Lookout Valley to the area near La Fayette. And while Confederate cavalry was supposed to screen and block the gaps from the enemy, the mountain gaps further confounded Bragg's uncertainty as to the Federals' intentions. "A mountain is like the wall of a house full of rat-holes," Bragg later wrote. "The rat lies hidden at his hole, ready to pop out when no one is watching."[14]

Unbeknownst to Bragg, the Union army continued to press forward on three separate fronts after reaching the south bank of the Tennessee. Due to the nature of the mountainous terrain, Rosecrans determined it was best to divide his army through the narrow roads and passes that marked the vicinity south of Chattanooga. The three-pronged advance had Maj. Gen. Thomas L. Crittenden's Twenty-first Corps marching eastward toward Chattanooga through the gap between Sand and Raccoon Mountains; Maj. Gen. George Thomas's Fourteenth Corps advancing toward Lookout Valley via Stevens' Gap on Sand Mountain, about twenty-four miles south of Crittenden; and Maj. Gen. Alexander McCook's Twentieth Corps advancing toward Alpine, Georgia through the gaps on Sand and Lookout Mountain even farther to the south.[15] Bragg was worried that he would be trapped on the road from Chattanooga to La Fayette. Various reports warned him that the Federals were advancing toward the Army of Tennessee from the west. Finally, by the evening of September 9, Bragg began to get a picture of the Yankee movements. The commanding general had received reports that the Federals had bivouacked in McLemore's Cove, a heavily forested area between Lookout and Pigeon Mountains, to the northwest of La Fayette. The lead division of Thomas's force, Maj. Gen. James S. Negley's division of approximately 5,000 men, had reached McLemore's Cove through Stevens' Gap on Lookout Mountain. The Federals were thus less than ten miles from the Confederate concentration at La Fayette, via Dug Gap in Pigeon Mountain, and in a vulnerable position close to the Rebel army. Moreover, thanks to some well-coached Confederate deserters, the Federals were unaware that Bragg's army had stopped its retreat and was now ready to face the Union advance. It seemed that Bragg now had the opportunity to ensnare Negley's division.[16]

Bragg hoped to concentrate a superior force on the isolated Union force and annihilate it. To this end, the commanding general summoned Hindman to his headquarters on the evening of September 9 and outlined his plan to entrap the portion of Thomas's force in McLemore's Cove, a natural cul-de-sac. Bragg directed Hindman to cross Pigeon Mountain through Worthen's Gap, enter the northern end of the cove, before moving south until he reached Davis's Crossroads, where the road between Stevens' and Dug Gaps intersects with the north-south road running through the cove. Meanwhile, Maj. Gen. Patrick Cleburne's division of Hill's Corps would march across Pigeon Mountain through Dug Gap and meet with Hindman at the crossroads. Upon converging, General Hindman would assume command of the Confederate force and strike the Federal army. At midnight a written copy of Hindman's instructions was sent to Hill, who was further directed either to send Cleburne or take command of the attack column himself. The double envelopment, if successful, would thus put Rosecrans at a severe disadvantage as he maneuvered toward Bragg's army.[17]

Bragg's tactical dispositions were sound. Hindman was a mere dozen miles from McLemore's Cove from his headquarters at Lee and Gordon's Mill near Chickamauga Creek. Cleburne's division, on the other hand, was just seven miles across Dug Gap from Davis's Crossroads. It was thus feasible for both forces to converge at the designated time, the morning of the tenth. Yet in the Army of Tennessee nothing was as easy as it appeared. For one thing, Bragg's instructions, while reasonable, were too imprecise for the men under his command. Bragg's written orders failed to provide a specific hour outlining the march, they did not include particular directions for Hindman to communicate with Hill prior to the arrival at Davis's Crossroads, and they contained no additional instructions as to how to deal with a reported Federal force near Cooper's Gap, on Hindman's right-rear. The discretionary orders thus constituted a critical failure, for the culture of the Army of Tennessee demanded precision. As the historian of the Tennessee army, Thomas Lawrence Connelly, noted, "Bragg's tendency to blame subordinates for failures had already created a reluctance in the high command to take initiative without specific instructions from the commanding general."[18]

It did not take long before Bragg's lieutenants began to unravel the commanding general's plans. Shortly after 1 A.M. on the tenth, Hindman's force advanced toward its objective, marching nine miles in five hours. But at 6

A.M., they were still four miles shy of Davis's Crossroads. Since Hindman had not heard from Hill, he halted at Morgan's House along the Cove Road and ordered pickets to probe southward, toward the crossroads, and to his right, along Lookout Mountain.[19]

Hill, on the other hand, had also found reasons to delay his march toward McLemore's Cove. In what would ultimately become a tragicomedy of errors involving Bragg's couriers failing to find Hill to deliver the commanding general's written orders, Hill did not receive a copy of the instructions until 4:30 A.M. By that point, he found it difficult to meet Hindman at Davis's Crossroads at the designated time for a number of reasons. Hill complained that Cleburne, who was supposed to lead the spearhead of the entire assault, had been bedridden with illness the previous day (a claim not supported by Cleburne himself); that the majority of his division was still spread out along the three gaps on Pigeon Mountain (Catlett's in the north, Dug in the center, and Bluebird in the south); and that Dug Gap was heavily obstructed by timber, preventing Hill's force from arriving at the rendezvous point in a few hours. Hill sent an additional note to Hindman informing the Arkansan of his failure to cooperate with him at the designated time. In his report, Hill pointed out that Bragg accepted his explanation for the delay and dispatched orders for Buckner to support Hindman. Buckner, whose force was stationed at Lee and Gordon's Mill, did not reach Hindman's position until 5 P.M. on the tenth. At that point, Hindman ordered Buckner to halt about a half mile north of his corps in order to hold the road through Worthen's Gap, along the northern end of Pigeon Mountain.[20]

Meanwhile, to the east, Hindman's 6 A.M. dispatch finally reached Hill at noon. Lamenting Hill's previous failure to communicate with him in regards to their joint assault on McLemore's Cove, Hindman pointed out that he would wait until Hill could verify the rumors of a Federal presence to his front as he advanced through Dug Gap. Hill, for his part, responded to Hindman at that time and finally started to move toward Dug Gap at around 1:30 P.M.[21] The delays of his subordinates likely worried Bragg, who also happened to be ill at the time. Reports continued to reach the commanding general of Federal movements to his front and rear. Bragg sent orders to Hindman urging him to move forward. The commanding general even ordered Polk, who was covering Hindman's rear at Lee and Gordon's Mill, to be prepared for a Union advance from Crittenden. Yet Hindman interpreted these instructions broadly, calling for a council of war and suspending further action. Hindman wrote Hill once more asking him if he could alter the plans to ensnare the Federals, even suggesting that they ignore the operation in McLemore's Cove altogether. Bragg's lieutenants had effectively ended the offensive movement for the tenth. If the Confederates had any chance to capture Thomas's isolated force, it would have to wait until the next day.[22]

Even though the assault on the tenth had failed, the opportunity to destroy Negley's division was still there the following day. On the evening of the tenth, as Bragg rode to investigate Hill's delays, he was approached by Hindman's messenger, Maj. James Nocquet. Nocquet relayed some of Hindman's apprehensions, namely that he suspected the Federal movements to the south were a ruse and that all operations towards McLemore's Cove should be suspended. Bragg was emphatic that the opportunity must not be wasted. He specifically notified Hindman through his emissary on the night of the tenth that "plans could not be changed" and that he was expected to "carry out his orders" and attack the Federals in McLemore's Cove the following morning. To emphasize the significance of the situation, Bragg followed up his verbal instructions with written orders a few hours later. Also, to support the coordinated assault, Bragg ordered additional troops to reinforce Cleburne. For his part, Cleburne had his division ready for the assault, one of his brigades having cleared the obstructions from Dug Gap during the night. Additional scouts were sent to the crest of Pigeon Mountain to notify Hill's force as to when Hindman launched his assault. If the assault came to fruition, the Confederates would pit more than 25,000 men against Negley's small force.[23]

Yet on the morning of the eleventh, as the lead elements of Cleburne's division made their way through Dug Gap and within half a mile of the crossroads to await Hindman's assault, there was no sound of gunfire, only silence. It was not until 7 A.M. that Hindman's force started moving southward toward the crossroads, still about four miles away. The reluctance Hindman had demonstrated to his commanding general regarding the planned assault was reflected in his operations that day, which were slow, hesitant, and halting. The sun was setting before Hindman ordered his men to attack, only to be checked by a single Federal volley. Later, the Confederates found the bulk of Negley's force gone. With darkness settling rapidly on McLemore's Cove, Hindman ordered his men to halt.[24]

Hill, on the other hand, ordered his men forward upon hearing the sound of musketry north of Davis's Crossroads. As he was prone to do in the Virginia theater, the corps commander personally led his men into action. Some stiff resistance from the Nineteenth Illinois halted Hill's advance as well. Within hours, Thomas's troops had retreated westward, toward Stevens' Gap on Lookout Mountain. The Confederate opportunity to strike was lost.[25]

While Thomas's force escaped near destruction at McLemore's Cove, Bragg had devised a plan to strike at Crittenden's Twenty-first Corps to the north on the twelfth. For his part, Rosecrans was still unaware of the gravity of his situation, instead lamenting that the Confederates had eluded capture. Bragg's plan consisted of Leonidas Polk's corps advancing against Crittenden with Hindman and Walker supporting. At nightfall, Bragg directed Polk to attack at dawn on the thirteenth. In a follow-up message, Bragg emphasized the need for swiftness. "Let no time be lost," he implored. Like Hindman before him, Polk balked at the opportunity to destroy the Federal contingent and hesitated. When Bragg arrived to reconnoiter the field of battle, he found that the Federal Twenty-first Corps had retreated to the west bank of Chickamauga Creek, near Lee and Gordon's Mill. Another opportunity was thus lost.[26] The Confederates had failed on two occasions to destroy Rosecrans's divided army, which had now maneuvered to protect its supply line in Chattanooga. Although Bragg had devised a sound strategy to defeat the divided Federal army, his subordinates failed to carry out his orders. Hill and Hindman played lead roles in the lost opportunities at McLemore's Cove. Hal Bridges, Hill's biographer, argued that Hill simply lost his initial reluctance to join in criticism of his commanding general from his fellow lieutenants. In effect, Hill joined the other disgruntled commanders of the Tennessee army, convinced that their commanding officer had issued discretionary orders and that anything Bragg recommended was certain to place the Army of Tennessee at risk. Dissatisfied with his senior officers, Bragg issued new orders to maneuver around the newly reconcentrated Federal army's left flank, hoping to force Rosecrans to retreat. Perhaps emboldened by the news that the lead elements of Longstreet's reinforcements from Virginia had begun to arrive on September 15, Bragg decided to concentrate his army near La Fayette, attempt to outflank the Union's left, and advance toward Chattanooga. This plan, if successful, would have forced Rosecrans to fall back to protect his line of supply. On the evening of the sixteenth, Bragg ordered an advance against the Federals, but then reversed himself the next day, issuing new orders to maneuver around the Union left the next morning.[27]

Although only one of the three divisions Longstreet brought from Virginia had arrived on the field of battle, Bragg issued orders to his subordinates to cross the Chickamauga and advance on the Federals on the nineteenth. Throughout the day, Hill's troops stood idle, but advanced half a mile by nighttime. "It was desultory fighting from right to left," Hill later wrote, "without concert, and at inopportune times."[28] That evening, as Longstreet arrived with the rest of his troops, Bragg reorganized his command, dividing his army into two wings: the right, or northern, wing would be commanded by Polk, and the left, or southern, wing by Longstreet, in deference to his rank. Hill, under the direction of Polk, would lead a daybreak assault on the twentieth with attacks launched in echelon, from right to left. If successful, the Confederates would drive the Federal army southward and away from Chattanooga. Bragg's restructuring of command in the midst of battle may have been correct procedure, given Longstreet's rank and prestige, but it grated at least one of Bragg's subordinates. Though Hill would still command the two divisions of his corps, he would now be reporting not directly to army headquarters but rather to Polk, who until that moment had been his fellow corps commander.[29]

The expected assault by Polk did not occur at the designated time. Given the responsibility of launching the echelon formation attack, Polk went to bed on the night of the nineteenth without giving Hill any instructions for the next morning's advance or even notice that such an advance was planned. Hill, for his part, made minimal effort to locate Bragg's headquarters for further details. Although he missed the commanding general, one of his staff officers received instructions for Hill to report to Polk, whose headquarters were nearby. For reasons unknown, Hill decided to rest until 3 A.M. before departing to find Polk. By the time Hill arrived, Polk's guides had left. Inexplicably, Hill simply returned to his headquarters, unaware that his troops were the spearhead of Polk's assault. Amid the reorganization of the Confederate army in the wake of Longstreet's arrival, Polk, as commander of the right wing, was responsible for guaranteeing that his units received proper orders for the assault the next day. Yet he neglected to ensure that Hill's troops stood ready to launch the attack. For his part, Hill failed to find the location of Polk's headquarters to inquire further instruction. Both generals neglected to execute Bragg's orders.[30]

Incensed to find that his planned daylight assault failed to materialize, Bragg set out to find Hill. The comedy of errors and misunderstandings that surrounded Hill and Polk delayed the opening of Confederate army's planned "day-dawn" attack until about 10:30 A.M.[31] Dissatisfied with the tardiness of his assault, Bragg ordered a general advance all along his lines. Under the pressure of repeated thrusts against the Union army's left, Rosecrans inadvertently created a gap in his line that allowed Longstreet's troops to pour through, causing the Union right flank to collapse. After repeated attacks from Polk's and Longstreet's wings, the Union force retreated toward Chattanooga, where it set up a formidable defense inside the city.

The Battle of Chickamauga cost the Army of Tennessee more than 18,000 casualties and ended a string of disheartening losses for Bragg's army. Although the Confederates routed a third of Rosecrans's army, no further pursuit or exploitation of the victory was possible. The Confederates suffered heavy casualties, their units remained in disarray, and they struggled with a lack of adequate transportation. Rosecrans's defeated Federals, on the other hand, had a clear line of retreat to Chattanooga. Hill and the other senior officers nevertheless criticized what they saw as Bragg's reluctance to pursue the defeated enemy, however, and stood ready to resume the offensive. Hill later claimed that on September 21 his "corps was ready to march or fight at dawn in the morning, with thinned rank, it is true, but with buoyant spirits."[32]

While Bragg blamed Chickamauga's lost opportunities on his corps commanders Polk, Hindman, and Hill, the Army of Tennessee's senior officers conspired against him. Dissatisfied with their previous failures, Bragg suspended Polk and Hindman on September 25 and ordered them to Atlanta to await further orders.[33] The following day, Hill, along with Generals Longstreet, Breckenridge, and Buckner met to discuss the "mismanagement manifested in the conduct of military operations in this army."[34] At the meeting, Hill and the other generals urged Longstreet to write the war department and request the removal of Bragg from command. While the anti-Bragg cabal maneuvered along mutinous lines, morale in the Army of Tennessee continued to decline. The suspension of Polk, a popular figure in the Confederate army, caused further insubordination in the high command. Bragg's attempt to order the bishop-general to Atlanta, apparently to suppress further rancor in his army, only escalated the discontent. On October 4, Longstreet, Hill, Buckner, and Breckenridge met a second time. Dissatisfied with conditions in the army and the removal of their fellow corps commanders, Hill and his fellow generals wrote a petition to be circulated among the ranking officers requesting Bragg's removal.

The October 4 letter to President Davis reiterated their earlier assertions that Bragg was incompetent. Declaring Bragg's health "totally unfits him for the command of an army in the field," the petitioners pointed out that the Federals gained strength while the Confederate army vacillated. Acknowledging their action might seem "unusual among military men," they claimed the condition of the Army of Tennessee compelled them to act.[35] Moving through Buckner's, Hill's, and finally, Longstreet's corps, the petition collected twelve signatures of corps, division, and brigade commanders. Wary of the effects of the circular letter on the army, Col. James Chesnut, Davis's envoy to the Army of Tennessee, wrote the president on October 5 and asked him to come to Tennessee.[36] Davis departed for Missionary Ridge, the site of Bragg's headquarters, on October 6, intent on eliminating the growing mutiny in the Tennessee army. Dismissing the reports of discontent as products of nervous anxiety, Davis remained unwavering in his support of Bragg. The president, in fact, planned to gather the army's senior officers and ask them personally to declare their allegiance in front of their commanding officer.

He felt that in the presence of Bragg and himself, the generals would have no choice but to comply. Davis had underestimated the near-mutiny in the Tennessee army's high command.

Arriving at Bragg's headquarters on October 9, Davis called a meeting with the corps commanders. Assembling in Bragg's office, the four corps leaders, Longstreet, Buckner, Hill, and Maj. Gen. Benjamin F. Cheatham (Polk's replacement) sat nervously. Davis, with Bragg present, spoke first, addressing the issue at hand, the conduct of the Chickamauga campaign. He asked Longstreet for an opinion, and after an initial hesitation, received an unflattering portrait of Bragg as a commanding officer. Longstreet's criticism of Bragg, however, paled in comparison to Hill's scathing assessment. "Hill had carefully taken a seat off in a corner of the room, apparently trying to be overlooked," Longstreet later wrote. "But when forced to speak, took his chair up and moved out almost to the centre of the circle" and offered his candid opinion of Bragg. Although Hill confessed to having admired Bragg when he first served under him during the Mexican-American War, he concluded "he was never so mistaken in his estimate of a man's character as a soldier."[37] Disappointed with the results of the meeting, Davis dismissed the generals and planned his next maneuver.

If Hill and the other dissident generals believed that their testimonies would influence Davis to remove Bragg, subsequent events proved otherwise. Davis remained adamant that Bragg maintain command of the Army of Tennessee. Determined to support his commanding general, the president resumed his inspection of the army and met separately with Longstreet and Buckner. The separate interviews elicited the same results, criticism of Bragg's leadership. In addition, Davis heard from Colonel Chesnut that the command of the Army of Tennessee should go to Joseph E. Johnston, a political adversary of the president.[38] Determined not to allow the command of the army to fall into the hands of Johnston, and disappointed with the conduct of Hill and Longstreet at the military conference, Davis increased his support of Bragg. Yet someone had to take the blame for the failures of the Chickamauga campaign. On October 11, Davis authorized Bragg to remove any officer who failed to cooperate with him. Thriving on the president's steadfast support, Bragg proceeded to reorganize his army, and immediately relieved Hill from command. Explaining his decision to remove Hill, Bragg wrote: "Possessing some high qualifications as a commander, he still fails to such an extent in others more essential that he weakens the morale and military tone of his command. A want of prompt conformity to orders of great importance is the immediate cause of this application."[39] Before he left the army on the fourteenth, Davis authorized Bragg to remove Hill from command.[40]

Accompanied by his adjutant general, a despondent Hill went to Bragg's headquarters to demand an explanation for his removal from command. In reality, the commanding general had no specific charges against Hill as he had against Polk and Hindman. Bragg, however, "distinctly disclaimed making any charge or imputation of military offense." Instead, his "request to relieve Genl Hill was based upon the idea that a commander could not successfully conduct operations, if he was not sustained by the cordial co-operation of his Subordinates," which Hill himself had made clear in Davis's meeting. Hill was unwilling to accept Bragg's allegations at face value. Figuring his removal had something to do with the petition requesting Bragg's removal, Hill admitted to signing "that paper with great reluctance." As the conversation grew heated, Hill demanded that the reasons for removal be placed in writing so he could defend himself in a court of inquiry. Bragg declined, maintaining that any requests must be made in writing through the "proper official channel."[41] Bragg's responses to Hill's effort to defend himself reflected his antagonism toward Hill. Although he had no specific charges against Hill's conduct in the Chickamauga campaign, Bragg sought to eliminate the person he believed initiated the October 4 petition against him.[42] In a postwar letter, Bragg confessed that he removed Hill for his participation in the army's "mutinous assemblage." Yet at the time, a possible consequence of Hill's being removed from command would be at least to lay the blame for the campaign's failures at his feet. Consequently, Hill's tenure with the Army of Tennessee came to a close.[43]

Hill would languish for months without a command while trying to ascertain specific reasons why he was removed from command. Southern newspapers blamed Hill for the hollow victory at Chickamauga. Even though Hill would obtain an interview with Davis, he would not succeed in salvaging his professional reputation nor return to active field duty. In fact, in November, Adjutant General Samuel Cooper informed Hill that there would be no command to offer him "without displacing other officers already in command." Then in February the war department failed to confirm Hill's provisional promotion to lieutenant general, thus, essentially demoting the North Carolinian to his previous rank of major general. Despite the aspersions on his reputation, Hill sought to obtain duty in Charleston, South Carolina, requesting President Davis to provide a statement of "undiminished confidence" to offset his demotion to major general. Davis refused. Failing to receive the president's approval, Hill felt as if Davis endorsed the notion that he was responsible for the debacle at Chickamauga. So, with Davis silent on the matter, Hill left Charleston and returned to North Carolina. As Hill's biographer noted, "No other Confederate officer had been so humiliated."[44]

Clearly, Hill faltered in the Chickamauga campaign. On two occasions—at McLemore's Cove and before the second day of battle on September 20—Hill was nowhere to be found when critical messages from the commanding general were sent his way. Even upon receiving each directive, Hill offered a litany of complaints as to why they were impractical before moving his troops to the desired point against the enemy. While Hill effectively led his troops when in action on the battlefield, his grousing, vituperative nature led him to fall in with Bragg's disgruntled officers, for which he ultimately received the war department's wrath, his removal from active field command, and his demotion to the rank of major general. And despite the fact that Hill wrote extensive reports and a postwar essay explaining his role at Chickamauga, he failed to address fully how he erred as a corps commander in Bragg's army by flirting with insubordination and conspiring with his fellow officers to sign a petition urging the removal of their commanding general. Hill's comportment in Tennessee and northern Georgia was simply deplorable. But the basis of Hill's failings could be traced to the simple fact that he, along with Longstreet, Polk, Hindman, and the other members of the anti-Bragg cabal, had allowed his pride to override his sense of duty.

When Hill prepared to go west at Davis's urging in the summer of 1863, Bragg had been struggling with dissension in his army for more than half a year. Entering into that maelstrom of criticism and dissatisfaction, Hill found himself forming biases and opinions about his new commander that were thus reinforced by the carping and condemnation of Bragg's critics in the army. As such, Hill was likely convinced that anything Bragg ordered or proposed was wrong. Hill held onto these notions and failed to give his commanding general the benefit of the doubt and to offer him his unequivocal cooperation. Thus when ordered to move against the Federal division in McLemore's Cove, Hill balked, disappearing from his headquarters before eventually claiming that Cleburne was ill and the proposed movement would be delayed. Then on the night of September 19, Hill failed to make every effort to ensure he received directions for the following day's action and to maintain an open line of communication with his superiors. In sum, Hill failed to take his responsibility as a corps commander in Bragg's army seriously, putting personal biases and animosity ahead of his duties.

Yet Hill did not deserve to be made the scapegoat of the Confederacy's lost opportunities at Chickamauga. When he was relieved of duty from the Army of Tennessee, despite his protests, Hill was shelved from further duty while his co-conspirators and fellow Bragg critics remained in active field command. Polk and Hindman, in particular, despite being the focus of Bragg's ire in the days following the Battle of Chickamauga, escaped the harsh castigation meted out to Hill. Instead, Polk received a transfer, and Hindman was eventually restored to command. Even Longstreet, despite his prominent role in attempting to oust Bragg from command, avoided censure at the time. Hill ultimately became the focal point of the war department's ire because he was outspoken and had few political connections. Unlike Polk and Longstreet, who maintained close friendships with the authorities in Richmond, or Hindman, who received letters of support from prominent citizens, Hill did not receive the kind of support that would give Davis or Bragg pause.[45]

When Hill did return to active duty in the war's final campaigns, his commanders recognized his strengths and weaknesses. And while the stigma of Chickamauga likely haunted Hill during the war's final months, he remained a capable officer that could at times serve effectively. Unfortunately for the Confederacy, he did not serve effectively during his tenure with the Army of Tennessee.

Notes

1. Daniel Harvey Hill, "Chickamauga—The Great Battle of the West," in Clarence Buel and Robert Johnson, eds., *Battles and Leaders of the Civil War*, 4 vols. (New York, 1885), 3:638.

2. Hal Bridges, *Lee's Maverick General: Daniel Harvey Hill* (Lincoln: University of Nebraska Press, 1991), 193–94.

3. Lee to Jefferson Davis, 17 August 1862, 6 January 1863, in Clifford Dowdey and Louis H. Manarin, eds., *The Wartime Papers of Robert E. Lee* (New York: Da Capo, 1961), 258, 388. In a postwar conversation with William Allen, Lee complained of Hill's temperament. "D. H. Hill had such a queer temperament," Allen later wrote, "he could never tell what to expect from him, & that he croaked." See William Allen, "Memoranda of Conversations with General Robert E. Lee," in Gary Gallagher, ed., *Lee the Soldier* (Lincoln: University of Nebraska Press, 1995), 7–8.

4. Quoted in Jeffry D. Wert, *General James Longstreet: The Confederacy's Most Controversial Soldier; A Biography* (New York: Simon and Schuster, 1993), 93.

5. Hill, "Chickamauga," 641.

6. Ibid., 639.

7. See Grady McWhiney, *Braxton Bragg and Confederate Defeat* (Tuscaloosa: University of Alabama Press, 1969), 375–78; Steven E. Woodworth, *Jefferson Davis and His Generals: The Failure of Confederate Command in the West* (Lawrence: University of Kansas Press, 1990), 194–96; Thomas Lawrence Connelly, *Autumn of Glory: The Army of Tennessee, 1862–1865* (Baton Rouge: Louisiana State University Press, 1971), 69–75.

8. Bragg to Leonidas Polk, 30 January 1863, U.S. War Department, *The War of the Rebellion: Official Records of Union and Confederate Armies*, 128 vols. (Washington, D.C.: U.S. Government Printing Office, 1880–91), series 1, vol. 20, pt. 1: 701. All citations are from Series 1.

9. Alexander Mendoza, *Confederate Struggle for Command: General James Longstreet and the First Corps in the West* (College Station: Texas A&M University Press,

2008), 60–61; Steven E. Woodworth, *Six Armies in Tennessee: The Chickamauga and Chattanooga Campaigns* (Lincoln: Nebraska University Press, 1998), 44–46.

10. Connelly, *Autumn of Glory*, 152–54.

11. Diane Neal and Thomas Kremm, *The Lion of the South: General Thomas C. Hindman* (Macon: Mercer University Press, 1993), 107–8, 164–66; Arndt D. Stickles, *Simon Bolivar Buckner: Borderland Knight* (Chapel Hill: University of North Carolina Press, 1940), 224–25; Thomas Connelly and Archer Jones, *The Politics of Command: Factions and Ideas in Confederate Strategy* (Baton Rouge: Louisiana State University Press, 1973), 68–70; *OR*, vol. 23, pt. 2: 962.

12. See Steven E. Woodworth, "Braxton Bragg and the Tullahoma Campaign," in Steven E. Woodworth, ed., *The Art of Command in the Civil War* (Lincoln: University of Nebraska Press, 1998), 157–78.

13. Woodworth, *Six Armies in Tennessee*, 68.

14. Connelly, *Autumn of Glory*, 172–73; Peter Cozzens, *This Terrible Sound: The Battle of Chickamauga* (Urbana: University of Illinois Press, 1992), 30; Woodworth, *Six Armies in Tennessee*, 59, 66 (quote).

15. Woodworth, *Six Armies in Tennessee*, 60.

16. Connelly, *Autumn of Glory*, 174–75; Woodworth, *Six Armies in Tennessee*, 67.

17. Cozzens, *This Terrible Sound*, 66; Connelly, *Autumn of Glory*, 175.

18. *OR*, vol. 30, pt. 2: 28, 138; Connelly, *Autumn of Glory*, 177.

19. *OR*, vol. 30, pt. 2: 292–93.

20. Ibid., 138, 293; Connelly, *Autumn of Glory*, 177–78; Hill, "Chickamauga," 641; Glenn Tucker, *Chickamauga: Bloody Battle in the West* (New York: Bobbs-Merrill, 1961), 67. In a postwar account, Hill was scathing in his criticism of the commanding general's shortcomings, arguing that Bragg's "lack of knowledge of the situation" and his "lack of personal supervision of orders" were the reasons why the assault on McLemore's Cove sputtered. See Hill, "Chickamauga," 641.

21. Cozzens, *This Terrible Sound*, 67.

22. Judith Lee Hallock, *Braxton Bragg and Confederate Defeat*, vol. 2 (Tuscaloosa: University of Alabama Press, 1992), 60; Woodworth, *Six Armies in Tennessee*, 70; Connelly, *Autumn of Glory*, 180–81. Hallock, Bragg's biographer, argues that imprecise reports from his cavalry influenced Bragg's hesitation and "lack of confidence" in the McLemore's Cove operation.

23. Neal and Kremm, *Lion of the South*, 167–68; *OR*, vol. 30, pt. 2: 29.

24. Cozzens, *This Terrible Sound*, 72; Neal and Kremm, *Lion of the South*, 168–69.

25. Cozzens, *This Terrible Sound*, 75.

26. Woodworth, *Six Armies in Tennessee*, 74–77 (quote on 75).

27. Bridges, *Lee's Maverick General*, 204; Woodworth, *Six Armies in Tennessee*, 79; Mendoza, *Confederate Struggle for Command*, 36; Hallock, *Braxton Bragg and Confederate Defeat*, 59–60.

28. Hill, "Chickamauga," 650.

29. Woodworth, *Davis and His Generals*, 235.

30. Mendoza, *Struggle for Command*, 40–41; Cozzens, *This Terrible Sound*, 303–5.

31. For a detailed discussion on the Confederate delays of September 20, see Cozzens, *This Terrible Sound*, 300–310; Connelly, *Autumn of Glory*, 211–22; Woodworth, *Jefferson Davis and His Generals*, 235–36.

32. D. H. Hill to Samuel Cooper, August 1, 1864, *OR*, vol. 30, pt. 2: 45.

33. Bragg to Samuel Cooper, September 29, 1863, ibid., 55.

34. Polk to Jefferson Davis, October 6, 1863, ibid., 67.

35. Generals to Jefferson Davis, October 4, 1863, Daniel Harvey Hill Papers, Library of Virginia, Richmond, Va.

36. James Chesnut to Jefferson Davis, October 5, 1863, OR, vol. 52, pt. 4: 538.

37. Longstreet to Edward Porter Alexander, August 26, 1902, Edward Porter Alexander Papers, Southern Historical Collection, University of North Carolina, Chapel Hill.

38. C. Vann Woodward, ed., *Chesnut's Civil War* (New Haven: Yale University Press, 1981), 482. Chesnut wrote that although "every honest man he saw out west thought well of Joe Johnston," the "president detests Joe Johnston for all the trouble he has given him. And General Johnston returns the compliment with compound interest."

39. Bragg to Davis, October 11, 1863, OR, vol. 30, pt. 2: 148.

40. Davis to Bragg, October 13, 1863, ibid. In addition to removing D. H. Hill from command, Bragg reduced Buckner from corps to divisional command and transferred troops from Cheatham's corps to reduce his influence. See Special Orders No. 33, October 15, 1863, Archer Anderson Collection, Eleanor S. Brockenbrough Library, Museum of the Confederacy, Richmond, Va..

41. "October 16, 1863 Memorandum of Archer Anderson," Anderson Collection, Museum of the Confederacy.

42. Although Longstreet did not publicly accuse Hill of writing the document until he published his memoirs in 1896, Bragg believed Hill remained the petition's author. "It was written by General D. H. Hill," Longstreet wrote, "as he informed me since the war." James Longstreet, *From Manassas to Appomattox: Memoirs of the Civil War in America* (New York: Konecky & Konecky, 1959), 465. In an 1886 letter to Jefferson Davis, Hill writes: "I had nothing to do with the petition to the President of the Confederate States for the removal of Gen. Bragg, save that I signed it willingly." Hill to Jefferson Davis, October 30, 1886, in Dunbar Rowland, ed., *Jefferson Davis, Constitutionalist: His Letters, Papers, and Speeches*, 10 vols. (Jackson: Mississippi Department of Archives and History, 1923), 9: 498–500.

43. Bragg quoted in Cozzens, *This Terrible Sound*, 533.

44. OR, vol. 53, 313 (first quote), OR, vol. 42, pt. 3: 1165; Bridges, *Lee's Maverick General*, 250–51 (second quote), 254, 257–61.

45. Neal and Kremm, *Lion of the South*, 179–80.

4

A. P. STEWART AT CHICKAMAUGA

Lee White

The Battle of Chickamauga was the only victory of the ill-starred Army of Tennessee. It was a vicious, chaotic, and hard-fought battle in a thick old-growth forest that was only occasionally broken by a cedar glade or a poor farmer's field that had been cut out of the surrounding hardwood timber. For three days in September of 1863, the Confederate Army of Tennessee would fight the Federal Army of the Cumberland in a seesaw fight that had very few examples of effective high-level leadership on either side. Even such notables as Nathan Bedford Forrest and Patrick Cleburne had lackluster, if not poor, performances. However, there were exceptions, and newly minted major general Alexander Peter Stewart and his brigade commanders of the "Little Giant Division" were such a case.

Stewart had been promoted to major general on June 2, 1863, having displayed solid and effective leadership on the battlefields of Shiloh, Perryville, and Murfreesboro. The *Chattanooga Daily Rebel* had described him as possessing "the essential qualities for a commanding officer . . . Coolness and skill coupled with a thorough acquaintance of the art militaire, a firm disciplinarian, but with thorough, even temper, that never suffers itself to be exerted or betrayed into any rash or intemperate expression, always the same calm, unmoved demeanor."[1] Stewart had acted as a division commander on a temporary basis several times and was respected by his peers and his men. He also had the wisdom to stay out of the vipers' pit of political infighting that seemed to be the curse of Braxton Bragg's Army of Tennessee. Stewart was able to stay on good terms with both Bragg and Lieutenant General Leonidas Polk, the chief voice of the anti-Bragg sentiment in the army. Stewart was a professional both on and off the battlefield, and this would serve him well in what was to unfold in the thickets of the Chickamauga battlefield.[2] The division that Stewart would command at Chickamauga was also a new entity in the Army of Tennessee, having been put together during the late spring of 1863.

The division consisted of Brigadier Generals Bushrod Johnson's Tennessee brigade, Henry Delamar Clayton's Alabama brigade, John Calvin Brown's Tennessee brigade, and William Brimage Bate's mixed brigade of Tennesseans, Alabamians, and Georgians. Johnson's brigade had been detached a few days before Chickamauga and would not rejoin Stewart until several days after the battle had concluded.

The most inexperienced brigade in Stewart's command was General Henry Clayton's Alabama command. It consisted of the 18th, 36th, and 38th Alabama Infantry Regiments and Captain John T. Humphrey's 1st Arkansas Battery. The 18th Alabama and Humphrey's battery were the veterans of the lot, and the 18th, although it had fought on the first day at Shiloh, had not seen action since June of 1862, having been in garrison in Mobile since then. The 36th and 38th had only done garrison duty in Mobile since their formation. They were all sent to Middle Tennessee in the spring of 1863, where they were put under General Clayton's command.

Before the war, Henry Clayton had been a lawyer in Barbour County, Alabama, and a strong secessionist. He led proslavery colonists to Kansas in 1857 and fought in some of the skirmishes there, before returning to Alabama to serve two terms in the state legislature from Barbour County until 1861, when he was elected colonel of the 1st Alabama Infantry. Clayton resigned from the regiment in January 1862 and returned home to organize a new regiment, the 39th Alabama Infantry, which he led through the Kentucky campaign and then at Stones River, where he was severely wounded. While Clayton was home recovering, General Bragg recommended that he be promoted to brigadier general, and in April, he received the promotion and took command of recent arrivals from Mobile.[3]

General Brown's brigade had seen action before. The 18th, 26th, and 32nd Tennessee had fought and been captured at Fort Donelson, Tennessee. After they were exchanged, they fought at Stones River, but had not performed well. The 45th Tennessee had fought at Shiloh, Baton Rouge, and Stones River. Major Taz Newman's 23rd Tennessee battalion had not seen action, and Captain T. H. Dawson's Georgia battery had fought at Stones River. Brown had been a lawyer in Giles County, Tennessee, and had opposed secession. When Tennessee finally left the union, Brown cast his fortunes with his state and was elected colonel of the 3rd Tennessee Infantry. They were ordered to Fort Donelson, where they were taken prisoner when the fort surrendered in February of 1862. After his exchange in August, Brown was promoted and given command of a brigade of Floridians and Mississippians, which he led into the battle of Perryville, where he was wounded. Upon his recovery three months later, he was placed in command of a brigade of Tennesseans who had also been captured at Fort Donelson and recently fought at Stones River.[4]

General Bate's brigade was Stewart's crack unit. Made up of the 37th Georgia Infantry Regiment, 20th Tennessee Infantry Regiment, 4th Georgia Sharpshooter Battalion, 58th Alabama, the Consolidated 15th and 37th Tennessee Infantry Regiments, and Captain Oliver's Eufaula (Alabama) Light Artillery. Though smaller in size than the other brigades, it made up for its size in quality and leadership. The 37th Georgia had been formed in the spring of 1863 by the consolidation of part of the 3rd Georgia Battalion and the 9th Georgia Battalion, both of which had fought in East Tennessee and at Stones River. The 20th Tennessee had fought at Shiloh, Baron Rouge, and Stones River. The 4th Georgia Sharpshooter Battalion had been created from the extra companies of the 3rd Georgia Battalion. The 58th Alabama had originally been the 9th Alabama Battalion, which had fought at Shiloh and Farmington, Mississippi. In the spring of 1863 two companies were added to the battalion and it was redesignated. The 15th Tennessee had fought at Belmont (Missouri), Shiloh, Perryville, and Stones River, after which, due to heavy losses, it was consolidated with the 37th Tennessee, veterans of Perryville and Stones River. The battery of the brigade, the Eufaula Light Artillery, had fought at Tazwell, Tennessee, and Stones River. Although mismatched in composition, Bate's division had great potential, and with strong leadership at all levels, in the hands of a commander who could appreciate its strengths and weaknesses, it made for a strong command.

William Bate was also a lawyer by training, but had also been a newspaper editor and a state congressman. He served in the war with Mexico and, like Clayton, was a strong supporter of secession. When Tennessee finally left the Union, Bate enlisted as a private but was soon elected colonel of the 2nd Tennessee Infantry. Bate led his men into battle at Shiloh and was severely wounded in the left leg. Bate's leg would have been amputated, but he refused and had to rely on a crutch from then on, but the loss of the use his leg was not enough to slacken his ambition.[5] Bate became known as "Fighting Billy" to his men, although not necessarily meant as a compliment, Sgt. Richard M. Gray of the 37th Georgia noted: "He had too little of the milk of human kindness in his composition to make an officer for whom men would cheerfully sacrifice life and limb, [because] his management and idea seemed to be that soldiers were mere machines to dance when he worked the wires. At Chickamauga . . . he knew as well as we and much better that a Maj Genls Baton lay in his success and he would have sacrificed every member of his Brigade to attain it . . . Fighting Billy shared the danger."[6]

Stewart's division was assigned to Hardee's corps, then encamped near Wartrace, Tennessee. Stewart had very little time to familiarize himself with his new command before their first campaign began. On June 24, General William Starke Rosecrans would lead his Army of the Cumberland out of its winter encampments around Murfreesboro and strike at Bragg's Confederates. The first blow came at Hoover's Gap, near Beech Grove, Tennessee. There, Bate's brigade would see its first action together, and in a very one-sided battle they would face Colonel John Wilder's Mounted Infantry Brigade, who were armed with the seven-shot repeating Spencer Rifles. Bate, needless to say, was driven back with heavy losses, and the Tullahoma campaign began. In a series of lightning quick feints and maneuvers, Rosecrans forced Bragg to fall back out of Middle Tennessee. Bragg retreated back to Chattanooga, arriving there in early July, and remained there for the next couple of months as he awaited Rosecrans's next move. It came in early September when Rosecrans once again flanked Bragg, forcing him to give up Chattanooga, the "Gateway to the Deep South." Bragg did not fall back far though, halting at the small town of La Fayette, Georgia, having been reinforced by troops from General Joseph E. Johnston's army in Mississippi and by Major General Simon Bolivar Buckner's Department of East Tennessee, to which Stewart's division was assigned to give Buckner a corps on September 1. Knowing that Lieutenant General James Longstreet had been dispatched from General Robert E. Lee's Army of Northern Virginia with 12,000 men., Bragg looked for a way to strike back at Rosecrans, who had separated his army into three columns. Bragg found several opportunities, but due to insubordination and just plain bad luck, he was not able to capitalize upon them, until September 16, when he devised a plan to attack Major General Thomas Crittenden's 21st Corps near Lee and Gordon's Mill on Chickamauga Creek.

Early on the morning of September 17, Buckner's corps marched north from its encampments near La Fayette toward Rock Springs Church, eight miles distant, and only a few miles south of Lee and Gordon's Mill. Lieutenant George W. Dillion of the 18th Tennessee described the day in his diary: "We were ordered out north about 8 miles, formed line of battle just before night with orders to build no fire, keep all musical instruments quiet and sleep just in rear of our guns."[7] Stewart's division moved out with high spirits, the day before Bragg issued his famous General Order 180, which stated:

The troops will be held for an immediate move against the enemy. His demonstration on our flank has been thwarted and twice he has retired before us when offered battle. We must now force him to the issue. Soldiers, you are largely reinforced; you must now seek the contest. In so doing I know you will be content to suffer privations and encounter hardships. Heretofore you have never failed to respond to your general when he has asked sacrifice at your hands. Relying on your gallantry and patriotism, he asks you to add the crowning glory to the wreath you wear. Our cause is in your keeping. Your enemy boasts that you are demoralized and retreating before him. Having accomplished your object in driving back his flank movement, let us now turn on his main force and crush it in its fancied security. Your generals will lead you. You have but to respond to assure us a glorious victory over an insolent foe. I know what your response will be. Trusting in God and the justice of our cause, and nerved by the love of the dear ones at home, failure is impossible and victory must be ours.[8]

Eighteen-year-old Lieutenant Bromfield Lewis Ridley Jr., an aide-de-camp on Stewart's staff, remembered that just before the order was issued, Captain Humphreys had a premonition about the nearing battle. He told several members of the staff that he had a dream the night before that they "would soon battle with Rosecrans and a brilliant victory would follow."[9] With such reassurances the morale of the men soared; they were going to have their revenge and an opportunity to regain the losses of the previous months. Stewart's division would camp that night near the banks of Pea Vine Creek, about two miles east of Rock Springs Church.[10]

About dawn on the morning of Friday, September 18, orders were received for Buckner's corps to cross Chickamauga Creek "at Thedford's Ford, [where it] will join the movement to the left, and press the enemy up the stream from Polk's front at Lee and Gordon's Mills." In conjunction with this move, Bushrod Johnson, now commanding a provisional division, would move out of Ringgold to cross the Chickamauga at Reed's Bridge and sweep up the creek toward Crittenden's position at the mills. There he would be joined by Brigadier General William Henry Talbot Walker's reserve corps, which was to cross Alexander's Bridge and "push vigorously on the enemy's flank and rear." Polk's corps was to confront Crittenden at Lee and Gordon's Mill and "if met by too much resistance to cross will bear to the right and cross at Dalton's Ford, or at Thedford's . . . and join the attack wherever the enemy may be."[11]

Although a sound plan, Bragg's luck seemed to turn against him as usual. Johnson's advance ran into trouble almost from the moment that he left Ringgold, when he was confronted by Colonel Robert Minty's cavalry brigade. Minty's men would fight an impressive delaying action against Johnson, making his advance a mere crawl. Johnson would not reach Reed's Bridge until late in the afternoon, hours behind the time that Bragg had envisioned in his plan. Walker's and Buckner's men tangled with each other as they tried to move forward on the same road. After finally getting his men free, Walker made his way to Alexander's Bridge with no opposition, but there he was greeted by part of Colonel Wilder's brigade, now known as the "Lightning Brigade." Walker tried to storm the brigade and suffered heavy casualties from Wilder's repeaters. Walker was forced to bring up his whole corps before he finally forced Wilder to withdraw; however, when his men tried to cross the bridge they discovered that Wilder's men had stripped the plank flooring from the bridge and thrown it into the creek, making the bridge unusable. Walker had to spend more time finding a place to ford the Chickamauga.

After the roads were cleared, Buckner's corps made good time, with Bate's brigade leading the column. Soon the booming of cannon and crack of musketry sounded to the north. Ridley recalled, "Tramp, tramp, tramp, the boys are marching—no guying of each other, and no frivolous flings at passing horsemen. The rapid step toward the scene of the conflict indicated but the determination that was written on every brow, and remarks to each other such as, 'Boys, we have retreated far enough; we will whip 'em this time or die,' were figured on every tongue."[12] Lieutenant Dillion noted that as they neared the ford, "Cannons were booming on our right, left and in front (12 o'clock). About 1 or 2 o'clock P.M., the roar of musketry was very rapid for a short time."[13]

Nearing the Chickamauga, Buckner ordered Stewart to advance on Thedford's Ford, sending his chief engineer, Major James Nocquet, to assist in the crossing.[14] Major General William Preston's division was sent further upstream to cross at Dalton's Ford. Stewart reached the ford about 2 P.M. and found a small force of Federals on the opposite bank, a detachment of the 98th Illinois Infantry of Wilder's Brigade.[15] With the assistance of Major Nocquet, Stewart deployed Bate's and Clayton's brigades on a ridge that overlooked the ford. As soon as they were in position Bate ordered Major Caswell to advance his sharpshooters toward the ford to probe the Federal position. Bate also ordered Captain Oliver to deploy his battery in support of Caswell. As the men were deployed, Captain Eli Lilly's 18th Indiana Battery of Wilder's brigade, on a hill near the Alexander house to the north, took notice of them and opened a long-range fire. One shot struck near General Stewart and ricocheted over Brown's brigade. Other shells exploded among Clayton's brigade, injuring several men.[16] Captain Oliver swung his guns around to confront Lilly and exchanged a few shots with the Federals, until they limbered up and withdrew to the southwest with Wilder at about 4:30 P.M.

With Lilly gone, Oliver now focused his guns on the Hoosiers at the ford, adding to the pressure that the 4th Georgia Sharpshooters had put on them.

With their attention drawn to their front, the Federals did not notice when three companies of the 18th Alabama under the command of Major Peter F. Hunley waded across the creek a short distance upstream. The Alabamians where accompanied by General Clayton, who positioned them on a hill that commanded Thedford's Ford,[17] making the Federals' position untenable. The Federals quickly ran back to their mounts and northward into the forest to rejoin their brigade, as Caswell and his men stormed across the creek and took up position on the opposite bank at 5 P.M.

Buckner decided against crossing his divisions until he learned what had occurred with Johnson's and Walker's advances, so Stewart was told to hold on to the foothold that he had gained. Stewart then ordered the Eufaula Light Artillery to cross to support the 4th Georgia Sharpshooters and then sent across the rest of Clayton's brigade to secure the crossing. The rest of the division was ordered to go into bivouac in line of battle on the south side of the creek. Clayton's men would spend a miserable night along the banks of the creek as the temperature dropped and a thick mist rose over them. A soldier in the 18th Alabama would remember it years later: "The weather became quite cold, and though the men were wet, they could not have fire on account of the nearness of the enemy."[18] So the men huddled together and tried to catch what sleep that they could through the cold and miserable night.

Early the next morning, Buckner, having learned the dispositions of Johnson and Walker, ordered his command across the creek. Stewart crossed the rest of his command over, forming them in the rear of Clayton's brigade, as Preston crossed his division at Dalton's Ford, a little further to the south. Bragg arrived and told Stewart and Buckner that the troops that had advanced further downstream had established a line just northwest of them. Buckner then ordered Stewart to move his division northward and form on the left of that line. Stewart's men left the large field that bordered the creek, entering into the dark and gloomy forest. Clayton soon came upon the left of Johnson's division and formed his brigade on line with Brigadier General Evander McNair's Arkansas brigade. Stewart formed the rest of the division in a column behind Clayton, with Brown being next, and with Bate being in the rear.[19] This formation was different than what the Army of Tennessee usually used, which was a single line of brigades. It offered Stewart better command and control, and although presenting a narrow front, he would have a lot of power along that front, and in the fight that he was about to go into that would made a huge difference. Preston's division came up and formed on Stewart's left with his left resting on a bend in Chickamauga Creek. Bragg had intended to continue his movement from the day before, but as

Buckner's men went into line, that plan was falling apart. Unbeknownst to him Union general George Henry Thomas's 14th Corps had made an all-night march and moved beyond Crittenden's flank at Lee and Gordon's Mill to the area of the Kelly farmstead about three miles further north. On the morning of September 19 he would unexpectedly run into Forrest's cavalry near Jay's Saw Mill, east of the Kelly farm. Forrest would then drag Walker's corps into the fight, and Thomas would send in more of his men. The battle would seesaw back and forth, and like a giant zipper being drawn together the forces of both armies brought more men to bear.

Stewart's men settled into their positions and waited. The men took the opportunity to write letters to their families, in some cases for the last time; others smoked their pipes, or remained silent, contemplating their future. As the morning wore on, the sound of distant gunfire echoed down from the north and grew steadily in intensity, but the only action happened about 9 o'clock when General Buckner ordered Captain Oliver to advance his Eufaula Light Artillery, which fired two rounds on part of Crittenden's position that was visible to the south before returning to its position in the rear of Bate's brigade.[20] Around noon, with the battle spreading into the farm fields of the Brock family, General Polk ordered Major General Benjamin Franklin Cheatham's division into the fight to protect Walker's left flank, which was then being hammered by Brigadier General Richard Johnson's division. Cheatham's five brigades marched forward, pushing into Brock field and the ridge to the north, stopping Johnson. However, their moment of success was short lived, as Cheatham soon found himself confronted by Major General Joseph J. Reynolds and two divisions of Crittenden's corps under the commands of Major General John Palmer and Brigadier General Horatio Van Cleve. The tide of battle quickly turned against Frank Cheatham, and he faced the real threat of being overwhelmed, particularly on his left flank, where the brigade of Brigadier General Marcus Wright had attempted to flank Reynolds and instead found itself facing a superior force in his front and on his flank. Wright was in a trap that was closing fast.

At about 1 P.M. Stewart was smoking his pipe and listening along with his staff to the roar of gunfire from Cheatham's fight, when Major Pollock B. Lee of Bragg's staff rode up and handed Stewart orders from Bragg "to move to the point where firing had commenced, which seemed to be a considerable distance to the right and somewhat to the rear of us."[21] Stewart wasn't comfortable with the vagueness of the orders and rode back to find General Bragg to get more specific instructions. Stewart found Bragg near his headquarters at Thedford's Ford, and in the conversation that followed, Bragg told Stewart, "that Walker was engaged on the right, was much cut up, and the enemy threatening to turn his flank, that General Polk was in command on that wing, and that I must be governed by circumstances."[22] Stewart then rode back to his command, still not clear as to what was expected of him, but determined to make the best of any circumstances that might develop. Stewart quickly had his troops moving northward by the right flank toward the sound of the guns, keeping his division in column of brigades.

Lieutenant Ben Lane Posey of the 38th Alabama Infantry remembered, "we soon started off to the right, and, generally at a double quick."[23] The division made its way behind Johnson's and then Brigadier General Evander Law's divisions, through heavy woods for about a mile. As they neared the sound of the battle, leaves began to fall in increasing volume, then limbs began to fall, being ripped from the trees by artillery. Finally, Stewart's columns arrived at the south end of the Brock field and viewed the pandemonium laid out before them. Stewart quickly dispatched several of his staff to find General Polk to ascertain the situation and find out where he was most needed. His course of action was soon decided for him as men of Wright's broken brigade began to stream out of the woods on the western side of the field. Stewart determined to go into action there. His decision was soon confirmed when Lieutenant William B. Richmond, aide-de-camp to General Polk, arrived and told Stewart, "From what he knew of the nature of the ground and the situation of the enemy, a better point at which to attack them could not be found."[24]

Stewart rode to Clayton at about 2 P.M. and ordered him to advance his Alabamians, telling him "that after having more definitely located the enemy I would have to act for myself and be governed by circumstances."[25] Stewart would report with pride that they advanced "with great spirit and alacrity, and in admirable order." Still concerned about the inexperience of the brigade, he ordered his assistant adjutant general, Major Robert A. Hatcher, to keep an eye on them and to send intelligence back to keep him apprised of the Federal positions as well as how the brigade was doing.[26] Lieutenant Posey later remembered that as they advanced they

> found our brethren, who preceded us in the fight, in much confusion and in considerable panic. The woods—it was all woods—was full of stragglers and skulkers and wounded. Whole companies, regiments and brigades seemed scattered to the winds—officers, even, with their tinsel on them, seemed to be hunting a safe place in the rear. The fugitives told the wildest tales of flight and massacre of regiments, and brigades, "cut all to pieces." Of course, they exaggerated the facts as an excuse for their own flight, but the actual state of the case was bad enough without exaggeration. The scene was disgraceful to our army, and at one time, I thought the battle lost, for it seemed that

everybody had run, or was running from the enemy. Worst of all, we were in a woods of dense undergrowth, and could not see the enemy 100 yards off. We only knew of their presence and position by the sound of their guns, and this only when they fired. A danger that can be seen frightens less than one that is invisible . . . fancy and fear create phantoms, more terrible than any reality.[27]

Among the stragglers was Colonel John Carter of the 38th Tennessee Infantry, who reported both to Clayton and then Stewart that his brigade, Wright's, had been flanked, overwhelmed, and had lost its battery, under Captain William W. Carnes.[28]

Clayton's brigade moved steadily northwestward, up the stair-step terrain, toward Van Cleve's unseen Federals, and soon the whine of minié balls filled the air and followed by the sickening thud of the balls as they struck flesh and bone. Observing Clayton from Brown's brigade, Lieutenant Ridley would later graphically describe the fire Clayton faced: "Did you ever note the thickness of raindrops in a tempest? Did you ever see the destruction of hail stones to growing cornfields? Did you ever witness driftwood in a squall? Such was the havoc upon Clayton."[29] In the ranks of the 38th Alabama, Lieutenant Posey would note that the first volley killed Major Orgin S. Jewett and Captain William R. Welsh and "brought down about a score of the companies of Welsh and Bussy. The regiment then fronted itself by impulse without 'undoubling,' and stood in many places in four ranks, which soon increased to five, six, or seven, as there was a scramble for the rear rank. This was natural, unavoidable under the circumstances. . . . They were . . . fighting a still unseen enemy. The truth is, that no regiment stands firmly, fights coolly, and without disorder in its first encounter. . . . the entire line was under fire, and soon a scene of dire confusion ensued—the men kept up a wild fusillade, though they did not see the enemy."[30]

The fight was similar throughout the rest of the brigade. In the 18th Alabama, Colonel James T. Holtzclaw was thrown from his horse and injured, passing command of the regiment to Lieutenant Colonel Richard F. Inge, who pressed the men onward. Edgar W. Jones of Company G remembered, "Standing in line the firing began, seemingly without any command, and in three minutes the engagement was something awful. The slaughter was dreadful. We discovered that we were within perhaps fifty paces of the enemy's main line. Company G had fifteen men wounded in less than that many minutes. Lieut. Col. R. F. Inge was shot and fell from his horse."[31]

Command now passed to Major Hunley, as Clayton ordered his men to lie down and find what cover they could on the leaf-covered forest floor as the leaden hail continued to rain down upon them. The men withstood the fire well and kept up a brisk fire of their own, "about 35 killed and 175 wounded. S. K. Fielder, first lieutenant Company H, was mortally wounded while gallantly cheering onward his men. Pollard and Harper, first and second lieutenants Company A, were wounded—the first mortally, the last very severely. Captain Wilkerson was slightly wounded in the heel, being struck by a fragment of shell, and left the field."[32] Clayton had decided to make a bayonet charge, but learned that the men were nearly out of ammunition, so he was forced to withdraw them to resupply. Clayton left nearly 400 men behind on the ground though,[33] and if there had been any question about how they would hold up in action, it had now been answered. Stewart now ordered Brown to advance to the front as Clayton passed to the rear.

Brown's men had lain on the ground behind Clayton, so close that several men were wounded or killed by overshots from Clayton's fight. When Brown ordered his men forward, they leapt to their feet with a yell and rushed into the fight at the double quick. They were greeted with the same reception that Clayton had received, which one soldier in the 32nd Tennessee described as "a cyclone of fire."[34] Many officers fell during the first volley. George Dillion of the 18th Tennessee remembered, "the engagement was the most severe contest of any that I ever witnessed in my life."[35] As Brown reached Clayton's former position, the men were shocked by the hellish scene: the ground was covered with the dead and wounded almost in a solid line, and small brush fires burned in front of them, filling the air with acrid smoke that mixed with the sulfuric black powder smoke that still hung in the air. Brown's men did not have long to take in the scene—their general kept the movement going forward—so they stepped over the bodies and moved closer to the Federal line, where the fighting became severe and "the dead and dying of both sides covered the ground."[36] Brown pushed the Federal line back toward the La Fayette Road, "the double quick was ordered, and then the 'charge.' When our men raised the 'rebel yell' and pressing on in fine order [we] soon found ourselves on the ground which had just been occupied by the enemy. Pressing on again, we drove the enemy before us, inflicting terrible damage . . . the situation was so grave, and the struggle so fierce, we did not look to right or left; but the commands, 'Steady!' 'Forward!' 'Aim Low!' 'Make every shot count!'—there were heard as the deadly conflict was urged on."[37] Brown soon was among the remains of Carnes's battery, which he was able to secure and send to the rear. Brown's men now came under canister fire from Federal artillery posted along the La Fayette Road and the Brotherton Ridge beyond, as well as from Colonel William Grose's brigade of Palmer's division, who were posted in line along the Brotherton Road to the north and in a fine position to enfilade Brown's right through the open woods.

The woods seemed to explode with iron balls, bark, and splinters around Brown's men. Colonel Palmer of the 18th Tennessee rode along his line, "waving his sword for the encouragement of his men," when he was struck by a ball that went through his right shoulder, severing a large artery, and only the "application of an improvised tourniquet" saved his life.[38] His command was then passed to Lieutenant Colonel William R. Butler, who had no more taken command when he was also wounded, although slightly, and passed command to Major W. H. Joyner, who was then hit. Command then passed on to Captain Gideon Lowe. Colonel John M. Lillard of the 26th Tennessee was also struck and fell from his horse, mortally wounded, as his men charged into the 26th Pennsylvania Independent Battery, killing its commander, Captain Alanson J. Stevens, nephew of Thaddeus Stevens, and capturing three cannon.[39] Brown tried to steady his men, when he was also hit by a spent ball that knocked him from his horse and left him with a painful bruise. The 75th Indiana was rushed from reserve and counterattacked Brown's right flank and sent the 18th and 45th Tennessee running to the rear. With his right flank turned and broken, Brown was then forced to withdraw the rest of his regiments to the rear to regroup and resupply with ammunition. Like Clayton before him, Brown had suffered heavy losses, particularly among his officer corps, but he had recovered Carnes's four guns, captured five cannon from the Federals, and drove the Federal line back westward almost to the La Fayette Road, nearly breaking the Federal line.

As Brown fell back, Stewart, unwilling to lose the momentum, unhesitatingly ordered Bill Bate to send his brigade in. Bate's brigade had been ordered to lie down near the edge of Brock field while first Clayton and then Brown were ordered into the battle, and they had to lay there listening to "roar after roar of musketry and artillery, and rebel yells that could be heard for miles."[40] Bate rode along his lines with his crutches strapped to his saddle shouting for his men to rise up, which they did with a yell. Bate came up to Colonel Thomas Benton Smith, the twenty-five-year-old commander of the 20th Tennessee Infantry, and excitedly called, "Now Smith, now Smith, I want you to sail on those fellows like you were a wildcat."[41] The men of the brigade jumped to their feet, fixed bayonets, and started to the front at the double quick. Bate's men rushed forward at 3:30 P.M. and wheeled their line slightly to the right to confront both Van Cleve's brigades and Grose's. Canister and shells greeted Bate as he came within view of the gunners. "We pressed steadily forward, unchecked by the murderous discharges of their small howitzers, loaded with canister and grape, and drove the first line from their position,"[42] recalled Sergeant James Litton Cooper of the 20th Tennessee. The assault of Bate's men carried them up the slope where

Brown had faltered. Although they received flank fire, the men kept up the attack, nearing the Brotherton Road. Cooper would later recount, "Here occurred the prettiest fighting during the whole war. We rushed up on a little hill, and the enemy were just below us, all crowded together in a deep hollow. Our rifles were in prime condition and our ammunition so good that I really enjoyed the fight."[43]

As Bate's men pressed closer to the Federals of Palmer's division, they were joined on their right by the 44th Alabama Infantry of Law's brigade, which had become separated from their brigade a short time earlier and had moved toward the sound of the fighting. Finding Bate, they moved onto line with him and helped drive Grose's line back from Brotherton Road. It was at this time, about 4 P.M., that Stewart ordered Clayton back into the fight. Lieutenant Posey remembered that "General Clayton galloped along the line, waving his hat, and shouting, 'forward.' St. John Vidmer, who had previously done much to check the retreat and restore order, rode in front, and said, 'The enemy are retreating—now is the time to charge.' Confidence was restored. Enthusiasm replaced the recent dejection. Forward we went, with now firm step, more and more rapid, until it became a double quick, then a run."[44] As Bate veered toward the north, Clayton moved around his left and headed west back into Van Cleve's men. Having been hammered by all three of Stewart's brigades, and now facing Clayton for a second time, Van Cleve's division began to crack and fell back across the La Fayette Road to the Brotherton Ridge. Lieutenant Posey continued, "We raised a loud yell and on we went, driving the fugitive enemy before us. Many of our men fell in this charge, but we pressed on over our fallen comrades. We went now like a tornado."[45] At the same time, Colonel John S. Fulton's brigade of Johnson's division appeared out of the woods on the south end of the ridge. This new threat added to the remounted attack of Clayton was more than Van Cleve's federals could stand and they broke, fleeing to the north and west. Clayton surged over the La Fayette Road, being joined by the 58th Alabama and the 15th and 37th consolidated Tennessee regiments, the left wing of Bate's brigade, which seemed to split apart as they pushed forward, and the 4th Alabama, another stray regiment of Law's brigade. Together they captured two cannon and then moved up the ridge Lieutenant Posey remembered:

> We swept by and over the abandoned cannon of the enemy. Their muzzles still pointed toward us, but they were now hushed. It was a sad picture. There lay the Yankee cannoneers dead around their guns, and there lay the dead artillery—horses piled one upon another. There, too, lay the dead Confederates, showing how close and desperate had been the contest for the battery. But we still pursued

the flying enemy in a mad, wild, reckless charge. Only once were we momentarily checked, when a few stepped to the front and urged on the charge, which was again renewed.[46]

Clayton's brigade continued westward and disappeared into the woods beyond. As Clayton's men went back into battle, Bate finally drove Grose out of position, and continued to move northward, recapturing the battle flag of the 51st Tennessee of Wright's brigade,[47] with the 37th Georgia, 4th Georgia Sharpshooters, and 20th Tennessee. The 44th Alabama would halt on the Brotherton Road, before being forced back by the fire from the rest of Palmer's division. As the shadows of the forest darkened in the hours of the late afternoon, they burst from the forest into the southern edge of the Poe field. Along the northern edge could be seen a line of federal artillery, four batteries, totaling 24 cannon altogether. As Bate had mounted more pressure on Grose and Van Cleve had begun to collapse, Brigadier General William Babcock Hazen of Palmer's division had foreseen the coming storm and quickly gathered the guns together. The 37th Georgia entered into the field led by Colonel Anthony François Rudler, born in Alsace, a veteran of the war with Mexico and William Walker's Filibuster campaigns in Central America.[48] Rudler ordered his men to charge, as did Colonel Smith with his 20th Tennessee. The Federal gunners were waiting for them, Lieutenant Ambrose Bierce, a topographical engineer on Hazen's staff, later recounted in his usual graphic style:

The field was gray with Confederates in pursuit. Then the guns opened fire with grape and canister and for perhaps five minutes—it seemed an hour—nothing could be heard but the infernal din of their discharge and nothing seen through the smoke but a great ascension of dust from the smitten soil. When all was over, and the dust cloud had lifted, the spectacle was too dreadful to describe. The Confederates were still there—all of them, it seemed—some almost under the muzzles of the guns. But not a man of all of these brave fellows was on his feet, and so thickly were all covered with dust that they looked as if they had been reclothed in yellow. "We bury our dead," said a gunner, grimly.[49]

The fire had indeed been terrific. A soldier in Smith's regiment, W. J. McMurray, gave the Confederate perspective, "Double charge after double charge of grape and canister plowed through our ranks, and the only words to be heard above the roar of battle were, 'Close up and forward, men!' . . . the Twentieth carried into action one hundred and forty men, and lost in killed and wounded ninety-eight, most of whom fell around this battery. . . . How any human being could live through such a conflict, the good Lord only can tell."[50] Bate would report that he lost 25 percent of his force in the attack in Poe field, including Colonels Rudler and Smith and Major Caswell, who all fell wounded leading their men.[51] Bate ordered his men back into the cover of the forest, where they began to re-form.

Clayton's men pushed on through the woods and emerged in the Dyer field near an old tanyard. There Clayton halted, although no opposition was in front of him. "A staff officer reporting the enemy advancing in strong force from the right, and it also having been reported to me, through my assistant adjutant general . . . that the enemy's cavalry had been seen in force upon the left as if preparing to advance, my brigade fell back across the road at leisure, where I halted and reformed it in connection with the portion of General Bate's brigade."[52] The fight on September 19 was now over for Stewart's division. The men were re-formed and settled into a defensive position to await what came next.

General A. P. Stewart had broken through the center of the Federal army, and although unable to get support to exploit it, he had saved Cheatham's division and taken the offensive away from the Federals. With his division of three brigades, he had attacked two Federal divisions and broke one of them, recaptured Carnes's battery and the flag of the 51st Tennessee, captured twelve pieces of artillery and between 200 and 300 prisoners.[53] However, it had taken a heavy toll; Stewart paid heavily, with Clayton's brigade losing 400 men alone in their first engagement. The loss of field-grade officers had been staggering: Colonels Palmer, Rudler, Holtzclaw, Tyler, and Smith had been wounded, Colonel Lillard had been killed, Lieutenant Colonels Butler, Inzer, Frayser, Inge, and T. H. Herndon were wounded, Majors Newman, Caswell, Wall, Kendrick, Shy, and Thornton were wounded, and Major Jewett was killed.[54] The battle would continue for another day of killing and the casualties continue to add up for Stewart, and in the end the victory would come at a heavy price. Indeed, the 18th Alabama would have the highest loss of any regiment in the Army of Tennessee in the battle, losing 297 of the 527 men who had gone into battle.[55]

As the sun set on September 19, Stewart and his brigadiers could be proud of their performance in the worst of situations. They not only saved Wright's beleaguered brigade, but stalled out all of the Federal initiative in the center of the field and then created a crisis just as grave for the Federals. Unlike many other commanders on both sides, Stewart had exercised strong command and control, as well as a keen understanding of his command from the quality of the men in the ranks and the abilities of its leadership. He had kept a close eye on Clayton's green troops by sending Major Hatcher with them and later by following behind them himself as they finally broke the Federal line. He had judged how much Brown's men could endure and the proper time and place to play his ace, Bate, in the fight. Then he used the rested and resupplied Clayton to finally tip the scales in his favor. The constant hammering blows he had delivered against Van Cleve had stopped the Federal advance, then pushed them back, and finally broke through and pushed well into the Federal rear. Unlike many commanders on the field that day who merely reacted to events, Stewart was able to quickly develop a plan and did everything in his power to ensure that it worked. Buckner would later compliment Stewart, saying, "No commendation from me can add to the well earned reputation of Major General Stewart and his able brigadiers."[56] Indeed Stewart was well served by his team of brigade commanders. Clayton had proved himself a capable leader, Brown had done well, and Bate had lived up to his nickname of "Fighting Billy."

However, the battle was not over for them. September 20 proved to be another hot day for Stewart's command, but not one that would see the kind of opportunities that were presented before. Stewart's command, as part of Longstreet's Wing, would make desperate but futile attacks against prepared Federal positions, ironically having to attack over part of the very ground that they had pushed the Federals from the day before. As the fighting finally neared its end, Stewart would have the honor of seeing his command drive the Federals from the south end of Kelly field in the closing moments of the battle. It can be said that Stewart made some of the first and last shots of the Chickamauga Battle.

Ironically, what had been their first battle as a division would be their last. At Chattanooga the "Little Giant" division would be dismantled when General Bragg reorganized the army. Bushrod Johnson's brigade would rejoin and then in a short time be transferred to Buckner's Division. Brown would be transferred to Major General Carter Stevenson's division, Bate would be transferred to Major General John Cabell Breckinridge's division, and after Breckinridge's move to corps command, Bate would take command of the division. Clayton would stay with Stewart and be joined by three other brigades. In a short time though, both Clayton and Brown would join Bate as division commanders and Stewart became a corps commander. On September 19 at Chickamauga all of them had proved that they had great potential. It is fitting that when Joseph Johnston surrendered his forces in April of 1865, what was left of the Army of Tennessee would be under the command of Alexander P. Stewart, the only division commander in that army to have delivered a good performance at Chickamauga, the only battle that the Army of Tennessee ever won.

Notes

1. *Chattanooga Daily Rebel*, July 8, 1863.

2. Ezra J. Warner, *Generals in Gray: Lives of the Confederate Commanders* (Baton Rouge: Louisiana State University Press, 1987), 293–94; Sam Davis Elliot, *Soldier of Tennessee: General Alexander P. Stewart and the Civil War in the West* (Baton Rouge: Louisiana State University Press, 1999), 80–81.

3. Warner, *Generals in Gray*, 52–53; Henry James Walker, "Henry Clayton and the Secession Movement in Alabama," *Southern Studies* 4, no.4 (Winter 1993): 342–60.

4. Warner, *Generals in Gray*, 35–36.

5. Dennis Kelly, "Back in the Saddle: The War Record of William Bate," *Civil War Times Illustrated*, December 1988, 27–28.

6. R. M. Gray Memoir, 62–63, Southern Historical Collection, University of North Carolina.

7. George W. Dillion diary, September 17, 1863, George Washington Dillion Papers, Tennessee State Library and Archives, Nashville.

8. *War of the Rebellion: A Compilation of the Official Records of the Union and Confederate Armies*, 70 vols. in 128 parts (Washington, D.C.: Government Printing Office, 1880–1901), ser. 1, vol. 30, pt. 2: 37–38 (hereafter cited as *OR*; all citations are to ser. 1, vol. 30, pt. 2.)

9. Bromfield Lewis Ridley, *Battles and Sketches of the Army of Tennessee* (Dayton, Ohio: Morningside House, 1995), 207.

10. Ibid.

11. *OR*, 31.

12. Ridley, *Battles and Sketches of the Army of Tennessee*, 208–9.

13. Dillion diary, September 18, 1863.

14. Ridley, *Battles and Sketches of the Army of Tennessee*, 209.

15. William Glenn Robertson, "The Chickamauga Campaign: The Armies Collide; Bragg Forces His Way across Chickamauga Creek," *Blue and Gray* 24, no. 3 (Fall 2007): 47.

16. Ridley, *Battles and Sketches of the Army of Tennessee*, 209.

17. *OR*, 401.

18. Jones, Edgar W. Jones and Zane Grier, eds., *The Eighteenth Alabama Infantry Regiment* (Mountain Brook, Ala.: L. Z. Grier, 1994), 7.

19. *OR*, 361.

20. *OR*, 400.

21. *OR*, 361.

22. Ibid.

23. "Ben Lane," *Mobile Advertiser and Register*, October 25, 1863.

24. *OR*, 361.

25. *OR*, 401.

26. *OR*, 362.

27. "Ben Lane."

28. *OR*, 362, 401.

29. Ridley, *Battles and Sketches of the Army of Tennessee*, 219–20.

30. "Ben Lane."

31. Jones and Grier, *Eighteenth Alabama*, 7.

32. *OR*, 405.

33. *OR*, 401.
34. T. I. Corn., "Brown's Brigade at Chickamauga," *Confederate Veteran* 21 (1913): 124.
35. Dillion diary, September 19, 1863.
36. Corn, "Brown's Brigade at Chickamauga," 124.
37. John Berrian Lindsley, ed., *The Military Annals of Tennessee: Confederate* (Nashville: J. M. Lindsley, 1886), 474–75.
38. Lindsley, *Military Annals of Tennessee*, 364.
39. *OR*, 376.
40. W. J. McMurray, "The Gap of Death at Chickamauga," *Confederate Veteran* 2 (1894): 329.
41. Ibid.
42. James Litton Cooper, "Service with the Twentieth Tennessee Regiment," *Confederate Veteran* 33 (1925): 138.
43. Ibid.
44. "Ben Lane," *Mobile Register and Advertiser*, October 25, 1863.
45. Ibid.
46. Ibid.
47. *OR*, 384.
48. *August (Ga.) Daily Chronicle and Sentinel*, October 14, 1860.
49. Ambrose Bierce, Russell Duncan, and David J. Klooster, eds., *Phantoms of a Blood-Stained Period: The Complete Writings of Ambrose Bierce* (Amherst: University of Massachusetts Press, 2002), 196.
50. McMurray, "Gap of Death at Chickamauga," 329.
51. *OR*, 384.
52. *OR*, 402.
53. *OR*, 362–63.
54. *OR*, 372, 386–87.
55. *OR*, 406.
56. *OR*, 359.

5

"A MINUTE NOW IS WORTH AN HOUR TOMORROW"
CLEBURNE'S NIGHT ATTACK

John R. Lundberg

A s the September sun began to set in the west, the men of Major General Pat Cleburne's division approached the freezing water of Chickamauga Creek and began to pull off their boots in preparation for the crossing. With the sounds of battle ahead and impressed with a sense of urgency, Cleburne called out to them: "Boys, go through that river, we can't wait!" With this exhortation, the men splashed through the waist-deep cold water, holding their rifles and ammunition above their heads, unaware of what lay before them. This crossing of the Chickamauga on the evening of September 19 initiated an often overlooked but crucial aspect of the Battle of Chickamauga; the night attack of Cleburne and his division.[1]

In the western theater of the Civil War, the Confederacy won only one major battle—Chickamauga. But Chickamauga became largely a Pyrrhic victory, barren of any benefit and at great cost. This thesis is mostly correct in that the Confederates were unable to follow up on their accidental victory, but it did not have to turn out that way.

The chief shortcoming of the Confederates at Chickamauga consisted in the failure to break the Union left under Major General George Thomas on September 20, thus allowing Thomas to save the Army of the Cumberland from complete defeat. This episode might have turned out very differently if not for Cleburne's assault on the night of September 19. If Cleburne had been prepared to make a dawn assault on September 20, as ordered by Bragg, Thomas and his men would have been unprepared, and the attack probably could have overwhelmed the Union left and destroyed the Army of the Cumberland. The confusion following Bragg's reordering of the army on the night of September 19 did not help matters any, but it seems unlikely, even if Bragg's orders had been conveyed in time to Cleburne, that the Irishman and his division could have done any good the next morning, considering the shape they found themselves in following the night attack.

The Battle of Chickamauga opened on September 18, 1863, when the advance forces of Bragg's Army of Tennessee began pushing back the advance elements of Rosecrans's Army of the Cumberland across Chickamauga Creek and toward the La Fayette Road. Bragg had made the road his main objective. As the only practical lifeline running north to south between Rosecrans's Federals and Chattanooga, Bragg intended to push across the Chickamauga and take possession of the road, cutting off the Union army and destroying it. At the end of the first day's battle, the Confederates found themselves reasonably close to the La Fayette Road in several places, but the Federals still retained possession of the thoroughfare.

September 19 dawned cold and frosty for both armies, and Bragg began the day with assaults against the Union right, around the Brotherton farm. The confusion among the troops of both armies reached an unimaginable extreme during the desperate fighting on the nineteenth, as the two sides seesawed back and forth in the dense woods, obscured all the more by the smoke and fog of battle. Bragg planned to turn the Union northern or left flank, and as he rushed troops in that direction, Rosecrans moved troops north, extending his flank. Patrick Cleburne and his men, coming from Pigeon Mountain to the south, crossed Thedford's Ford across the Chickamauga at about 4 P.M. on September 19, headed for the Confederate left.[2]

Patrick Cleburne and his division comprised one of the hardest fighting and best-led divisions in the Army of Tennessee. Born in Ireland, Cleburne served in the British army before immigrating to the United States, where he worked as an apothecary first in Ohio and then Helena, Arkansas. Reading law, Cleburne managed to pass the bar and began practicing law in Arkansas before the outbreak of the war. Although he did not fully understand slavery and the Southern attachment to the institution, when the war broke out he sided with his friends in Arkansas to fight for the Confederacy. After raising a company of infantry, Cleburne rose rapidly through the ranks, from colonel to brigadier general prior to the Battle of Shiloh. Following the Battle of Perryville in the fall of 1862 Cleburne received a promotion to major general, and by the time of Chickamauga, he had whipped his division into such a fine combat unit that it would have been the envy of Her Majesty's regiments of foot in his native Ireland.[3]

At Chickamauga, Cleburne's division consisted of three brigades. The first, containing six regiments of Alabamans and Mississippians, was commanded by Brigadier General S. A. M. Wood. The second, commanded by Brigadier

General Lucius Polk (nephew of Lieutenant General Leonidas Polk), had five regiments of Tennesseans and Arkansans, and finally, the third brigade, commanded by Brigadier General James Deshler, was composed of Texas and Arkansas regiments, the survivors of the Battle of Arkansas Post. Also attached to Cleburne's division were three batteries of artillery; Calvert's Arkansas Battery, Douglas's Texas Battery, and Semple's Alabama Battery, all under the command of Major Thomas R. Hotchkiss. With these three brigades and three batteries, Cleburne splashed across the Chickamauga at dusk on September 19.[4]

Several historians have put forward the notion that at that moment, Bragg possessed an excellent opportunity to crush the Union right. Major General John Bell Hood's Confederates were driving back the Union forces in their front around the Brotherton farm along the La Fayette Road, and two uncommitted brigades, those of Brigadier General Archibald Gracie Jr. and Colonel John H. Kelly, lay just behind Hood. With Cleburne's division now on the scene, Bragg could use it to spearhead an assault that would crush Rosecrans's left and secure the La Fayette Road. It is indeed probable that Bragg could have accomplished this objective, but it would have done him no good. His goal remained to cut the Union forces off from Chattanooga, to the north. Crushing Rosecrans's right would merely allow the Army of the Cumberland to retreat north toward Chattanooga, destroying any Confederate success. Bragg, with these goals in mind, ordered Cleburne and his men north, to report to Polk, commanding the right wing of the Army of Tennessee, around the Youngblood farm.[5]

The footsore, wet, shivering soldiers marched north and finally arrived around the Youngblood farm at 5:30 P.M. After his orders to report to Polk, Cleburne did not see any need for urgency, as darkness had almost fallen and night attacks in the Civil War remained rare, both because of the difficulty of maneuvering in the dark and the potential for friendly fire incidents. Neither Cleburne nor his men expected anything more that evening than to go into bivouac for the night. Captain Coleman of the 15th Mississippi Battalion of Sharpshooters in Woods's brigade wrote: "The sun was nearly down. . . . I had no idea of meeting the enemy that evening."[6] The Texans of Deshler's brigade also complained about their disposition that night, after having the "pleasure" of wading the Chickamauga with their boots on.

When Cleburne arrived, he aligned his division with the right flank resting on Jay's Mill, and his left extending due southward, facing west. The Irishman placed his men behind the remaining fragments of the divisions under Major Generals Frank Cheatham and St. John Liddell. On the right, nearest Jay's Mill, he placed Polk's brigade, in the center Wood's brigade, and finally on the left flank he ordered James Deshler's Texans and Arkansans into line.[7]

Cleburne prepared his division to bivouac for the night when St. John Liddell intervened. Liddell's men had fought all day against the First Division, Fourteenth Corps under Brigadier General Absalom Baird and the Second Division, Twentieth Corps under Brigadier General Richard Johnson. Liddell's men fared badly in the fighting, but Liddell convinced himself that the Union forces were preparing to build breastworks and hold their ground for the night. In his memoirs, Liddell wrote: "They [The Federals] were halted in the woods, not far before us, probably to secure ground gained and to rest for the night. . . . If Cleburne's attack was delayed till morning, the enemy would be found entrenched and fully prepared. I told him [Cleburne] that no time was to be lost to give us room between our position and the Chickamauga, only some four hundred yards in our rear."[8]

There are several problems with Liddell's logic. First, he assumed that Johnson and Baird would stay where they were for the night and not try to solidify their position after the long day's fight. Second, he apparently feared a Union counterattack that would push his men into the Chickamauga, when Cleburne's fresh and organized division would seem to provide the best Confederate defense in that eventuality. It is also unclear why he thought the Federals would counterattack in the dark with such badly cut up and disorganized forces. Third, he underestimated the time necessary to prepare Cleburne's men for a twilight attack over unfamiliar ground. By the time Cleburne could get his men into position, it would be dark, and night attacks in the Civil War proved a rarity—no more than half a dozen were attempted—and for good reason. A night attack, in addition to the logistical as well as command and control nightmares it presented, also ran the risk of incurring friendly fire. And yet, Liddell seems to have ignored all this when he began urging Cleburne to attack. Cleburne hesitated, because he obviously grasped many of the implications Liddell did not, and refused to move forward without orders from Lieutenant General Daniel Harvey Hill, their corps commander.

On the Union side of the field, Major General George Thomas, commanding the Union left wing, dispatched orders to Baird to communicate with Johnson and withdraw their men a half-mile to the rear, to high ground in the vicinity of the Kelly field. Baird received these orders by his own reckoning just at 5 P.M. However, he did not withdraw, nor did he communicate the orders to Johnson.[9] Had he done so, and his and Johnson's divisions had withdrawn, there would have been no basis for Liddell's insistence that Cleburne attack at once.

Shortly after Liddell began urging an attack, Hill rode up, and Liddell made his case for an attack. Hill agreed and ordered Cleburne forward.

Liddell, with supreme arrogance, then told Cleburne, "General, I hope you will be quick, for a minute now will be worth an hour tomorrow." With that, Cleburne rode off to align his division for the assault.[10]

A few hundred yards in front of the Confederates, Thomas arrived after 5:30 P.M. and found Baird and Johnson conferring in the rear of Colonel Benjamin Scribner's brigade. Thomas rode with the two to show them personally the ground he had selected for their redeployment; a ridge a half-mile in their rear around the Kelly field, guarding the La Fayette Road. Before their ride, Johnson sent out handwritten orders to his brigade commanders to withdraw, but Baird waited until after the ride to inform his brigade commanders of their orders. This delay again kept Johnson's and Baird's men in position for Cleburne to attack. Johnson's brigade commanders received the order to fall back just at the moment Cleburne's men began engaging them through the Winfrey field.[11]

On the Union side, Johnson had his brigades arranged with Colonel Philemon Baldwin's brigade on the left, Brigadier General August Willich's brigade in the center, and Colonel Joseph Dodge's brigade on the right. In front of Baldwin's and Willich's men lay open ground, the Winfrey field, about 175 yards wide, through which any attacking Confederates would have to advance. To the left and rear of Baldwin's men lay Baird's division, with Brigadier General John Starkweather's brigade on the right and Scribner's brigade on the left. If Baird's men came to the aid of Johnson's men to their front, they would have to move almost directly through them, a fearful prospect in a night attack.[12]

At 6 P.M., with scarcely ten minutes of daylight remaining, Cleburne's brigades moved forward. They advanced due west, with Wood's brigade in the center, moving through the Winfrey field, Polk on the right, north of the field, and Deshler on the left, south of the field. As they moved through the ranks of the prone brigades of Liddell's and Cheatham's divisions, the latter sent up a yell, though one private in Brigadier General Daniel Govan's brigade warned some of Polk's Tennesseans that they would have some hard fighting ahead.

Wood aligned his brigade with the regiments in a single line, the 18th Alabama on the left, followed by the 33rd and 16th Alabama regiments, the 45th and 32nd Mississippi, and finally the 15th Mississippi on the right. Directly in the rear of Wood's men, Major Thomas Hotchkiss placed Douglas's, Semple's, and Calvert's batteries in position to support the advancing infantry. As Wood's men advanced toward the worm fence on their side of the Winfrey field, the 5th Kentucky, 1st Ohio, and 32nd Indiana of Baldwin's and Willich's brigades hunkered down with hasty breastworks of logs and rocks behind the fence on the opposite side of the field.[13]

Company A, 1st Ohio, had just begun to deploy as skirmishers in the field when Wood's men popped out of the woods to their front. Most of the skirmishers fled, while some stopped to give a parting shot first. The 1st Ohio began firing even before they could see the Confederate line, much to the chagrin of their commander. The woods had become quite dark by this point, but there remained enough light in the open Winfrey field for both sides to see each other. But with the fading visibility, the sound of battle became more important to the defending Federals as well as the Confederates groping their way forward. A heightened sense of sound seems to have affected almost everyone, as they all reported it to be some of the loudest and fiercest firing they had ever experienced.[14]

Wood's regimental commanders remained trepid as they entered the Winfrey field. Halfway across the field, the commander of the 16th Alabama halted his regiment for no apparent reason, and Colonel Samuel Adams of the 33rd Alabama to his left did the same. They remained halted for ten minutes before resuming the advance toward the muzzle flashes of the Union defenders opposite them. Some stragglers from the 33rd Alabama even began firing into the ranks of their own regiment, causing the death of, among others, the regimental adjutant. Only a steady stream of curses in the dark induced them to cease fire.[15]

In the dark, the attack began to stall. Up to this point, Wood's men had suffered relatively few casualties from enemy fire, as the defenders tended to overshoot their targets in the dark. Nevertheless, Wood's men began to falter in the dark and confusion. As their advance ground to a halt, Thomas Hotchkiss came to the rescue. He moved Semple's Alabama battery through the ranks of Colonel Mark Lowrey's 32nd and 45th Alabama and opened fire at short range on the Union defenders. Hotchkiss also brought up Calvert's battery on the right, which also unlimbered and began firing at the Union defenders. This fire sent many men of the 5th Kentucky, 1st Ohio, and 32nd Indiana scrambling to the rear for cover.[16]

On the left, Brigadier General John K. Jackson had brought his brigade up on the right flank of Wood's brigade just after the Alabamans cleared his ranks. Now, Jackson's brigade swept forward, driving the 32nd Indiana and 49th Ohio of Willich's brigade backwards. Colonel Sam Adams of the 33rd Alabama led his men across the now-vacant breastworks toward the 6th Indiana in the second line of Baldwin's brigade. Even as Adams had his men going forward, the commander of the 16th Alabama inexplicably ordered a precipitous retreat, and his men tumbled back through the Winfrey field after they had reached the cusp of victory.

When Adams's Alabamans rushed toward the 6th Indiana, Baldwin attempted to rally the regiment even as the remnants of the 1st Ohio dashed through their ranks toward the rear. Shortly, Baldwin reeled in the saddle and dropped dead, as the Indianans and Alabamans engaged in hand-to-hand fighting in the dark. Before long, the Hoosiers decided that discretion was indeed the better part of valor and withdrew to the rear.[17] This largely ended the fighting in the center, as the Winfrey field caught fire from the artillery blasts, and the blaze lit up the dark Georgia night. On either flank, Cleburne's other two brigades had not fared any better than Wood's Alabamans and Mississippians.

On the Union left, north of the Winfrey Field, Baird's and Johnson's men ended up mostly firing at one another in the dark, leaving Polk's Confederates to reap the benefits. As Polk and his men began to advance, Johnson, seeking a way to shore up his left flank, sent a note to Baird, asking him permission to bring Starkweather's brigade forward on the left of Baldwin's men, at that time engaged with Wood's Confederates. Baird consented, and Johnson then made the error of sending a note to Benjamin Scribner, whose troops lay on Starkweather's left, to move forward in a right wheel. Apparently Johnson hoped to catch the attackers in the flank as they advanced, but he only ended up causing more friendly fire incidents.[18]

As Scribner's 38th Indiana advanced, one private in the regiment noted: "Under the shadow of the pines it was very dark and most of the light was made by the flashes of musketry and artillery. The aim of the rebel artillery was too high to do much damage. Tree-tops, limbs and twigs were clipped off over our heads and fell all around us. The men who took a hand in that night fight will not soon forget it. It was a display of fire-works that one does not care to see more than once in a lifetime."[19]

To the right, as Starkweather advanced, his right flank regiment, the 79th Pennsylvania, encountered the rear of the 5th Kentucky on Baldwin's left flank. The Pennsylvanians fired into the Kentuckians, and the Kentuckians returned fire, causing massive confusion and casualties. Eventually, the two regiments realized their mistake, and ceased firing. Starkweather wrote: "No blame can be attached to any of the troops for these mistakes; they were unavoidable."[20] Just as Starkweather's men began firing into the rear of Baldwin's men, Starkweather executed a right wheel to try and get around the troops to his front. Unfortunately, Scribner executed his left wheel, which Johnson had ordered, at exactly the same moment. Scribner's men then began firing into the left rear of Starkweather's men.

Just as chaos reigned in the Union ranks, Lucius Polk's Tennesseans struck both brigades in the front. Initially moving forward, Polk reported that the right of his brigade came under heavy fire, but that the left encountered almost no resistance, thanks to the Federal mistakes. With this little resistance, Polk's men swept forward, carrying the field in front of them. Scribner and Starkweather remained unable to rally their commands until they reached the ridge east of the Kelly farm, where Thomas wanted them three hours earlier. Polk reported that he lost just sixty men in the fighting, and captured fifty prisoners, three pieces of artillery, and three caissons.[21]

On the Confederate left, south of the Winfrey field, Deshler's Texans and Arkansans experienced more success than Polk's men. As Deshler's men advanced, they veered to the left, opening a gap between the right flank of Colonel Frank Wilkes's 17th, 18th, 24th, and 25th Texas and the left flank of the 18th Alabama in Wood's brigade and slid completely past the right flank of the 77th Pennsylvania into the rear of Dodge's brigade.[22]

Just as the Texans stepped off, Brigadier General Preston Smith's Tennessee brigade of Cheatham's division moved forward into the gap created between Deshler's right and Woods' left. Thinking that he was advancing behind Deshler rather than to his right, Smith rode into the ranks of the 77th Pennsylvania and demanded to know what regiment it was. At that point one of the Pennsylvanians, realizing that he was a Confederate, fired at Smith, who fell lifeless from his horse. The brigade command then fell to Colonel Alfred Vaughn of the 13th Tennessee, and he too narrowly escaped capture.[23] While the drama of Smith's advance played out, Deshler realized his mistake and aligned his brigade to attack the 77th Pennsylvania and 79th Illinois in the front, flank and rear simultaneously, destroying them.[24] South of the main Winfrey field, a smaller, cleared glen contained the Winfrey house itself and a small orchard. Through this field, Deshler's men advanced toward the two unsuspecting regiments. "It was now quite dark," remembered Lieutenant Robert Collins of the 15th Texas Dismounted Cavalry, "but we struck the Federal line and moved it."[25] One of Collins's comrades, Private William Oliphant of the 6th Texas, remembered the night:

> It was now quite dark but just ahead of us was a bright light. A field was burning and we were ordered to charge through it. A battery had been stationed in the field and it was still there. It had been captured and then recaptured and then abandoned. The guns had set fire to the high sedge grass of the field. The fence was on fire and the tall dead trees were blazing high in the air. Dead and wounded men were laying in great danger of being consumed and the Federals occupying the opposite side of the field were pouring a deadly fire of shot and shell through the smoke and flames. Bowing our heads and grasping our guns firmly we plunged into that vortex of hell. On emerging from

the fire and smoke yelling like demons, we dashed at the Federals and soon had them flying.[26]

As the Texan skirmishers advanced, the skirmish line of the 17th, 18th, 24th, and 25th Texas Regiment stumbled into Union lines and were taken prisoner. However, the rest of the regiment, coming up from behind, charged forward, and surrounding the 77th Pennsylvania and 79th Illinois, freed their own men. While some Federals escaped into the woods, the rest surrendered. According to the regimental historian of the 77th Pennsylvania, seventy-three members of his regiment fell into enemy hands, sixty-four enlisted men and nine officers. Among the officers captured were Colonel Rose, commanding the regiment, and Corporal Woolsair, the color-bearer. The colors of the 77th Pennsylvania and 79th Illinois both fell into the hands of Deshler's Texans.[27]

A great deal of controversy has arisen regarding who captured the battle flag of the 77th Pennsylvania. In his history of the regiment, John Obreiter recalls that "The flag was captured . . . and passed through the ranks of the 17th and 18th Texas." Likewise, Sergeant W. W. Heartsill recalled, "our Brigade immediately charged the enemy and captured 250 and recaptured our skirmishers that were taken a few moments before, [and] we also got their flag which is a beautiful one." In his report of the engagement, Colonel Frank Wilkes, commanding the 17th, 18th, 24th, and 25th Texas, reported that the honor of capturing the flag of the 77th Pennsylvania should go to Private Lewis Montgomery of Company B, 18th Texas, and that the honor for capturing the banner of the 79th Illinois should go to Privates C. C. Martin and Benjamin Pippin of Company K, 18th Texas.[28]

Despite these claims, Colonel Alfred Vaughn of Smith's brigade also claimed to have captured the battle flag of the 77th Pennsylvania. In his report, Vaughn went into detail regarding the event. About the time Smith was killed by a member of the 77th Pennsylvania, Vaughn was in front of his regiment, the 13th Tennessee, accompanied by a Captain Donelson of his staff. Vaughn wrote:

> Riding up to a soldier, I asked to what command he belonged. Discovering that I was a Confederate officer he fired at me, missing me, but killing Captain Donelson, who was by my side. I immediately ordered some files [infantrymen] from the Twelfth Tennessee Regiment to shoot him, which they did, killing him instantly. The line in front, seeing their situation, cried out, "Do not shoot, we surrender." I then rode forward and found them in the act of grounding their arms. Discovering a stand of colors in my front, I asked, "Who has those colors?" The

reply was "The color bearer." I then said, "Sir, to what command do you belong?" He replied "To the Seventy-Seventh Pennsylvania Regiment." I then took from him the stand of colors and handed them to Captain Carthel, Forty-seventh Tennessee Regiment, and ordered him to turn them, with the prisoners captured . . . over to General Cheatham. The reason I have been thus explicit in detailing the facts connected with the capture of the stand of colors [is because] they were claimed to have been captured by General Deshler's command.[29]

Vaughn's claim remains unverified because the colors did end up with the 17th Texas, leaving the question of how the Texans acquired them unanswered. Vaughn offers no explanation for that. The most likely scenario is that Vaughn took possession of the colors just as Deshler's men dashed through the darkness and surrounded the Pennsylvanians, freeing Vaughn from potential capture and claiming the battle flag themselves. If this is in fact the case, Vaughn never had a rightful claim to the colors, because without the timely intervention of Wilkes's 17th, 18th, 24th, and 25th Texas, he would have been a prisoner himself and forced to return the flag. In any event, regardless of Vaughn's claims, it appears that Lewis Montgomery of Company B, 17th Texas, holds the honor for capturing the battle flag of the 77th Pennsylvania.

The capture of the 77th Pennsylvania largely put an end to Cleburne's night attack. The soldiers on both sides, confused and decimated, finally laid down to rest for the remainder of the night. Neither side would be in a position to move for quite some time. "The night wore slowly and sadly away," wrote a Union soldier of Johnson's division. "The pale-faced moon shone faintly over the field of carnage, and silently performed her nightly voyage. The two sides lay near each other, weary, wan, and terribly decimated, waiting for sunrise that they might renew the struggle." Things seemed just as bleak in Cleburne's ranks. "We lay in line of battle all night," recalled Lieutenant Collins. "We could hear the wounded men between ours and the federal lines calling for some of their comrades by name and begging for water. The night was cold and crisp and the dense woodland was dark and gloomy; the bright stars above us and flickering light from some old dead pine trees that were burning in an old field on our left and front, giving everything a weird, ghostly appearance."[30]

That night Lieutenant General James Longstreet and his First Corps, Army of Northern Virginia, arrived as reinforcements to aid Bragg and his Army of Tennessee. Bragg then faced a difficult decision: how should Longstreet fit into the army's infrastructure? Concluding that he should give Longstreet a large command, Bragg decided to restructure his army into two grand wings, the left under Longstreet, and the right under the second-highest ranking officer under his command, Lieutenant General Leonidas Polk. Bragg's restructuring of his army in the face of the enemy and in the midst of a battle probably stands out as one of the strangest decisions made by a Civil War army commander throughout the course of the war, but in view of the circumstances, it seems that Bragg made the best possible decision. The restructuring, though, left Lieutenant General Daniel Harvey Hill, Cleburne's corps commander, out of the loop and suddenly subordinate to Polk, whom he disliked.[31]

Still, Bragg's restructuring of the army did not necessarily prove fatal to the next day's efforts to destroy the Army of the Cumberland and capture the La Fayette Road. Instead, the execution, or lack thereof, of the orders, coupled with the state of Cleburne's division, did prove fatal. Bragg envisioned a series of hammer blows against Rosecrans's line, starting on the right with Hill's corps, and proceeding south, until Longstreet led the last attack against the Union right. This meant that Polk would be in charge of beginning the battle the next day, and Bragg instructed him at a midnight conference to attack at dawn, so as to give the Union troops less of an opportunity to fortify their positions around the Kelly field. Despite these orders, Polk did not try very hard to find Hill to give him the orders, and Hill, upset about being placed under Polk's command, did not make much of an effort to find Polk. Thus, as dawn approached, Polk had not communicated to Hill that he was to spearhead a daylight assault.[32] However, even if Hill and Polk had communicated immediately, it is unlikely that Hill and Cleburne could have gotten Cleburne's men organized and into position for a daylight assault. The night fighting had disorganized and cut up Cleburne's men so badly that it would have been almost impossible to awaken them in the dark, organize them, and get them into position on time.

As the sun rose on Sunday, September 20, it became clear that Polk could not carry out Bragg's orders, even as the Union troops made the best of their time. Shortly before dawn, George Thomas solidified his positions around the Kelly field and soon had his men fortifying those positions. Thomas Dodge, a Union soldier in Johnson's division, remembered the day: "Towards morning all was activity. Our army fell back to a better defensive position, contracting its lines and preparing for battle. . . . Prudence dictated ample preparations to meet the assault, and so the army was busily engaged from daylight until eight o'clock in erecting rude breastworks of logs and stones." Colonel Benjamin Scribner, commanding a brigade in Johnson's division, wrote: "Before daylight on the morning of the 20th we took up a position on the left . . . of our division. . . . Here we built temporary breastworks . . . and got all things arranged, when the enemy advanced upon us in strong force." Brigadier General John Starkweather reported that he got his men into position by three in the morning and immediately commenced felling trees for building breastworks, though this work would have taken several hours. Brigadier General John Palmer, commanding a Union division to the right of Johnson's men, wrote after the war that if the Confederate assault had started at dawn, "'the battle would not have lasted an hour; we would have gone to Chattanooga on the run.'" It seems abundantly clear from these statements that had Polk been able to carry out a dawn assault as ordered by Bragg, the Confederates could have turned Chickamauga into a complete victory by routing the Union left and cutting off the bulk of Rosecrans's forces from Chattanooga.[33]

But all of this became a lost opportunity for the Confederates. It was not until shortly before dawn that Polk even bothered to try and find Hill, and when he again failed, he sent orders directly to Cleburne and Major General John Breckenridge, another of Hill's division commanders, to attack as soon as possible. When the courier found Hill, he was seated with Cleburne, still unaware that Bragg had ordered a daylight assault. Even then, Polk's orders merely stated that Cleburne and Breckinridge should attack immediately. Hill, still upset about being relegated to a command under Polk, counter-manded the orders until Cleburne, Breckinridge and their men could cook and eat breakfast, thus wasting at least another hour. When Bragg arrived a little later, he discovered that even had Polk conveyed the orders to Hill and Hill had obeyed, there was little chance that the attack could have been carried out in time. Cleburne's men remained too out of position and worn down after the night fighting to move quickly at all. Finally, at 9:30 A.M., Cleburne and Breckinridge got their attacks underway, but by then it was too late. Thousands of Confederates fell in a vain attempt to dislodge Thomas's now entrenched veterans. Cleburne's night assault had not only cost the Confederates a chance for total victory at Chickamauga, but also a great many of his men their lives as well. Even though Longstreet broke through the Union right later in the day, Thomas's men, still intact, were able to stave off complete defeat for the Army of the Cumberland.[34]

In the end, it appears that St. John Liddell's admonition to Cleburne that "a minute now is worth an hour tomorrow," proved all too true, but not in the way Liddell meant it. Rather, every minute spent in the useless, unwarranted attack by Cleburne's men on the night of September 19 trans-lated into Confederate disaster the next day. Every minute on the night raid cost many of Cleburne's men their last hour on earth the following day and squandered an important opportunity for the Confederates to win a total victory at Chickamauga.

Notes

1. Craig L. Symonds, *Stonewall of the West: Patrick Cleburne and the Civil War* (Lawrence: University Press of Kansas, 1997), 144.

2. Peter Cozzens, *This Terrible Sound: The Battle of Chickamauga* (Urbana: University of Illinois Press, 1992), 263.

3. Symonds, *Stonewall of the West*, 7–120.

4. Cozzens, *This Terrible Sound*, 546.

5. First, Glenn Tucker in his 1961 monograph *Chickamauga: Bloody Battle in the West* (New York: Konecky & Konecky, 1961), 176, argued that Bragg should have used Cleburne to crush the Union right. Then in 1992 Peter Cozzens in *This Terrible Sound*, 263, echoed Tucker in this criticism, but the argument still does not appear to hold up under the weight of Confederate objectives.

6. Coleman quoted in Cozzens, *This Terrible Sound*, 263.

7. Ibid.; W. W. Heartsill, *Fourteen Hundred and Ninety-one Days in the Confederate Army: A Journal Kept by W. W. Heartsill for Four Years, One Month and One Day; or, Camp Life, Day by Day, of the W. P. Lane Rangers from April 19, 1861 to May 20, 1865*, ed. Bell Wiley (Jackson, Tenn.: McCowat-Mercer, 1953), 152; *The War of the Rebellion: A Compilation of the Official Records of the Union and Confederate Armies*, 70 vols. in 128 parts (Washington, D.C.: Government Printing Office, 1880–1901), ser. 1, vol. 30, pt. 2: 154. (Hereafter cited as *O.R.*; unless otherwise noted, all citations are to series 1, volume 30.)

8. St. John Liddell, *Liddell's Record: St. John Richardson Liddell, Brigadier General, C.S.A. Staff Officer and Brigade Commander Army of Tennessee*, ed. Nathaniel Cheairs Hughes Jr. (Baton Rouge: Louisiana State University Press, 1985), 143.

9. *O.R.*, pt. 1: 278–79. Baird claimed he did not withdraw his men because he anticipated an imminent Confederate assault, but this looks like wishful thinking in hindsight, because he knew as well as anyone the rarity of night attacks.

10. Liddell, *Liddell's Record*, 144.

11. Cozzens, *This Terrible Sound*, 265; William Sumner Dodge, *History of the Old Second Division, Army of the Cumberland Commanders: McCook, Sill, and Johnson* (Chicago: Church and Goodwin, 1864), 545.

12. Cozzens, *This Terrible Sound*, 267.

13. Ibid.

14. Ibid., 268.

15. *O.R.*, pt. 2: 165–66; Cozzens, *This Terrible Sound*, 269.

16. *O.R*, pt. 2: 173–75.

17. Cozzens, *This Terrible Sound*, 270–72.

18. Ibid., 272–73.

19. Henry Fales Perry, *History of the Thirty-eighth Regiment Indiana Volunteer Infantry: One of the Three Hundred Fighting Regiments of the Union Army in the War of the Rebellion, 1861–1865* (Palo Alto, Calif.: P. A. Stuart, 1906), 90.

20. *O.R.*, pt.1: 301.

21. Ibid., 176; Cozzens, *This Terrible Sound*, 275.

22. John Obreiter, *The Seventy-seventh Pennsylvania at Shiloh: History of the Regiment*, (Harrisburg, Pa.: Harrisburg Publishing, 1908), 162.

23. Ibid.; *O.R.*, pt. 2: 161.

24. Federal accounts confirm that the Texans struck the front, flank, and rear simultaneously. See: Dodge, *Old Second Division*, 549.

25. Robert M. Collins, *Chapters from the Unwritten History of the War between the States; or, The Incidents in the Life of a Confederate Soldier in Camp, on the March, in the Great Battles, and in Prison* (Dayton, Ohio: Morningside Press, 1988), 150.

26. James M. McCaffrey, ed., *Only a Private: A Texan Remembers the Civil War; The Memoirs of William J. Oliphant* (Houston, Tex.: Halcyon Press, 2004), 45.

27. Obreiter, *Seventy-seventh Pennsylvania*, 164.

28. Ibid., 164; W. W. Heartsill, *Fourteen Hundred and Ninety-one Days*, 152; *O.R.*, pt. 2: 194.

29. *O.R.*, pt. 2: 108.

30. Dodge, *History of the Old Second Division*, 551–52; Collins, *Chapters*, 151–52.

31. Steven E. Woodworth, *Six Armies in Tennessee: The Chickamauga and Chattanooga Campaigns* (Lincoln: University of Nebraska Press, 1998), 102–3.

32. Ibid., 103–4.

33. Dodge, *History of the Old Second Division*, 552, 554; *O.R.*, 287, 301; Palmer as quoted in Woodworth, *Six Armies in Tennessee*, 107.

34. Woodworth, *Six Armies in Tennessee*, 104–5.

6
—

BULL OF THE WOODS?
JAMES LONGSTREET AT CHICKAMAUGA

William G. Robertson

One of the best-known Confederate general officers in the American
Civil War is James Longstreet, "Lee's old war horse." His fame stems
from his substantial record in the eastern theater of the conflict and the
postwar controversy revolving around his role in the Battle of Gettysburg
on 2–3 July 1863. Long reviled in Confederate historiography, Longstreet has
enjoyed a renaissance in assessments of his performance for the last several
decades. As the aura surrounding Robert E. Lee and his generalship has
gradually waned in recent years, James Longstreet's stock among Civil War
scholars and popular writers has risen proportionately. Some of the reversal
in Longstreet's reputation has been driven by scholarship, some by a desire
to demolish the Lee "cult," but more has been fueled by the success of the
late Michael Shaara's novel *The Killer Angels* and the film derived from it.
Shaara's work, wildly successful as fiction, has become the iconic image of
the real James Longstreet as well, an outcome never intended by its author.
That image has now become the standard theme in all things Longstreet-
related: a stalwart and intelligent officer, who could see the future of warfare
better than his army commander, who wished to conserve the lives of his
men by protecting them from insane frontal attacks, and who recognized a
better path to victory but was denied the opportunity to follow it. Carried
to extreme, such an image does as much violence to the historical record
as the original image of James Longstreet as the man who single-handedly
lost the Battle of Gettysburg. What is needed is a more balanced portrayal
of this man, a portrayal that sees him as neither hero nor villain, but simply
analyzes his performance dispassionately. A useful place to begin such an
appraisal is the Battle of Chickamauga in September 1863, where Robert E.
Lee does not appear but James Longstreet does. Thus the controversies of
Gettysburg need not cloud the analysis of Longstreet's performance, which

can simply be seen in terms of the situation in which he found himself, his actions in response to that situation, and an assessment of those actions.[1] The man who arrived on the banks of Chickamauga Creek in north Georgia late on the evening of 19 September 1863 brought a great deal of experience with him. Born on 8 January 1821 in South Carolina, Longstreet graduated from the United States Military Academy at West Point, New York, in 1842 with a dismal academic record. Prior to the outbreak of the Civil War, he saw service on the frontier as an infantry officer and won two brevets in the Mexican War. Nevertheless, advancement in the combat arms was slow in peacetime. Ever ambitious and seeing a path to faster promotion by becoming a paymaster, he transferred to that specialty in 1858. April 1861 found him serving as a paymaster in Albuquerque, New Mexico Territory, with the rank of major. Two months later, he resigned his United States commission and threw in his lot with the Confederate States of America. In the new nation, promotion came rapidly for Longstreet: brigadier general in June 1861, major general in October 1861, and lieutenant general in October 1862. For the first two years of the war, he served in the eastern theater, where his battle experience was extensive. Present at First Manassas in a minor role, he soon rose to prominence during the battles of the Seven Days, Second Manassas, Sharpsburg, Fredericksburg, and Gettysburg. Absent in a semi-independent command in southeastern Virginia in April–May 1863, he missed Lee's triumph at Chancellorsville. Otherwise he was closely identified with the Army of Northern Virginia, where he led the First Corps. Indeed, by late summer 1863 James Longstreet was Robert E. Lee's senior corps commander. With Stonewall Jackson dead, Longstreet was indeed "Lee's old war horse" and a bulwark upon which Lee depended heavily. By August 1863 he was forty-two years old, strong, in good health, and supremely ambitious. That ambition caused him to seek his fortune elsewhere than the Army of Northern Virginia.[2]

The idea of drawing Confederate units from elsewhere to reinforce the Army of Tennessee did not originate with James Longstreet, but was something of a feature among participants in what historians have called the "western concentration bloc." Longstreet himself had suggested a generic version of such a transfer to Lee in January 1863. After preparing the ground through private correspondence with his patron, Senator Louis Wigfall of Texas, and a chance meeting with Secretary of War James Seddon, Longstreet again broached the subject with Lee in May. All of these proposals were politely but firmly rejected by Lee. Although Longstreet usually expressed his wish to go West in terms of a simple, altruistic desire to serve the Confederacy in a different venue, he was also driven by far more personal motives.

Three themes run through his private correspondence on the subject: he saw no more opportunity to assuage his ambition in the Army of Northern Virginia as long as Lee remained at its head; the Army of Tennessee's commander, Braxton Bragg, had suffered a long series of reverses; and Longstreet was supremely confident that he could be victorious if only he could be in untrammeled command of a field army. Following the unpleasantness of the Gettysburg Campaign, these thoughts could no longer be contained, and Longstreet began another lobbying effort to engineer a transfer for himself to the West. Again he began writing private letters to powerful politicians. To Senator Wigfall he confided on 18 August: "If I remain here I fear that we shall go, little at a time, till all will be lost. I hope that I may get west in time to save what there is left of us." While the idea of going was firm, the manner was negotiable. As the circumstances and the addressee dictated, Longstreet variously proposed to exchange places with Bragg, to serve under Joseph E. Johnston, to take his entire corps, or to take only a smaller contingent. The key goal was to remove James Longstreet himself from under Robert E. Lee's control.[3]

Longstreet's most recent biographers have placed a rather benign interpretation on the various letters he sent to Richmond in support of his campaign to leave Virginia. William Piston, for instance, suggests that Longstreet may have simply desired to serve under Joseph E. Johnston again, while Jeffry Wert denies that ambition was Longstreet's controlling motivation. Johnston seemed to understand otherwise, writing to Wigfall in March 1863 that "It is, indeed, a hard case for him, the Senior Lieut. Genl. & highest in reputation, to be kept in second place." Johnston, however, did not directly command the Army of Tennessee during this period, maintaining instead a nebulous and distant oversight of that command from Mississippi. As Longstreet was well aware, Braxton Bragg commanded the Army of Tennessee and generally operated without reference to Johnston. If Longstreet went to Bragg's army, he would have to supplant the North Carolinian in command if he were to gain the position he desired. Also, Bragg was a full General, while Longstreet was only a Lieutenant General, making a one-for-one swap impossible for reasons of rank alone. Still, as the days began to grow shorter and Longstreet grew more dissatisfied with his situation, a simple change of scenery might have seemed sufficient, for the moment. Ever since his switch from infantry officer to paymaster, if not even earlier, Longstreet's ambition had been on display as a bright thread in the tapestry of his career. One can deny that more was at play than a patriotic desire to serve the Cause, but a careful analysis of his letters that touch upon this subject in 1863 and the wording within them permits another interpretation entirely. Indeed, such analysis clearly delineates a disgruntled subordinate with a high opinion of his own abilities vigorously seeking an opportunity to enhance his personal reputation through transfer to another venue. It is the ambition, not the patriotism, which is most on display in Longstreet's private correspondence during this period, his own protestations to the contrary notwithstanding.[4]

Unknown to Longstreet, events in Richmond in late summer gradually made his transfer to the West more and more likely. On 24 August, President Jefferson Davis called Robert E. Lee to Richmond for several days of discussions in hopes of resolving critical issues of Confederate strategy. Lee initially favored taking the offensive again in Virginia, but as other dignitaries like Secretary of War Seddon joined the talks, reinforcement of the Army of Tennessee from the eastern theater came to be viewed more and more favorably. When Lee wrote Longstreet for detailed planning figures for just such a contingency, Longstreet begged off on furnishing the numbers. Nevertheless, he continued to argue strenuously for such a movement and offered to lead smaller numbers than heretofore proposed if transfer to the West could be arranged. Even before Longstreet's curious answer was received in Richmond, Davis made his decision, probably on 5 September. Braxton Bragg's Army of Tennessee would be reinforced by troops temporarily transferred from the Army of Northern Virginia. Those troops would consist of two divisions from James Longstreet's First Corps, and Longstreet would lead them. There was no talk, however, of Longstreet replacing Bragg; he would serve under Bragg's direct command. The movement would be by rail, with the units traveling by the direct route via Richmond, Lynchburg, Bristol, Knoxville, and Chattanooga. Total travel time was estimated to be approximately four days, over a distance of 540 miles.[5]

By the time the first of Longstreet's men were ready to board their trains in central Virginia, beginning on 8 September, their relatively easy and direct route had been denied to them. On 2 September, Federal forces under Major General Ambrose Burnside had severed it by capturing Knoxville, Tennessee. Army planners now had to scramble to cobble together a new routing, covering more than 800 miles. The original plan used five railroad companies of common gauge south of Richmond; the new one utilized as many as fourteen railroads of varying gauges, split into two alternate paths. Instead of arriving at Chattanooga within four days, the troops now would require more than a week to reach Bragg's army. Though the movement was now exponentially more difficult, it proceeded according to the new timetables worked out by Major Frederick W. Sims' Railroad Bureau. The decrepit state of the Confederacy's railroads meant that Longstreet's nine infantry brigades and one artillery battalion would travel piecemeal, with brigades split among several trains. For the troops the journey represented something of a triumphal tour through much of the South, with huge welcomes being the norm at virtually all stations passed en route. Although the practice was discouraged, many men seized the opportunity to pause long enough to visit families and friends before resuming the trip to north Georgia. By the time the leading element, Brigadier General Jerome Robertson's brigade, reached the vicinity of Bragg's command, the Army of Tennessee was no longer in Chattanooga. Forced from the mountain city about the time Longstreet's men began gathering at their Virginia railheads, Bragg had concentrated around La Fayette, Georgia, and was preparing to advance northward against Major General William S. Rosecrans's Federal Army of the Cumberland.[6]

When Bragg precipitated the Battle of Chickamauga by crossing the creek of the same name on 18 September, only Robertson's brigade of Longstreet's command and Major General John B. Hood participated in the initial skirmishes. On the next morning, the brigades of Brigadier Generals Henry Benning and Evander Law reached the field and joined Robertson's Texans before going into battle. Because Longstreet had not yet arrived, Bragg assigned Hood to the command of his own and Brigadier General Bushrod Johnson's divisions. Brigadier General Evander Law assumed command of Hood's division, consisting of the brigades of Robertson, Benning, and Colonel James Sheffield, who had replaced Law. Thus configured, Law's troops on 19 September participated fully in the heavy fighting in the Brotherton and Viniard fields. Longstreet, meanwhile, was just arriving in the area, having left Richmond on 14 September, well after most of his troops were on their way. Major Osmun Latrobe of his staff had reached Bragg's headquarters at 3:00 A.M. on 17 September, but Longstreet did not dismount at Catoosa Platform, Bragg's railhead several miles short of Ringgold, Georgia, until 2:00 P.M. on 19 September. According to Longstreet, no one met him at the platform with either news of the ongoing battle or directions to the fight. This lapse, if lapse it were, is usually blamed on Bragg, but Bragg and his staff were fully engaged all day in a serious battle. Why Major Latrobe was not there to meet his chief is unknown, as he seems to have spent the morning of 19 September with Bragg and the afternoon with Hood. Nevertheless, by some means, Bragg eventually learned that Longstreet had arrived in the area.[7]

Somewhat peeved at the lack of a suitable welcome, Longstreet and two staff officers, Lieutenant Colonels Moxley Sorrel and Peyton Manning, waited until 4 P.M. for the arrival of their horses, then started west toward the distant sounds of battle. According to Longstreet, they took the "main road," which could have been any of three roads leaving Ringgold in a westerly direction. Along the way, the party encountered troops bearing wounded men entering their path from the right, the same direction as the firing. If true, these statements would indicate that Longstreet's party was on a road that led southwest from Ringgold and would eventually encounter Chickamauga Creek at Lee and Gordon's Mill. Night fell before they reached the vicinity of the creek, where both Longstreet and Sorrel later claimed they were accosted by pickets presumed to be Federal. Employing a ruse, they withdrew safely by loudly announcing their intentions to cross farther down the stream and fading back into the woods. While it is highly likely that Longstreet encountered suspicious pickets, they could hardly have been Federal soldiers since none of Rosecrans's men were on the east side of the creek on the night of 19 September. Probably any pickets met east of the creek were elements of Major General Joseph Wheeler's Cavalry Corps facing the Federal brigade still holding the creek crossing at Lee and Gordon's Mill. Having possibly escaped a serious situation, Longstreet and his two friends retraced their steps until they reached a well-traveled road leading to Alexander's Bridge over the Chickamauga. Finally crossing the creek at that point, Longstreet's party took the current Viniard-Alexander Road toward the vicinity of Bragg's headquarters. En route, they met Lieutenant General Leonidas Polk and Major General John C. Breckinridge heading in the opposite direction. Exchanging no more than pleasantries, the two parties went their separate ways, Polk and Breckinridge to Polk's headquarters at Alexander's Bridge and Longstreet to Bragg's headquarters near Thedford's Ford.[8]

When Longstreet reached Bragg's camp around 11 P.M., he found the army commander asleep in an ambulance. Rousing quickly, Bragg proceeded to apprise the visitor of the situation and the plan for the next day. First, Bragg had divided the army into two wings, with Polk taking the right and Longstreet the left. Longstreet's new command consisted of six divisions. Major General John B. Hood led the divisions of Brigadier General Bushrod R. Johnson, Hood's own division under Brigadier General Evander M. Law, and two brigades of Major General Lafayette McLaws's division under Brigadier General Joseph B. Kershaw. Major General Simon B. Buckner contributed two divisions, led by Major General Alexander P. Stewart and Brigadier General William Preston. Finally, Major General Thomas C. Hindman's division from Polk's corps rounded out Longstreet's left wing. As for the plan, Polk's right wing would initiate an attack at "day-dawn" with the goal of turning the Federal left flank and driving Rosecrans's forces southward across the front of the Confederate left wing. Longstreet's command would then join the fight, and together the two wings would push the Army of the Cumberland southward into the mountains, away from Chattanooga. Although he would control one more division than Polk, Longstreet had the simplest task and would wait for Polk's troops to bring the battle to him. Polk's right-hand division would initiate the fight, and divisions would join the action sequentially from right to left until all were engaged.[9]

Having described Longstreet's command and explained the simple plan, Bragg gave Longstreet a map, promised him a guide, and bade the visitor good evening around midnight. Sunrise was less than six hours away and "day dawn" little more than five. Longstreet had already endured a long train trip from Atlanta, had ridden at least twenty miles, had nearly been fired upon, and had probably had little to eat. Now, in the middle of the night, he had been given an ad hoc command of nearly 23,000 troops, only five of whose seventeen brigades came from his old First Corps. At this point, Longstreet had two choices. First, he could spend the remaining hours of darkness searching in the foggy, smoky woods for his senior subordinates, hoping to learn enough about their commands and situations to use them effectively when the battle at last came his way. Second, he could lie down near a campfire for some fitful sleep until near daylight, leaving the necessary coordination to be done between dawn and the time the advance of Polk's left would trigger the advance of his right. To Longstreet the choice was easy. Weary from a long and arduous day of travel and with little ability to locate his subordinates in the dark woods, Longstreet decided to sleep until morning in the vicinity of Thedford's Ford. By so doing, he was taking something of a risk. If the battle began on time, Longstreet would have only a few moments to assimilate the location of his troops, and none to rearrange them. Still, Longstreet's experience was that battles seldom began on time. While some commanders drove themselves to a frazzle by going without sleep during a campaign, such was not Longstreet's way. Indeed, his decision proved to be eminently sensible for an officer in his situation.[10]

After no more than five hours of rest, Longstreet awoke on the morning of 20 September 1863 expecting to hear the roar of battle commence within the hour. He heard nothing because Polk's right-hand commander, Lieutenant General Daniel H. Hill had not received the order during the night to commence the attack at dawn, and was thus unprepared to do so when the order finally reached him some time after 6 A.M. Unaware of the reasons for the delay, but no doubt grateful for the additional time available to visit his divisions and adjust his lines, Longstreet rode to the front. With him was Private Thomas Brotherton, of the First Confederate (Georgia) Regiment, whose modest log home lay several hundred yards west of the right center of Longstreet's line. Brotherton would be available to serve as a living map of the terrain upon which Longstreet's troops would be fighting when the battle finally began. Upon meeting Hood, Longstreet learned that his front-line trace consisted of the divisions of, from left to right, Hindman, Johnson, and Stewart. Preston's division of Buckner's corps lay to the left rear of Hindman's division and would serve as the pivot around which the entire army would maneuver. It was worrisome that Preston's division was on the far left of Longstreet's wing while the other division of Buckner's corps, Stewart's, was on the far right. There did not appear to be time, however, to reunite Buckner's command before the battle began. Even more worrisome to Longstreet was the fact that Johnson's division lay in front of Hood's division, now under Evander Law, and that Kershaw's command (two brigades of McLaws's division) had not yet reached the front. Thus the troops with which Longstreet was most familiar were not in the front line at all. Finally, when Longstreet reached Stewart's division on his right flank, he was told that no Confederate forces could be found within a half-mile of Stewart's right. There was no connection whatsoever between Polk's right wing and Longstreet's left wing.[11]Finding things not to his liking, but not knowing how much time he would have to rectify matters, Longstreet chose to make only a few adjustments of a seemingly simple nature. He judged that there was not time to reunite Buckner's corps, so Buckner would have to do the best he could with widely separated divisions. Unknown to Longstreet, Buckner had operated just that way during the previous day's battle. Unhappy with Bragg for a variety of reasons, both significant and petty, he had chosen to remain relatively inactive with Preston while Stewart executed a masterful attack that momentarily broke the Federal line. As a result of Longstreet's decision to leave Buckner's corps split, Buckner would again remove himself from a significant role in the coming fight by trailing behind Longstreet most of the day. Much more significant was Longstreet's determination to place Hood's troops from Virginia in the front line. In order to make a place for Law's division, while at the same time extending his right toward Polk's wing, Longstreet ordered Stewart to shift his division approximately five hundred yards to the right. Stewart dutifully marched his division northward the requisite distance. Unbeknownst to Longstreet, Bushrod Johnson also shifted rightward shortly thereafter in response to Stewart's move. He did so by calling forward several units from Colonel Cyrus A. Sugg's brigade in the division's second line to extend Colonel John Fulton's brigade in the first line. Thus there was no hole in the front line for Law's division to occupy, and it remained behind Johnson. The failure to achieve his design for the First Corps troops was apparently unnoticed by Longstreet, who wrote in both his after-action report and his memoirs that Hood's old division made it into the front line after all. In only one sense was that assertion true. On 20 September John B. Hood commanded three divisions (Johnson's, Law's,

Kershaw's). Part of Hood's new command was in the front line, but none of his old one was.[12]

The effort by James Longstreet to place the troops he had brought from Virginia in his front line, while seemingly innocuous, had large consequences. At the end of the previous day's fighting, the defensive line of the Army of the Cumberland was the product of two forces. First, Major General George H. Thomas had selected a defensive position east of the north-south La Fayette Road in the vicinity of the Kelly farm, thus forming the northern half of the Federal battle line. South of the Kelly farm, the Federal battle line had been shaped by the punishing attacks of a succession of Confederate divisions, which had driven the Federals west of the same La Fayette Road. Thus the Federal defensive trace represented a gigantic question mark, with part east of the north-south road and part west of it. The bulk of Polk's wing faced Thomas's perimeter around the Kelly farm, making its start line considerably farther east than Longstreet's, which faced the recessed southern half of Rosecrans's army. By moving his line five hundred yards to the north, Longstreet inadvertently placed Alexander P. Stewart's division in front of a considerable portion of Polk's wing. In fact, as events would soon prove, Stewart thus masked Major General Benjamin F. Cheatham's division, Polk's left-hand unit, and also part of Major General Patrick R. Cleburne's division of Harvey Hill's corps. Because Polk's attack would not begin until 9:30 A.M., instead of 5:30 A.M., Longstreet had just enough time to unwittingly slide his right in front of Polk's left. Unaware of the consequences of his shift to the right, which had yet to materialize, Longstreet believed that he had done all he could risk doing prior to the imminent attack. Stewart still did not touch Polk's command, but he refused his right brigade and hoped for the best. Longstreet meanwhile relaxed and awaited the opening of the battle.[13]

The final alignment of Longstreet's left wing after its commander's modifications was quite unbalanced. Beginning on the left, William Preston's division waited some distance in the left rear of Hindman's division, with its left on the Chickamauga. Preston was scheduled to be both the pivot for the entire army and the reserve of the left wing. On the left of the actual front line stood Hindman's division, arrayed with the brigades of Brigadier Generals Arthur M. Manigault and Zachariah C. Deas in the front line and Brigadier General Patton Anderson's brigade in a second line as a local reserve. To Hindman's right, Bushrod Johnson's division also formed in two lines, with Colonel John S. Fulton's and Brigadier General Evander McNair's brigades forward and Colonel Cyrus A. Sugg's brigade in reserve. Behind Johnson stood Law's division, also in two lines, but with a twist. Law's front line consisted of his old brigade, now under Colonel William F. Perry, with Brigadier

Generals Jerome B. Robertson's and Henry L. Benning's brigades behind it. In rear of Law, Joseph Kershaw's two newly arrived brigades waited in column as a reserve. Back at the front, Stewart's division formed on Johnson's right, with the brigades of Brigadier Generals John C. Brown and William B. Bate in front and Brigadier General Henry D. Clayton's brigade in reserve. Clearly, the right center of Longstreet's wing (the divisions of Johnson, Law, and Kershaw) represented a massive force, nearly half of the nearly 23,000 infantry troops under Longstreet's command. Indeed, as ultimately constituted, Hood's three divisions represented slightly more than 10,000 men, a number not terribly far removed from the number of troops in Pickett's Charge at Gettysburg. The questions a modern analyst must ask are: who created this column of three divisions and for what purpose?[14]

Postwar, with the results plain for all to see, Longstreet claimed that he had intended to create Hood's five-line-deep formation as a grand column to punch its way through the opposing Federal line. This supposedly represented a distillation of all the experience Longstreet had gained in assaults against rifle-musket armed opponents from First Manassas through Gettysburg. Yet, Longstreet's own after-action report, written in October 1863, makes no mention of any such rationale and indicates that Hood's old division under Law was in the front line, thereby reducing the five-line formation to three, at least in Longstreet's contemporary understanding. This error is repeated in Longstreet's memoirs. Further, Joseph Kershaw's after-action report casts more doubt on Longstreet's prescience. In that document, dated 15 October 1863, Kershaw noted that Longstreet had called his two brigades forward from their bivouac at Alexander's Bridge around 9 A.M., well after the right wing's attack should have begun. Had that attack started on time, Kershaw would not have been part of any column. As he understood his mission from the left wing commander, Kershaw was to serve as a reserve to Hood's (now Law's) division. Kershaw moved forward as directed, moving by the Alexander's Bridge and Brotherton Roads. The latter road brought him up behind the Johnson-Law column in marching formation, but not so close as to report to Hood. It was not until shortly after 11 A.M., when the general advance of the left wing was already beginning, that Kershaw was told by Longstreet to report to Hood. Doing so, Kershaw received orders from Hood to form a line of battle in his rear and follow Law's division, even then under hostile fire. Thus, rather than being a part of the grand column from early morning, Kershaw was a last minute addition to whatever troops were in front of him on the axis of the Brotherton Road. Contemporary evidence therefore tends to discount the idea that Lieutenant General James Longstreet was the author of the grand column idea. General happenstance was more likely responsible.[15]

While Kershaw was en route to the front, Lieutenant General Leonidas Polk finally initiated the long-delayed advance of his right wing around 9:30 A.M. According to Bragg's plan, the assault began with John C. Breckinridge's division on the Confederate right, followed a few minutes later by Patrick R. Cleburne's division. Next in line to the south was Benjamin F. Cheatham's division. As Cheatham moved forward, his brigade commanders soon found that their lines were masked by troops from Alexander P. Stewart's division of the left wing in their front. Riding personally to Bragg with the news, Cheatham was told to halt his division, which would go into reserve status. Such was not the case with the left side of Patrick Cleburne's division. The left brigade of Cleburne's command, Brigadier General James Deshler's, also found itself behind some of Stewart's men and was pinched out of line as Cheatham's men had been. Cleburne's center unit, Brigadier General Sterling A. M. Wood's brigade, was partially lapped by Brigadier General William B. Bate's brigade of Stewart's division, and the two brigades mingled in confusion, thereby halting the rippling of the Confederate attack southward. When he slid Stewart's division several hundred yards north earlier that morning in the failed effort to make room for Law's division in the front line, Longstreet thus inadvertently created chaos at the seam where the two wings met. The tangle created by the collision of Wood and Bate further stopped the smooth entry of units into the advance progressing from the army's right. Thus the left wing did not immediately take up the attack as Bragg had intended.[16]

Impatient that the left half of the army was not entering the fight, Braxton Bragg sent a staff officer, Major Pollock Lee, to reenergize the sequential attack from right to left. When Lee found Alexander Stewart and gave him Bragg's preemptory order to attack, Stewart responded with the original attack plan given him by Longstreet earlier that morning. Assured by Lee that Bragg's order superseded any of Longstreet's, Stewart sent his division forward without reference to what was happening to his right or left. Attacking alone, except for part of Wood's brigade of Cleburne, Stewart's division crossed the Poe Field and the La Fayette Road, shattered part of the Federal line, but was ultimately unable to hold its gains and receded to its start line. Seeing Stewart launch his forlorn hope, Longstreet held Hood's command before Major Lee could launch them also. Still, it was time to attack, so after a moment's delay Longstreet ordered the remainder of the left wing, minus Preston's division, to begin its own coordinated advance. Hood gave the order to Bushrod Johnson and at 11:10 A.M. that officer's first line stepped off in the direction of Tom Brotherton's cabin and the Federal line just behind it. As the divisions of Johnson and Law began to move, Longstreet sent Kershaw to Hood, who added the South Carolinian's two brigades to his command.

South of Johnson, Thomas C. Hindman's division also headed westward, seeking the Federals in the woods beyond the La Fayette Road. Having put his wing at last into motion, Longstreet and his handful of staff officers rode along behind Kershaw's men at the tail end of what momentarily had become the grand column. As Kershaw crossed the La Fayette Road and entered the woods beyond, Longstreet cautioned him to watch his right flank because Stewart's division was retreating in that sector.[17]

Because of circumstances neither Longstreet nor any other Confederate could have foreseen, there was no Federal battle line facing the bulk of Johnson's division as it advanced across the La Fayette Road at the Brotherton cabin. Only a few pickets from Brigadier General Thomas J. Wood's Federal division remained to dispute the passage of Johnson's left brigade, Colonel John Fulton's, because Wood had hastily withdrawn his command from the Federal line in response to a direct order from the Federal army commander. Johnson's right brigade, Brigadier General Evander McNair's, encountered slightly more resistance from Brigadier General John Brannan's division, but with his right brigade already mauled by Stewart's attack and his right flank open because of Wood's departure, Brannan too gave way quickly. Thus the grand column broke through the Federal line and into the Federal rear, not because of its great weight and its deep formation, but because of a brief lapse in William S. Rosecrans's understanding of the battle situation. Five lines weren't needed; a single line sufficed to crack the Federal army's right center wide open. James Longstreet could take no credit for the absence of formed troops in his front, but the battle was not yet over and there were yet decisions to be made as the Confederate column swept through a skirt of woods and into the wide fields of the Dyer Farm.[18]

For a few moments the advance of Longstreet's left wing bid fair to drive half the Federal army from the field. On the left, Major General Thomas C. Hindman's division smashed one Federal division and was only briefly held up by part of another in the south end of the Dyer farm. To Hindman's right Colonel John Fulton's brigade drove straight across the Dyer field without significant resistance, forcing Rosecrans himself to displace southward. On Johnson's right, Evander McNair received a serious wound, causing his brigade to halt at the east edge of the Dyer Field facing a line of cannon hastily assembled by the Federals. At that point, Law's brigade under Colonel William Perry reinforced McNair's men and all mounted a charge toward the gun line. While Fulton continued west unmolested, Brigadier General John Gregg's brigade, now under Colonel Cyrus Sugg, flanked the guns, forcing the capture of many of them. Advancing in Hood's fourth line, Brigadier General Jerome Robertson's brigade joined Perry's and McNair's men in claiming Federal guns as trophies. Back on the La Fayette Road, Brigadier General Henry Benning's brigade meanwhile turned north at the south end of the Poe field and formed a northern shoulder to the penetration. Yet the Federals were not yet done in the Dyer field, as a Federal brigade counterattacked from the north end of the field, causing a panicked retreat eastward by McNair's, Perry's, and Robertson's soldiers. Seeing the rout, Hood ordered Kershaw to take his own and Brigadier General Benjamin G. Humphreys's brigade to chase the troublesome Federals northward. After seeing Kershaw in motion, Hood rode to rally his former brigade, Robertson's Texans. While in the midst of his old command, Hood was seriously wounded in the right thigh and forced from the field. When Longstreet learned of Hood's incapacitation is unknown, but he appointed no successor. Nor did he seize the reins of command himself.[19]

Longstreet's exact location at this time is unclear, but he was probably still trailing the last of Hood's column as it reoriented toward the north end of the Dyer field. What is not in dispute is the situation facing the left wing. Shattered Federal formations were fleeing in all directions with triumphant Confederate units in rapid pursuit. In his heart of hearts, Longstreet could probably never have expected to be so successful so soon at so small a cost. What should be done next? Bragg's plan had called for a wheel to the left to drive the Federals away from Chattanooga, but Polk's right wing had clearly not been successful, and more Federals seemed to be heading northwest than south. Certainly the original plan had little relevance to the situation rapidly unfolding before his eyes. It was a critical moment that called for quick assessment of the options and a decisive response. With Hood down and Buckner momentarily shunning an active role, James Longstreet alone could orchestrate the movements of his six divisions to complete the victory. Yet Longstreet was not a commander that moved quickly, and he took no immediate action. Having fruitlessly asked for guidance from Longstreet, Bushrod Johnson halted his advance and sought reinforcements on his own. That search ultimately brought Thomas Hindman's division to Johnson's support. Although Longstreet claimed credit for reorienting Hindman northward, both Johnson and Hindman agreed that Hindman's move was made on Johnson's initiative. According to his memoirs, Longstreet about this time was distracted by the arrival of Henry Benning, who was distraught because he had become separated from his brigade after losing his horse. Soothing Benning sufficiently for the Georgian to regain his composure, Longstreet now paused to consider his situation. Calling for his lunch to be brought forward, he turned his horse to the northeast and headed off with Buckner on a personal reconnaissance of his right.[20]

Probing northward through the woods west of the La Fayette Road, Longstreet apparently got far enough forward to see the Federal positions still in place around the Kelly farm. Before he could be sure of what he had seen, he and his party were fired upon and forced to beat a hasty retreat. As soon as they had reached safety, Longstreet ordered Buckner, who had a spare battalion of artillery attached to his corps, to bring up several batteries to enfilade the Federal line. Satisfied that the Federals were beaten, he continued southward to the vicinity of the Brotherton house where his staff had laid out his lunch. Unknown to the Confederates, the area Longstreet had so cavalierly reconnoitered was essentially open to exploitation, with no large units between the Kelly Field perimeter and the rapidly forming Federal line of resistance on Snodgrass Hill. Leaving the half-mile gap unrecognized, Longstreet, Buckner and their staffs sat down to a tasty lunch of Nassau bacon and sweet potatoes. Several events occurred during this lunch. First, a Federal shell exploded nearby, striking Lieutenant Colonel Peyton T. Manning of Longstreet's staff. His mouth full of sweet potato, Manning began to choke to death until Longstreet noticed the problem and directed that Manning's mouth and throat be cleared. Second, when approached by Major William M. Owen of William Preston's staff, Longstreet offered Owen a number of captured cannon and teams. According to Owen, Longstreet was in an expansive mood and expressed the opinion that Federal resistance was dwindling and the battle would soon end in a Confederate victory. Meanwhile, the fight for Snodgrass Hill and Horseshoe Ridge had already begun as Johnson and Kershaw sent their tired troops up the wooded slopes.[21] Before he had left his lunch spot, Longstreet was summoned to meet Braxton Bragg, who had moved forward near the left wing. According to Longstreet, whose account of the meeting is the only one extant, he asked the army commander for reinforcements to build upon the gains already achieved. Longstreet did this notwithstanding the fact that he retained control of Brigadier General William Preston's division of approximately 4,000 enthusiastic but essentially untried troops. Buckner, to whose corps Preston's men belonged, had been reluctant for Longstreet to use them earlier, but they had been moved to a position just north of the Brotherton cabin by early afternoon. Making no mention of Preston, Longstreet asked for troops to be detached to his assistance from Polk's right wing. Bragg declined to grant Longstreet's request, believing it would make more sense to energize Polk's command for another effort in coordination with Longstreet's continuing attacks against the Federals holding the high ground northwest of the Dyer field. Rebuffed by the army commander, Longstreet tried another tack. This time he suggested that fresh troops could use the Dry Valley Road to gain the rear of those Federal units still resisting on Horseshoe Ridge and destroy them all. Unwilling to strip Polk's command to perform this movement, which flew in the face of the original battle plan, Bragg again demurred. The two men parted unsatisfactorily, with Bragg telling Longstreet that, as the latter remembered, he could next be found at Reed's Bridge, some distance behind the Confederate Right Wing. Indeed, after the meeting, Bragg did ride toward the right to energize Polk's command once again. He did not, however, go to Reed's Bridge. According to a staff officer of Buckner's, who spent the afternoon with Longstreet, the left wing commander returned to the vicinity of his earlier lunch site.[22]

If Longstreet indeed proposed to Bragg a flanking move via the Dry Valley Road, which cut through the hills just west of the Horseshoe Ridge/ Snodgrass Hill massif, he made no effort to implement it on his own with Preston's division of fresh troops. Just before 4:00 P.M. he told Buckner to employ Preston's command in what was essentially a frontal assault upon the hill mass over the ground earlier contested by Joseph Kershaw's battered brigade. The only fresh troops in the left wing represented a one-time shot to finish the battle in Longstreet's sector. Essentially, he was faced with three choices for Preston's employment: send the division along the Dry Valley Road in an effort to turn the Federal right; push the division into the gap between the two disconnected halves of the Federal army, thereby taking either the Kelly field perimeter or the Snodgrass Hill position in flank; or send the division straight uphill into the teeth of the Federal position on Horseshoe Ridge/Snodgrass Hill. For a man who later claimed that he had assimilated the lessons of Gettysburg, especially that of Pickett's Charge, it would seem that the last option should have been discarded immediately. Nevertheless, Longstreet chose to send Preston into a direct frontal assault against a position much stronger than Cemetery Ridge had been. There had already been at least twelve brigade-sized assaults against Horseshoe Ridge/ Snodgrass Hill, all of which had failed to carry the position. Because of his reconnaissance, his lunch, and his visit to Bragg, Longstreet was probably unaware of what had taken place since Bushrod Johnson had begun attacking the Federal position around 2 P.M. Joined by Hindman's three brigades and Kershaw's lone brigade, those assaults had regularly failed in a welter of shattered units and bleeding men. Now, with far better options available, James Longstreet simply decided to reinforce failure by sending three more brigades straight up the ridge.[23]

Throughout the afternoon of 20 September, the Confederate attacks against the Federal forces rallying on Horseshoe Ridge/Snodgrass Hill were brave but disjointed in the extreme. Brigadier General Bushrod Johnson began them around 2 P.M. at the west end of the hill complex and was joined shortly thereafter by Brigadier General Joseph Kershaw with his own brigade. Brigadier General Benjamin Humphreys supported Kershaw's right, but through an abundance of caution and an eventual order from Longstreet, he did not seriously assault the east end of Snodgrass Hill. Indeed, Humphreys's brigade lay in the gap between the two halves of the Federal army, the same gap that Longstreet had penetrated earlier but had not recognized. After Hood was wounded, there was great confusion in regard to who should coordinate the various brigade attacks then just beginning. Johnson met Kershaw in the Dyer field and asked for a date-of-rank check, which found Johnson to be senior by approximately three weeks. When one of Evander Law's staff officers brought a suggestion that Kershaw assume command of several of Law's brigades nearby, Kershaw was much embarrassed because Johnson's seniority stood in the way. A proposal by a member of Hood's staff that Longstreet be informed defused the tension. Both Johnson and Kershaw returned to their respective commands, doubtless expecting Longstreet to appear in person to resolve the issue. Following his command on foot, Kershaw was soon pinned down with his own brigade in a ravine at the foot of Snodgrass Hill, where he could not even communicate intelligently with his other brigade, Humphreys's. Law's division, meanwhile, did not again enter the fight, leaving the brigades of Perry, Robertson, and Benning to remain unengaged for the remainder of the afternoon. Resting behind Humphreys's brigade, they too faced the wide but unexploited gap between the two halves of the Federal line.[24]

While four Confederate brigades (Humphreys's, Perry's, Robertson's, and Benning's) dropped out of the fight on the eastern end of Longstreet's line, Bushrod Johnson resumed his attacks on the western end. When Major General Thomas Hindman appeared with his three brigades, Johnson was no longer the senior officer on that part of the field. Hindman formed two of his brigades on Johnson's left and sandwiched the third between Johnson and Kershaw. When all was ready, the attacks resumed, at considerable cost, and without success. Hampered by a wound received earlier in the day, Hindman nevertheless maintained what little control there was of the seven brigades attempting to drive the stubborn Federals from their positions atop the ridge. Although one junior officer later claimed that he saw Longstreet talking to Johnson at the foot of the ridge during the afternoon, it is far more likely that Longstreet advanced no nearer the fight than the Brotherton cabin, as described by Lieutenant Colonel Thomas Claiborne, who remained with Longstreet all afternoon. From that position, the left wing commander could see nothing of the desperate struggle occurring nearly a mile distant beyond two tree lines. At the very time that the Federals had been most in disarray and a firm hand controlling the exultant divisions of the left wing could have achieved victory, Longstreet was otherwise engaged, as recounted above. Now, at 4 P.M., he elected to commit Preston's division, the wing reserve, to assault over Kershaw's and Hindman's men in yet one more throw of the dice. Two of Preston's brigades assaulted the hill complex before the third arrived, and they were repulsed like all the attacks that had gone before. Fortuitously for the Confederates, Major General George Thomas, commander of all Federal forces remaining on the field, had been ordered to withdraw by the commander of the Army of the Cumberland. As darkness fell, the Federals slipped away, leaving three heroic regiments to be bagged by Preston's last brigade. At great cost in blood, Horseshoe Ridge/Snodgrass Hill finally belonged to the left wing.[25]

Longstreet's actions from 4 P.M., when he committed Preston's division, to the close of the battle are instructive. Lieutenant Colonel Claiborne, a member of Buckner's staff, suggested that Longstreet order Major General Joseph Wheeler's cavalry corps to join the fight on the Confederate left during this period. Wheeler had been operating all day south of the main battlefield and had already seized control of the vast Federal hospital complex at Crawfish Spring. It was unclear whether Longstreet's writ extended to Wheeler's command, and the wing commander initially hesitated to act. Pressed by Claiborne, Longstreet dictated two orders to Wheeler between 5 and 6 P.M., calling the cavalryman to assist the infantry. Even had Wheeler recognized Longstreet's authority, darkness and distance rendered the orders moot. Although he would later say that he knew of the Federal withdrawal and counseled immediate pursuit, Longstreet in actuality had no idea at the close of the action how far the Federals had gone. At 6:15 P.M., he wrote to Bragg, stating that the day's fighting was over and requesting a division to relieve Hindman's troops from the front line. He closed by saying that he hoped "to be ready to resume the conflict at an early hour to-morrow," hardly the sentiment of a man who knew that the enemy was in full retreat. Confirmation of Longstreet's ignorance of the location of the Federals on the evening of 20 September can be found in two messages sent by him early the next morning. In the first, timed at 5:30 A.M., Longstreet ordered Wheeler to scout forward to locate the enemy. In the second, timed at 6:40 A.M., he reported to army headquarters that he was engaged in sending forward infantry skirmishers to find the Federals and therefore could not immediately come to headquarters. Clearly, Longstreet knew no more than Bragg or anyone else at the end of 20 September where the Army of the Cumberland had gone. Only after many years of hindsight did the situation become obvious.[26]

As the hours passed on 21 September, it gradually dawned on the Army of Tennessee that its opponent had indeed left the immediate vicinity of the previous day's struggle. When Bragg met Longstreet that day, he requested Longstreet's ideas about subsequent movements. Longstreet, who had been on the ground little more than thirty-six hours, immediately proposed a bold movement to cross the Tennessee River upstream of Chattanooga, operate against the Federal rear, and force Rosecrans's army back into Middle Tennessee. If that proved impossible, he favored driving northeast to destroy Ambrose Burnside's command in Knoxville. Surprisingly for a man of Longstreet's experience, none of his grandiose schemes reckoned with several critical facts. First, the Confederate army had no pontoon train sufficient to cross the Tennessee River. Second, most of the troops that had recently joined Bragg by rail, including Longstreet's, had come without any transportation assets whatever. Third, the Army of Tennessee had incurred more than 17,000 casualties in the preceding two days, including numerous officers from major general to lieutenant. Fourth, Confederate movement across the Tennessee would open Bragg's line of communication southward to Rosecrans's interdiction and relinquish the booty scattered around the Chickamauga battlefield. With its ammunition supply depleted, its food stocks at dangerously low levels, and its single-track railroad lifeline collapsing under the strain, the Army of Tennessee, in Bragg's mind, was in no shape to mount such a campaign as Longstreet proposed. Perhaps Longstreet never expected it to do so; it was enough that he had placed a grander vision than Bragg's on the record, where it might later be revisited as evidence of his strategic ability. Over the next few days Bragg slowly pushed the Federals back into their Chattanooga defenses and settled into a semi-siege of the Army of the Cumberland. As that siege dragged on, the rancor that had long plagued the Army of Tennessee blossomed into full flower. Although he was a newcomer to the theater, James Longstreet played a prominent role in the ultimately unsuccessful cabal attempting to oust Braxton Bragg from command.[27]

Over the years, historians have generally been very kind to James Longstreet's performance at Chickamauga. A few samples from earlier times will suffice: Donald B. Sanger (1952): "His keen battle sense perceived the opportunity; his initiative and courage based on experience impelled the prompt action which brought success." Ezra J. Warner (1959): "At Chickamauga in September 1863, he was largely responsible for the Confederate victory." Building upon this view, Jeffrey Wert (1993) raised praise of Longstreet at Chickamauga to new heights:

Indisputably, Longstreet's presence on the battlefield on September 20 was the decisive factor on the Confederate side. He imposed his will and, most important, order on the Left Wing of the army. His tactical arrangement of the units—a narrow, deep column of attack—proved to be the ideal formation for the terrain and conditions on the field . . . The orderliness and the mode of attack rank him as one of the preeminent combat generals of the war. Few officers of that rank grasped the realities of or situation on a battlefield better than Longstreet. He saw what would not work at Gettysburg and fashioned what would work at Chickamauga. He had advocated the strategic combination that brought him and his troops to Chickamauga and then utilized his intellect and experience to formulate the tactical scheme that brought victory. It was the performance of a first-rate soldier, of a man who knew his trade.

While not ubiquitous, Wert's description of Longstreet's performance at Chickamauga is far more the norm than the exception.[28]

A careful reading of primary sources and a close analysis of just what Longstreet did after his arrival at Catoosa Platform on the afternoon of 19 September yields a far different picture than the now traditional view. It is clear that Longstreet came to the Army of Tennessee consumed by ambition and animosity toward Braxton Bragg. Reaching the field after a full day of battle had already occurred, he arrived too late to influence the development of the battle plan for 20 September. Contrary to his later statements, he was not responsible for the creation of the three-division grand column. He apparently never knew that Bushrod Johnson's division was at its head, and he gave Kershaw's command to Hood after the column began its advance. His efforts to place the troops from the Army of Northern Virginia in the front line, though not successful, inadvertently but directly resulted in the collision between his and Polk's wing, and the subsequent pinching out of more than six brigades from Polk's attack. He could not have known that Thomas Wood's Federal division would leave the line in front of him just as Hood's attack began. In all these things, Longstreet was hardly censurable, but neither was he prescient. Once the breakthrough occurred, he had a chance to display battlefield brilliance in a fluid and unexpected situation. Instead, he slowed the advance, did not aggressively probe for flanks and gaps, took a leisurely and expansive lunch break, and allowed four of his brigades to drop out of action for most of the afternoon. Most damning of all, through lack of attention and hands-on command techniques, he permitted a long series of uncoordinated and piecemeal frontal assaults against a position much stronger than the famous Cemetery Ridge at Gettysburg. George Pickett charged but once; Johnson, Kershaw, Hindman, and Preston charged multiple times up steep, wooded slopes against Federal troops with their backs to the wall.

James Longstreet, who later claimed to have known better, was responsible for all of those futile attacks and the resulting casualties.[29]

After Chickamauga, some Confederate troops called James Longstreet the "Bull of the Woods," a term of endearment. Careful, dispassionate analysis suggests that the "Bull" was remarkably passive in a situation tailor-made for brilliant improvisation. Such was not Longstreet's style, not at Chickamauga nor elsewhere. He did not—probably could not—change that style, and historians have been remiss in suggesting that he did in the dark woods bordering the "River of Death." As a result, he consciously employed no innovative methods and showed no tactical brilliance at Chickamauga, his postwar boasts notwithstanding. Instead, he employed the same slaughterhouse tactics used by his peers, tactics which the Confederate States of America could ill-afford. When Hood's wounding removed a key echelon of command, he took no action to repair the damage, leaving the outcome in the hands of the private soldier. That soldier deserved and had a right to expect a better leader. Many Civil War commanders would have performed far worse than James Longstreet did at Chickamauga in September 1863, some would have done as well, and a few would have done better. If historians are to make anything of the great Battle of Chickamauga, they must put aside hero-worship and coldly juxtapose actions taken against opportunities offered. Only by using that harsh calculus can a true assessment of a military commander be reached. By that calculus, James Longstreet's performance at Chickamauga is far less exceptional and far more average than many previous works have indicated.[30]

Notes

1. Michael Shaara, *The Killer Angels: A Novel* (New York: David McKay., 1974), xi, 52–73, 133–42, 191–216, 251–76, 300–318, 350–61, 370; conversations by William Glenn Robertson with Michael Shaara, Fort Leavenworth, Kans., 1–3 December 1986. For a critique of Shaara's counterfactual portrait of Longstreet in *The Killer Angels*, see D. Scott Hartwig, *A Killer Angels Companion* (Gettysburg, Pa.: Thomas, 1996), 2–5.

2. Important works on James Longstreet include: H. J. Eckenrode and Bryan Conrad, *James Longstreet: Lee's War Horse* (Chapel Hill: University of North Carolina Press, 1936); Donald Bridgman Sanger and Thomas Robson Hay, *James Longstreet* (Baton Rouge: Louisiana State University Press, 1952); William Garrett Piston, *Lee's Tarnished Lieutenant: James Longstreet and His Place in Southern History* (Athens: University of Georgia Press, 1987); and Jeffry D. Wert, *General James Longstreet: The Confederacy's Most Controversial Soldier; A Biography* (New York: Simon & Schuster, 1993). Longstreet told his own story in James Longstreet, *From Manassas to Appomattox: Memoirs of the Civil War in America* (Philadelphia: J. B. Lippincott, 1896; repr., Bloomington: Indiana University Press, 1960), although he apparently had some unacknowledged assistance in the writing. See William W. Hassler, "The 'Ghost' of General Longstreet," *Georgia Historical Quarterly* 14, no.1 (Spring 1981): 22–27.

3. United States War Department, *The War of the Rebellion: A Compilation of the Official Records of the Union and Confederate Armies*, 70 volumes in 128 parts (Washington, D.C.: Government Printing office, 1880–1901), ser. 1, vol. 18: 959, and vol. 29, pt. 2: 693–94, 699. (All subsequent references are to series 1, and will hereafter be cited as *OR*.); Thomas Lawrence Connelly, *Autumn of Glory: The Army of Tennessee, 1862–1865* (Baton Rouge: Louisiana State University Press, 1971), 100–101, 150–51; Thomas Lawrence Connelly and Archer Jones, *The Politics of Command: Factions and Ideas in Confederate Strategy* (Baton Rouge: Louisiana State University Press, 1973), 49–86; Piston, *Lee's Tarnished Lieutenant*, 42, 65–67; Wert, *Longstreet*, 226–28, 239–41, 300–303; Longstreet, *Manassas*, 327–28, 330–31, 433–35.

4. Piston, *Lee's Tarnished Lieutenant*, 44, 66–67; Wert, *Longstreet*, 302–3. On the other hand, Thomas Lawrence Connelly and Archer Jones had no doubt that Longstreet's motives were less than lofty: "Longstreet's peculiar interest in a western concentration seemed to be based on selfish ambitions—he hoped to obtain command of the Army of Tennessee." Connelly and Jones, *Politics of Command*, 52–53.

5. *OR*, vol. 29, pt. 2: 699–701; vol. 51, pt. 2: 759–61; Roger Pickenpaugh, *Rescue by Rail: Troop Transfer and the Civil War in the West, 1863* (Lincoln: University of Nebraska Press, 1998), 27–28. Secretary of War Seddon apparently played a key role in Davis's decision. According to a member of Longstreet's staff, John W. Fairfax, "the night before my going a brother of the Sec. of War called to see me, in my room in the Spottswood Hotel, Richmond. Mr. Seddon told me: 'When you get to the Army of the Tenn. you will find Longstreet in command of that army.'" John Walter Fairfax to Joseph Bryan, 1 August 1902, John Walter Fairfax Papers, Virginia Historical Society, Richmond, Va.

6. Robert C. Black III, *The Railroads of the Confederacy* (Chapel Hill: University of North Carolina Press, 1952), 184–91; Pickenpaugh, *Rescue by Rail*, 28–43.

7. *OR*, vol. 29, pt. 2: 713; vol. 30, pt. 2: 33, 287, 510–11, 517–18; William C. Oates, *The War between the Union and the Confederacy* (New York: Neale, 1905; repr., Dayton, Ohio: Press of Morningside Bookshop, 1985), 253–54; Longstreet, *Manassas*, 437; H. M. Drane to F. W. Sims, 15 September 1863, and J. H. Bowen to F. W. Sims, 16 September 1863, both in Telegrams to and from Frederick W. Sims, Valentine Museum, Richmond, Va.; Osmun Latrobe diary, 17 and 19 September 1863, Maryland Historical Society, Baltimore, Md.; George Brent diary, 17 September 1863, Braxton Bragg Papers, Western Reserve Historical Society, Cleveland, Ohio.

8. *OR*, vol. 30, pt. 2: 2: 287; Longstreet, *Manassas*, 437–38; G. Moxley Sorrel, *Recollections of a Confederate Staff Officer* (New York: Neale, 1905; repr., Dayton, Ohio: Press of Morningside Bookshop, 1978), 192–93; Frank A. Burr interview with James Longstreet, *Cincinnati Enquirer*, 1 April 1883. Longstreet's and Sorrel's accounts of the encounter with the hostile pickets differ slightly in the details, with Sorrel claiming that shots were fired.

9. Sorrel, *Recollections*, 193–94; Longstreet, *Manassas*, 438–39; *OR*, vol. 30, pt. 2: 33, 287–88; Burr interview.

10. Sorrel, *Recollections*, 193; Longstreet, *Manassas*, 439; *OR*, vol. 30, pt. 2: 290–91. Sunrise on 20 September 1863 at Chickamauga was at 5:47 A.M. William M. Polk, *Leonidas Polk: Bishop and General* (New York: Longmans, Green, 1894), 2:249–50n.

11. James Alfred Sartain, *History of Walker County, Georgia* (Dalton, Ga.: A. J. Showalter, 1932), 102–3; Glenn Tucker, *Chickamauga: Bloody Battle in the West* (In-

dianapolis: Bobbs-Merrill, 1961; repr., Dayton, Ohio: Press of Morningside Bookshop, 1972), 262–63; *OR*, vol. 30, pt. 2: 288, 363; Longstreet, *Manassas*, 439–40; J. B. Hood, *Advance and Retreat: Personal Experiences in the United States and Confederate States Armies* (New Orleans: Hood Orphan Memorial Fund, 1880; repr., Bloomington: Indiana University Press, 1959), 62–63.

12. *OR*, vol. 30, pt. 2: 288, 357, 363, 456; Longstreet, *Manassas*, 439–40, 447–48; Connelly, *Autumn of Glory*, 156–58. In his own memoirs, Hood claimed to have commanded five of Longstreet's six divisions, but that would have left Longstreet virtually without a command. In addition, one of the five division commanders, Hindman, outranked Hood, so the latter's claim is clearly spurious. Hood, *Advance and Retreat*, 63.

13. *OR*, vol. 30, pt. 2: 79, 155, 161, 363. According to the placement of unit markers on the battlefield, Longstreet's start line was approximately one-half mile forward (west) of Polk's wing.

14. According to Bushrod Johnson's report, Fulton's brigade numbered only 556 officers and men on 20 September, while Sugg's brigade totaled 858. McNair's brigade furnished no report for 20 September, but counted an aggregate of 1,207 on the previous day. Subtracting an estimated 200 casualties on 19 September from McNair's original number yields a brigade strength on 20 September of approximately 1,000 officers and men. Johnson's division thus mustered approximately 2,400 officers and men for the advance. *OR*, vol. 30, pt. 2: 467. According to tallies collected by Bragg's staff, Law's division consisted of 3,965 officers and men on 20 September, while Kershaw's two brigades numbered 3,670. Kinloch Falconer, "Tabular Statement showing the number of effectives in the Battle of Chickamauga, September 19th & 20th 1863," Joseph Jones Papers, Special Collections, Tulane University, New Orleans, La.. Thus Hood's eight brigades contained a few more than 10,000 troops. A recent and authoritative study of Pickett's Charge yields a total of 11,800 troops in that assault. Earl J. Hess, *Pickett's Charge: The Last Attack at Gettysburg* (Chapel Hill: University of North Carolina Press, 2001), 39, 57, 69.

15. James Longstreet to E. P. Alexander, 17 June 1869, quoted in Wert, *Longstreet*, 311–12; *OR*, vol. 30, pt. 2: 288, 503; Longstreet, *Manassas*, 440, 447.

16. *OR*, vol. 30, pt. 2: 79, 155, 161, 198, 385.

17. Ibid., 288, 303, 363–64, 457, 503; Longstreet, *Manassas*, 447.

18. *OR*, vol. 30, pt.1: 402, 409, 635, 656, 672; pt. 2: 474–75, 500; John J. Hight, *History of the Fifty-eighth Regiment of Indiana Volunteer Infantry* (Princeton, Ind.: Press of the Clarion, 1895), 189–90.

19. *OR*, vol. 30, pt. 2: 303–4, 474–75, 495, 498, 500–501, 503–4, 509, 511–12, 517–18; W. F. Perry Account of Chickamauga, Ezra Carman Papers, Library of Congress, Washington, D.C.; Joseph Q. Burton, *Historical Sketch of the Forty-seventh Alabama Infantry Regiment, C. S. A.* (University, Ala.: Confederate Publishing, 1982), 9; *OR*, vol. 30, pt. 1: 59–60, 636–37, 694; Hood, *Advance and Retreat*, 63–64.

20. Benjamin G. Humphreys, Manuscript History of the "Sunflower Guards," J. F. H. Claiborne Papers, Southern Historical Collection, University of North Carolina, Chapel Hill, N.C.; *OR*, vol. 30, pt. 2: *OR*, vol. 30, pt. 2: 288–89, 304, 358, 459–60; Longstreet, *Manassas*, 448–50.

21. Longstreet, *Manassas*, 450–51; *OR*, vol. 30, pt. 2: 289, 358, 360, 461–62, 503–4; John B. Turchin, *Chickamauga* (Chicago: Fergus, 1888), 140–42; William Miller

Owen, *In Camp and Battle with the Washington Artillery* (Boston: Ticknor, 1885), 281–82. While often placed in the vicinity of the Dyer house in Dyer field, the site of Longstreet's lunch is much more likely to have been near the Brotherton cabin on the La Fayette Road. Owen's description of his movements and the fact that Federal artillery was firing down the La Fayette Road lend credence to this view. See also Thomas Claiborne letter, 16 April 1891, Eyewitness Accounts Folder, Chickamauga and Chattanooga National Military Park, Ft. Oglethorpe, Ga.

22. Longstreet, *Manassas*, 451–52; Claiborne letter, 16 April 1891; Owen, *In Camp and Battle*, 278–81; *OR*, vol. 30, pt. 2: 34, 357–58, 415, 419. The location of the Bragg-Longstreet conference is unknown. It could have been at the site of the present marker for Bragg's headquarters in the woods east of the La Fayette Road, or it could have been on the road itself, where Major Owen saw Bragg as Preston's division moved toward Brotherton's. Owen, *Camp and Battle*, 279. Longstreet's call for reinforcements here seems to have been part of a more general pattern, as explained by Major General Lafayette McLaws: "You can follow Longstreet's career, from the First battle of Manassas to the close of the war, and you will see that the first act, in any engagement, was to call for reinforcements; not that any reinforcements were needed, but that was his policy." Lafayette McLaws to Charles Arnall, 2 February 1897, quoted in Robert K. Krick, "If Longstreet . . . Say So, It Is Most Likely Not True," in Gary W. Gallagher, ed., *The Second Day at Gettysburg: Essays on Confederate and Union Leadership* (Kent, Ohio: Kent State University Press, 1993), 65.

23. *OR*, vol. 30, pt. 2: 289, 304–5, 358, 415, 462–63, 504. The number of assaults is computed at twelve by crediting Kershaw's brigade with three, Johnson's three brigades with two each, and Hindman's three brigades with one each. If Humphreys's abortive efforts are counted, the number rises to at least thirteen brigade-sized assaults before Preston arrived at the base of the ridge.

24. *OR*, vol. 30, pt. 2: 304–5, 460, 462–63, 503–6, 509, 512, 518–19; W. F. Perry Account of Chickamauga, Ezra Carman Papers, Library of Congress, Washington, D.C.; Benjamin G. Humphreys, Manuscript History of the "Sunflower Guards," J. F. H. Claiborne Papers, Southern Historical Collection, University of North Carolina, Chapel Hill, N.C.

25. *OR*, vol. 30, pt. 2: 289, 304–5, 415–17, 462–64; "Reminiscences of Capt. William Henry Harder," Tennessee State Library and Archives, Nashville, Tenn.; Thomas Claiborne Letter, 16 April 1891, Eyewitness Accounts Folder, Chickamauga and Chattanooga National Military Park, Ft. Oglethorpe, GA; 30 *OR* 1: 253–254. Buckner certainly remained at the Brotherton cabin during this period, as Preston noted.

26. Claiborne letter, 16 April 1891; *OR*, vol. 30, pt. 4: 675, 682; Longstreet, *Manassas*, 453; *OR*, vol. 30, pt. 2: 520–21; Longstreet to Braxton Bragg, 6:15 P.M., 20 September 1863, George Brent to James Longstreet, 20 September 1863, and Longstreet to Braxton Bragg, 6:40 A.M., 21 September 1863, all in Braxton Bragg Papers, Western Reserve Historical Society, Cleveland, Ohio. In response to Longstreet's 6:15 P.M. message, Bragg asked the left wing commander to come to headquarters that night and provided guides to show the way. In his reply to Bragg of 6:40 A.M. the next day, Longstreet claimed that he had just received the request for a meeting and even then was too busy to visit the army commander. By 1883 everything was clear, as Longstreet explained: "I sent [Bragg] word that our victory was now complete, and the fruits of it should be rapidly gathered." Frank A. Burr interview with James Longstreet, *Cincinnati Enquirer*, 1 April 1883.

27. Longstreet, *Manassas*, 461–62, 464–68; *OR*, vol. 30, pt. 2: 24, 34–37, 289–90; Braxton Bragg Notes on Chickamauga, Braxton Bragg Papers, Western Reserve Historical Society, Cleveland, Ohio; *OR*, vol. 30, pt. 4: 705–6, 728, 742–43; "Statement of casualties in the Army of Tennessee in the engagements of the 19th and 20th September 1863," Joseph Jones Papers, Special Collections, Tulane University, New Orleans, La. Longstreet's key role in the anti-Bragg cabal is carefully documented in Hal Bridges, *Lee's Maverick General: Daniel Harvey Hill* (New York: McGraw-Hill, 1961), 233–39. Although Hill plainly stated to Longstreet in 1888 that he had not written the anti-Bragg petition prepared for Jefferson Davis, Longstreet after Hill's death claimed that Hill was the author. Longstreet to Marcus J. Wright, 22 August 1892, Eldridge Collection, Huntington Library, San Marino, Calif.; Longstreet, *Manassas*, 465.

28. Sanger and Hay, *Longstreet*, 207; Ezra J. Warner, *Generals in Gray: Lives of the Confederate Commanders* (Baton Rouge: Louisiana State University Press, 1959), 193; Wert, *Longstreet*, 321. In fairness to Wert, he does recognize several of James Longstreet's shortcomings at Chickamauga, but his summation of Longstreet's performance in that battle is difficult to support after close analysis.

29. Longstreet's most obvious mistake after penetrating the Federal line on the afternoon of 20 September 1863 was his failure to use four of his own First Corps brigades to good effect. For most of the afternoon, the brigades of Humphreys, Robertson, Perry, and Benning stood idle facing the half-mile gap between the disconnected halves of the Army of the Cumberland. Robertson's and Benning's brigades had suffered heavily on the previous day, but Perry's had not, and Humphreys's men were new to the battle and thus unbloodied. Movement of this battle-hardened force into the gap, whose terrain consisted solely of flat woods, would in all probability have led to the collapse of the four Federal divisions in the Kelly field perimeter facing eastward against Polk's right wing. Preston's division lay directly behind the four brigades before it was sent to charge frontally at Snodgrass Hill. Add Preston's troops to the four brigades facing the gap, and the destruction of the Army of the Cumberland most likely would have been complete. See Buckner's after-action report in *OR*, vol. 30, pt. 2: 357–58, for only a partial description of the mass of Confederate units doing nothing in the vicinity of the Poe house for most of the afternoon. The handful of anonymous Federals whose shots halted James Longstreet's reconnaissance in the gap early in the afternoon performed a far greater service for the Army of the Cumberland than they could possibly have imagined.

30. Fitzgerald Ross, *Cities and Camps of the Confederate States*, ed. Richard Barksdale Harwell (Urbana: University of Illinois Press, 1958), 125.

7

NEGLEY AT HORSESHOE RIDGE
SEPTEMBER 20, 1863

David Powell

Union Major General James S. Negley was uneasy. The time was 11:00 A.M. on September 20, 1863, the second day of the battle of Chickamauga. Due to tactical emergencies elsewhere, his command, the 2nd Division, 14th Army Corps, Army of the Cumberland, had largely been taken from him and dispatched to other points of the line. Now he was assigned a position on a high, open ridge, left with only one of his three infantry brigades, and ordered to assemble and protect an artillery reserve. He did not know the status of his other two brigades, or indeed, most of the army. So far, his role had been limited to a brief but hurried attack the evening before and a morning of impatient waiting. His corps commander, Major General George H. Thomas, had been sending repeated and urgent requests for Negley's command to be replaced by other troops in the Brotherton field so it could join the rest of the corps in the Kelly field. Then, when his men were finally replaced, he was given this new mission far from the fight. On top of everything else, he was sick: Very sick. He had no business being on a horse, let alone trying to command a division. In the opinion of Surgeon R. G. Bogue, the 2nd divisional medical director, Negley was "really unable to be on duty, being a fitter case for a bed patient."[1] Shortly, however, General Negley would be called upon to make the most fateful decision of his military career and with no guidance or help from his superiors. The battle was about to come to him.

James Scott Negley was one of Pittsburgh, Pennsylvania's, leading sons, with strong military credentials, at least for the citizen soldiers of the era. After graduating from the Western University of Pennsylvania, he joined the local militia and served through the length of the Mexican War.[2] He remained in the militia after returning home and by the time the Civil War erupted he was a brigadier general in the state forces. In October 1861 he was commissioned as a brigadier general of U.S. volunteers and served in

Kentucky and Tennessee for the next two years. When Confederate General Braxton Bragg invaded Kentucky in the fall of 1862, Negley successfully defended Nashville from various Rebel probes. He and his division next won noted acclaim for their gallant stand at Stones River. That fight also won him his promotion to major general, recommended by the army commander himself, William S. Rosecrans.[3]

Negley had begun the Chickamauga campaign as the senior divisional commander in Thomas's 14th Corps. The first week or so had been strenuous, crossing the Tennessee River near Stevenson, Alabama, on September 1, and climbing both Sand and Lookout Mountains over the next several days. On September 9, as his division descended Lookout Mountain into McLemore's Cove, Negley encountered Rebel cavalry. He was now leading the advance of Thomas's entire corps. Their objective was La Fayette, on the east side of Pigeon Mountain, a spur of the larger Lookout Mountain. Taking La Fayette would help reunite all three of Rosecrans's scattered infantry corps and signal the success of the first stage of the campaign to flank Bragg out of Chattanooga and bring him to battle. The town itself was only supposed to be lightly defended, with Bragg's main body in full retreat to Dalton, Georgia, much farther east.

Enemy resistance further stiffened the next day, and the reports filtering into Negley's headquarters suggested that, far from retreating, Bragg's whole army was instead concentrating at La Fayette. If so, Negley, with only one division, was marching into a trap. Fearing the worst, Negley halted at Davis's Crossroads and appealed to Thomas for reinforcements. A couple of miles ahead of him, Dug Gap provided access through Pigeon Mountain to La Fayette. The enemy had a cavalry division to screen their movements while Negley had only his escort, one company of mounted troops. Thomas, alert to the potential danger, hurried another infantry division forward under Brigadier General Absalom Baird, raising Negley's total force to about 11,000 men.

Negley's fears were well-founded. Bragg was assembling a force to crush the Federals, including no less than five Rebel divisions, numbering in all about 26,000 infantry. Confederates were ahead of him to the east, in Dug Gap, and to his north, the only way out of McLemore's Cove that did not require an arduous mountain crossing. Southward the cove pinched into a narrow valley where Pigeon Mountain joined Lookout Mountain, and the only escape there was up a narrow winding road through Daugherty's Gap. Retreating back west was no easier; Negley's now combined force of two divisions would have to climb back up Lookout Mountain via Stevens' Gap. Getting the trains and artillery up and through the gaps would create significant bottlenecks, making any retreat slow and very risky.

Throughout the eleventh, Negley orchestrated a controlled withdrawal toward Stevens' Gap, all the while hoping that the Confederates did not attack. His escape had as much to do with a series of command problems within the Confederate army as with Federal skill, but by dusk both divisions had retreated to defensible ground near Bailey's Crossroads. The only action was some limited fighting with the rear guard toward the end of the day. On September 12, a third division joined the force and the supply trains had largely escaped via Stevens' Gap. Better yet, the Rebels withdrew back to Dug Gap, having realized they missed their best chance to crush Negley's command. The crisis was over. The strain of the moment, however, had told on Negley.

That night he went to Surgeon Bogue, who diagnosed him with diarrhea and gave him medicine. By September 15, Negley was too sick to move, spending that day and the next in bed, unfit for duty. Fortunately the division remained stationary on both days waiting for other Federal units to catch up. September 17, however, required a march. Negley attempted to return to duty, riding his horse, but an ambulance trailed him wherever he went, as a precaution. Even this effort exhausted him. Nevertheless, when the division marched again on the eighteenth, Negley was back in the saddle. He was also up most of the night, seeing to the details of his command. The next three days would involve similar activity, as the armies came together along Chickamauga Creek.

When the battle began in earnest on the nineteenth, the 14th Corps was in the forefront of the fighting, all except Negley's command. His division, once in the lead, had become the rear of the corps when Rosecrans reversed course to retreat back to Chattanooga. On the afternoon of the eighteenth, Negley was ordered to move to Glass Mill, a mile or two upstream from Lee and Gordon's Mill, and relieve Brigadier General William B. Hazen's brigade so that force could join their own corps farther north. Once at Glass Mill, however, Negley discovered that Hazen had not been informed of the relief and had no orders to move. Arriving at the scene, Negley's troops halted and then marched back toward Crawfish Spring. Negley himself sent an aide to find Thomas and inform him of the confusion. Major J. A. Lowrie found Thomas at Rosecrans's headquarters and informed both generals of the problem. Major General John M. Palmer, Hazen's division commander, was also present and quickly re-sent the order to Hazen to move out. This new directive cleared up the confusion but not before Negley's men had shuffled around for several hours in pointless countermarching.[4] The mishap over the order to relieve Hazen did not ultimately affect the outcome of the battle but it was a foreshadowing of similar confusion and frustration over the next couple of days. The night itself was a tense one for the men of the division. Lieutenant

Colonel William D. Ward, commanding the Thirty-seventh Indiana Infantry, recalled that he was directed to form his unit in line, facing north, with what he thought was his back to the enemy. Ward noted, "I obeyed the order but could not, during the night, rid myself of the idea that we were facing in the wrong direction, and here passed the night very restlessly."[5] Over in the 19th Illinois, the men were completely exasperated. Their regimental history described the day's activity as "some marching here and there, [returning] to bivouac about a quarter of a mile from whence we had started."[6]

September 19 found Negley's three brigades deployed to cover the Glass Mill crossing. The main force remained on the west bank of West Chickamauga Creek. Pickets were sent forward to the east bank but they saw few Rebels.[7] Just before dawn, however, Confederate Major General John C. Breckinridge sent one brigade of his division across to the west bank of the creek at Glass Mill. Breckinridge's mission was to create a diversion.[8] Along with the brigade, two guns from Cobb's Confederate Kentucky Battery went to lend support. Throwing a few shells toward the Union line, Cobb's gunners drew fire in response from Captain Lyman Bridges's Illinois battery, but the action did not develop into a larger fight. After about five rounds, Cobb withdrew his section into cover and a lull ensued.[9]

That lull didn't last long. Breckinridge reinforced Cobb by sending another battery across the creek and renewed the artillery duel.[10] Union Brigadier General John Beatty, whose men now guarded this part of the line, called for more artillery support.[11] The resulting engagement lasted about an hour and caused a fair number of casualties, but produced no other result. Having found the Yankees in strength, late in the morning the Rebels were ordered back across the creek.[12] The fight ended when Breckinridge received orders to move farther north and replace another Confederate division facing Lee and Gordon's Mill. Rebel cavalry moved up to replace Breckinridge's infantry.

During the day, other Union troops had been moving north behind Negley's command and by midday Negley's division was holding the extreme right of the Union army. The battle of Chickamauga had by now developed into a major engagement, and at 3:00 P.M., Rosecrans ordered Negley to turn over defense of Glass Mill to Union cavalry and move his men to Rosecrans's current headquarters at the Widow Glenn's house, about three miles north. From there, they would be directed into the fight. Two of Negley's brigades, under Colonels Timothy R. Stanley and William Sirwell, started off right away. Beatty's brigade, still in contact with Confederate skirmishers, disengaged more cautiously and had only reached Crawfish Spring by about 5 P.M.[13]

Negley and his leading two brigades, marching hard, moved rapidly and arrived at the Widow Glenn's by approximately 4:30 P.M. On the way, they passed all the signs of a major battle in progress. Wounded and stragglers choked the roads. Just as they reached the house, Negley's men crested a ridge overlooking the battlefield. Members of the 78th Pennsylvania in Sirwell's brigade recorded the scene: "A panorama of war on a grand scale. The battle was raging fiercely in the forest along the Chickamauga; batteries of artillery and brigades of infantry were moving on double quick to the support of our forces on the battle lines. [W]e could see the smoke of battle rising above the trees, almost shutting out our view of the forest, while the roar of artillery and the rattle of musketry was deafening." The Pennsylvanians were watching Union Major General Jefferson C. Davis's division wage a desperate struggle around the Viniard farm a mile to their east. Nor did the scene suggest that the fight was going well. Out of the woods were also "pouring thousands of wounded soldiers and stragglers. It was a sight never to be forgotten."[14]

For Rosecrans, Negley's arrival was in the nick of time. The Union center had been ruptured and Confederates were swarming into the gap. Rosecrans ordered Negley to take his two brigades, locate General Thomas, and attack into the teeth of the Confederate advance to restore the Union line. Stanley's brigade was at the head of the column and the first to respond. In the lead, the 11th Michigan met General Rosecrans a few rods north of the Glenn cabin observing the fight. Here, as each company passed the commanding general, the 11th raised their rifles in salute, each time smartly returned by Rosecrans. "Make it warm for them, Michigan boys," Rosecrans called, provoking cheers in response.[15] James Martin, writing about the same incident, recalled that Rosecrans "told us if we had a fight with the Rebels to give them fits."[16] After passing the army commander, Stanley's men moved out into south Dyer field and formed a line of battle facing east. Sirwell's brigade was right behind. His lead regiment, the 37th Indiana, did not get cheering words from Rosecrans, but did have a short exchange with a wounded Federal heading for the rear. When asked how the fight was going, he replied, "well, it is about nip and tuck and d——d if I ain't afraid that tuck has the best of it."[17] With these somewhat unsettling words, the 37th advanced into the field and deployed with the rest of Sirwell's men on Stanley's right.

Atop the ridge behind the infantry, two of Negley's artillery batteries prepared to go into action. The high ground here was a perfect artillery position and in fact would become Rosecrans's chosen headquarters site the next day due to the excellent panorama if offered. Now, in the late afternoon of September 19, twelve Union cannon unlimbered here to support the attack.[18] With his line ready, Negley sent word back to Rosecrans that he could not find Thomas but he had located the Rebels. Should he hold his ground or advance? In a minute the courier returned with Rosecrans's instructions: "That is right, fight there, right there, push them hard."[19]

Everyone expected to face a terrific fight. The sense of urgency was palpable, and the crisis seemed at hand. With only six regiments and 2,450 bayonets on hand, Negley must have wondered if his command was being sacrificed to buy time for additional reinforcements.[20] If he could have waited, the other four regiments of Beatty's brigade and the 74th Ohio, then detailed as train guard, might have joined the attack. However, there was no reason not to expect the Rebels to press their advantage immediately and no time to wait for the rest of the division.

When the charge came, however, it was anticlimactic. In the ranks of the 78th Pennsylvania, J. T. Gibson recorded what happened next: "We seemed to be entering the center of the fiercest conflict," he recorded, "and we fully expected to bear the brunt of the battle that evening." Then, he added, "Instead of attacking our front . . . as expected, the enemy seemed to fall back."[21] Lieutenant Colonel Ward, his 37th Indiana following the 78th Pennsylvania in support, wrote, "it appeared that we would be very heavily engaged but, as we rapidly advanced, the roar of musketry in our front suddenly ceased. We gained and occupied the position to which we were ordered without firing a gun and with only one man wounded."[22]

Similarly, resistance abruptly collapsed in front of Stanley's brigade. Lieutenant John Young of the 19th Illinois dismissed the fight as "severe skirmishing."[23] For their part, the 11th Michigan charged, "driving the Rebels before them like chaff before the wind."[24] Despite the ominous gloom of the smoky woods, strewn with the dead and wounded from earlier fighting, the danger proved largely illusory. The Confederates were as disorganized by their success as the retreating Federals had been by defeat, and the arrival of Negley's fresh forces turned the tide abruptly.

Still, it was a very uncomfortable night for the men of the 2nd Division. Negley halted both his brigades inside the woods, just west of a small ridge that dominated the center of Brotherton field. Inside the tree line, Negley's men "threw up a slight breastworks of logs, rails and trash."[25] Due to the proximity of the enemy, fires were prohibited. The night was cold, and some of the men were short of blankets, having been forced to leave their packs behind at Davis's Crossroads a week earlier. Wounded men were all around, their cries producing a low chorus of pain and misery all night. Uncertainty about fighting in the distance also plagued the men. A little later that evening, a large fight erupted in the woods to their left-front. Unknown to them at the time, this action was a night attack by Rebel Brigadier General Patrick

Cleburne's division against a Union line in Winfrey field, about a mile to the east. Nothing could be seen of this fight except stabs of flickering light as musket fire split the night, but the roar of discharging rifles lasted by some accounts an hour or more. Negley reported that once in place, he could not locate troops to his left or right.[26] As far as he could tell, his six regiments were holding this isolated line all alone.

In the meantime, Beatty's brigade was looking for Negley. Major Lowrie had been assigned the task of bringing up Beatty's command when it could catch up, but Lowrie could not find Negley. Instead, he located Rosecrans and was just asking the commanding general where to go when Negley himself rode up. Beatty's men were still very scattered, and Negley elected to put the brigade in reserve near the Osborn house, about a quarter of a mile from Rosecrans's headquarters at the Widow Glenn's.[27]

Having placed Beatty's men, Negley returned to the ridge where his cannon were emplaced to watch Sirwell's and Stanley's advance. He remained there until 10 P.M. After the evening's action had subsided, he rode back to Rosecrans's headquarters, where most of the army's senior commanders had already been conferring. Negley arrived about the time that discussion had ended, and Rosecrans's chief of staff, Brigadier General James A. Garfield, drew up the next day's orders. Once written, Garfield read them to the assembled commanders, and finally, around midnight, army business was concluded.[28] No specific orders were given to Negley at this time, though a number of other divisions were to be shifted about during the night to better prepare for the expected enemy attacks the next morning.

This should have concluded the meeting and allowed Negley to get some rest. Rosecrans felt the need of some cultural activities, however, and asked Major General McCook to sing. While doubtless McCook had a fine singing voice, the music selection might have been a little questionable. The song, 'The Hebrew Maiden's Lament' was hardly cheerful, and to a man as sick and tired as Negley, the episode must have seemed excruciating.[29] Perhaps, like Major General Thomas, Negley managed to doze a little during the interlude. Finally, sometime well after midnight, the generals departed headquarters, and Negley finally lay down for a few hours of badly needed rest.[30] It had been another exhausting day. His command had been involved in two actions, marched several miles in between, and spent another confusing night trying to figure out where to deploy. Unable to locate friendly troops on either flank, Negley had two brigades holding a line without, as far as he could tell, any support at all, and one brigade some distance to the rear in reserve. He did not know the terrain he was ordered to defend, not yet having had a chance to look it over in daylight. And, of course, his physical condition had not improved. Under any other circumstances, he would have been in a sickbed, not leading a division into a night attack.

The next morning, on what would become the most fateful day of his military career, Negley was up early. Lieutenant William H. H. Moody, one of Negley's aides, went on duty at 3 A.M. and was promptly sent forward to ensure that the men in the front line were on alert and to obtain the latest reports from Stanley and Sirwell.[31] Closer to dawn, Captain Alfred L. Hough followed with a second message for Stanley. When Hough returned, he discovered that orders had arrived in the interim calling for the 2nd Division to join General Thomas and the rest of the corps a mile or so north.[32] After Rosecrans's conference broke up, Thomas had gone back to his own headquarters near Kelly field. His 14th Corps was responsible for defending the army's left flank and holding open the retreat route to Chattanooga. Thomas had previously posted Baird's division of his own corps on the left with orders to extend as far north as the Reed's Bridge Road. Sometime after Thomas reached his headquarters, however, he received a report from Baird explaining that the distance to Reed's Bridge road was too great for one division to defend properly.[33] Thomas sent a note to Rosecrans asking for Negley's division to cover the gap.

As soon as it was light enough, Rosecrans started for Thomas's position, to see the problem personally. On the way, he rode the length of the Union line and made several adjustments in deployment. He directed McCook to shift Davis's division, which was too far to the west. Palmer's division was also too spread out, and Rosecrans had it close up, which in turn moved Major General Joseph J. Reynolds's division over, and brought Brigadier General John M. Brannan's division into the front line alongside Negley's left—northernmost—flank. Once he reached Thomas, both generals rode to the McDonald house, half a mile north of Baird's current position, where Rosecrans agreed with the 14th Corps commander that more troops were needed there. Rosecrans told Thomas that Negley "would be sent immediately" to fill the hole on the left.[34] This was a rash promise. Negley was in the battle line, not in reserve, and some of his troops were scattered. The division could not simply be moved out of line and marched north. While at the McDonald house, Rosecrans issued two orders. The first, sent to Negley, was written at 6:30 A.M. It informed Negley both of the need to join Thomas on the left and to send a staff officer to General McCook to direct the replacing units into the right part of the line. The second, written five minutes later, was to McCook informing him of the intended movement.[35]

Why move Negley in the first place? Thomas was very specific in asking for the return of this division. While Negley was a part of his corps, Thomas had commanded divisions from other corps the previous day, and two of these divisions were now an integral part of his Kelly field line. Rosecrans had several divisions in reserve that could have filled the gap in question without the additional confusion of first pulling Negley out of the middle of his front. One of these reserve commands was Brigadier General Thomas J. Wood's division, the force that ultimately replaced Negley. It would have been simpler and safer to send Wood straight to the 14th Corps. Thomas was apparently under the impression that Negley was also in reserve, not the front line, but Rosecrans knew better and should have been more alert to the problems this request caused.

Negley also retrieved Beatty's brigade. "Before day break," recalled Adjutant Sharp of the 15th Kentucky, "we moved and joined our division at Brotherton's."[36] Negley placed these new arrivals somewhere in the south Dyer field, behind the other two brigades, who were still in line in the woods west of Brotherton's farm. Beatty's men would act as the divisional reserve. Sharp recalled that the brigade was in place around 5 A.M. on the morning of the twentieth.

When Rosecrans's order arrived, Negley promptly sent an aide to McCook and another to Thomas, with instructions to take some cavalry escorts and establish a courier line between his own and Thomas's headquarters in preparation for the march north.[37] Other officers were sent to the brigades, alerting them to be ready to move out at once. Now all that was needed was the replacement division. Instead, however, Negley began to be bombarded by a series of messages from various commanders, all urging haste to Thomas.

Thomas sent at least three different couriers. The first was Captain J. P. Willard. Sometime between 7 and 8 o'clock, Thomas became impatient with Negley's continued absence. Willard was ordered to tell Negley to move "without delay."[38] Negley informed Willard that he was complying, and Willard returned to Thomas to report that piece of good news. To ensure that no further delay resulted, Thomas sent Willard back to Negley to lead the division into the new position on the left. In the meantime, Negley had just received word from Lieutenant Colonel Fisher, of McCook's staff, to go to Thomas's assistance. Fisher was sent by McCook when he received his copy of Rosecrans's order.[39]

Impressed with the urgency in Willard's request, Negley had already decided to join Thomas without waiting for the replacements. He had pulled his brigades out of line and into column when Rosecrans himself rode up on his way back from Thomas's command post. Rosecrans met Lieutenant Alfred L. Hough of Negley's staff, who described the encounter. "[Rosecrans] asked what troops these were. I replied, 'General Negley's division.' He asked what they were doing there. I replied, 'going to join General Thomas.' He asked if they had been relieved. I answered 'No.'"[40] Quickly, Rosecrans ordered Sirwell and Stanley back into the line, and, with Hough, rode over to Negley. By his own admission, Rosecrans spoke "a little sharply" to Negley about the danger of withdrawing before he had been fully relieved, but did instruct him to send Beatty's brigade on ahead, since it was still in reserve.[41] Captain Willard, who had just arrived from Thomas the second time to act as Negley's guide, was directed to go ahead with Beatty. With at least one brigade started on the way to Thomas, Rosecrans next rode to find McCook and see why Negley's relief had not materialized.

The next messenger to arrive at Negley's command post was Lieutenant Charles C. Cooke, the aide Negley had dispatched earlier to find Thomas and establish the courier line. Having done so, Cooke was returning to Negley's side and carrying with him verbal orders from Thomas: the by now familiar "move immediately to the left and support of General Baird."[42] Hard on Cooke's heels, Captain J. D. Barker of the 1st Ohio Cavalry rode up at around 9 A.M. Barker commanded the 14th Corps's escort company and had been sent by Thomas to find out what was taking Negley so long. The by now harried division commander replied that he still had not been relieved, but Beatty's brigade was on the way, and he would be along with the others as soon as possible. Barker galloped back to Thomas with this news, which by now Thomas already knew, since Willard had appeared with Beatty's men in the interim. Next, Thomas sent Barker directly to Rosecrans, appealing to the highest authority he could to ensure Negley's speediest arrival.[43]

Rosecrans was by now at McCook's headquarters. Leaving Negley, he had noticed Wood's division in position several hundred yards to the rear. Rosecrans sent an aide to inform Crittenden that he wanted Wood's division to replace Negley, thus solving what had so far been the critical sticking point of finding men enough for the task. Now it was Rosecrans's turn to get bombarded with couriers.

First to arrive was Negley's man, Lieutenant William H. H. Moody. Moody had been instructed to tell McCook that Beatty's departure had left his (Negley's) line very weak and that the enemy was now "massing in our front." Rosecrans asked Moody to repeat that message and then told the young lieutenant, "Go to General Crittenden and tell him I say to make that line strong and good." Rosecrans then asked Moody if Wood had started arriving. "I know nothing of General Wood," replied Moody, who then galloped off on his errand to Crittenden.[44]

Next to arrive were two messengers from Thomas. The first was the aforementioned Captain Barker, and shortly afterward, Captain Willard again.

Barker had come via Negley, who still had seen no sign of the replacement troops. Rosecrans expressed surprise at this information and felt sure that by now, Wood should have come forward, since he was only a short distance to the rear. Willard, who had passed Wood, arrived just then and reported that Wood's men did not yet have their new orders and were still halted some distance to the rear per Crittenden's earlier instructions.[45] Rosecrans then sent one of his own aides, Captain Tomms, directly to Wood with orders to replace Negley "at once." Barker was sent back to Thomas, and Willard to Negley. On the way to Negley, Willard met Tomms returning, who informed him that the orders to Wood had been successfully delivered.[46] Some time between 9:00 and 9:30, Rosecrans personally encountered Wood and urged him to hurry.[47] Finally, troops were going to replace Negley.

Wood's men started to arrive around 9:30 A.M. By now Negley must have been completely frustrated, though he remained outwardly calm. Certainly some of his staff expressed their aggravation. To Lieutenant Moody's eyes, Wood's men deployed their skirmishers and advanced much too slowly, considering the urgency of the moment. He later wrote, "They advanced very leisurely across the open field."[48] All told, in the past two hours, Negley had received a half-dozen urgent messages, sent via four different couriers, all impressing on him the need for haste. Initially responding with alacrity, he had been verbally rebuked by Rosecrans for planning to leave before being relieved, and then saw his division split up as Rosecrans himself sent Beatty's brigade on ahead. As Beatty was being detached, Negley commented to Captain Hough that he was "anxious to keep [his] division together."[49] Now, just as it seemed that he would finally be on his way with the other two brigades, his command was further splintered.

Wood's orders were to cover Negley's front and connect with Brannan's troops on his right. For several reasons, this distance was too large for Wood to cover with his two brigades, and his men only filled the space currently occupied by Stanley's brigade. Negley took his place at the head of Stanley's column and was starting up the road. Behind Stanley came Sirwell. Sirwell's four regiments had proceeded only a few hundred yards when word came up the line that Wood's two brigades were not large enough to fully replace Negley's three and that Rebel skirmishers had come forward into the gap vacated by Sirwell. Negley had no choice but to dispatch Sirwell's troops back to their old breastworks, where they handily drove off the Rebels.[50] However, this movement finished fracturing the division, with Beatty gone ahead at least an hour previous, Stanley on the march northward, and Sirwell turned back to reoccupy his original position. Willard, riding alongside Negley to guide him to Thomas, was now sent to General Crittenden to ask for more troops. In response, Crittenden sent Colonel Sidney M. Barnes's brigade of Brigadier General Horatio P. Van Cleve's division to extend Wood's line and allow Sirwell to depart.[51] All of these travails meant that the thing Negley was most worried about preventing—his command being split up and scattered about the battlefield—had come to pass.

John Beatty's experience exemplified the problems inherent in this piecemeal commitment. Beatty reached Thomas at about 8 A.M. and was immediately sent to support Baird. Initially, Beatty deployed his brigade facing north astride the La Fayette Road, facing towards the rise where the McDonald house sat. While this position did not satisfy Thomas's desire to cover the ground all the way to the Reed's Bridge Road with a line facing east, it did manage to secure Baird's flank, and Beatty thought it was a strong defensive line. Thomas felt otherwise. Very soon his aide, Captain William B. Gaw, brought an order for Beatty to take the whole brigade forward to the McDonald house and face east as intended. Beatty protested, but Gaw insisted that the order "was imperative."[52] In Thomas's defense, the corps commander expected the rest of the division to arrive momentarily and fill in the gaps of Beatty's now badly attenuated line, but in the meantime this was little comfort to Beatty. Beatty's worst fears were made reality when, shortly after he took up the new line, Confederate Major General John C. Breckinridge's infantry division burst out of the woods to his front, shattering his command and precipitating the crisis Thomas had been envisioning all morning.

Negley, however, was only peripherally aware of what has happening to his brigades. He had advanced some distance with Stanley when, having received word that Beatty was under attack, he deployed Stanley's men into line facing north and ordered them forward to find the First Brigade. Negley himself halted with the remainder of his artillery (Marshall's and Swartz's batteries) to await Sirwell's arrival. Stanley pressed on and met Thomas a short distance up the path. Thomas gave him a more detailed picture of the situation on the left and ordered him to Beatty's aid.

While Negley was halted along the Glenn-Kelly road, Captain Gaw rode up with new orders. Negley was to take his own artillery, along with any other batteries he could collect, and place them all on a long, open ridge about twelve hundred yards due west of Kelly field, directly in the rear of the 14th Corps position. In the previous day's fighting, the artillery had been pushed forward into the woods alongside the infantry, and several Union batteries had been overrun. Today Thomas was trying to find positions from which he could mass his cannon and support the infantry now so desperately engaged, without risking the same gun losses. This open ridge, part of Snodgrass Hill, seemed ideal for that purpose.

Accordingly, Negley took Marshall and Schultz over and posted them as indicated.[53] From here, artillery could command the Glenn-Kelly Road below and also shoot as far as the McDonald house far to the northeast, where John Beatty's brigade was currently in action. Negley must have reached this position sometime after 10 A.M., perhaps as late as 10:30. Now, as he deployed the cannon, other troops started to join him. The first to arrive was another battery, Lieutenant Frank G. Smith's Battery 1, 4th U.S. Artillery. Smith belonged to Brannan's division of the 14th Corps, and when his brigade was ordered to Kelly field to help repulse Breckinridge, Smith's guns were intercepted on the road by Major James A. Lowrie, of Negley's staff, and sent up to join Negley.[54] At very nearly the same time, between 10:30 and 11:00 A.M., Sirwell's brigade reached the hill, marching in close column across the fields from the south via the Dyer house.[55] A short time later, the 42nd and 88th Indiana arrived from the north, a fragment of Beatty's command that had become separated during the enemy's attack.[56] Both regiments had suffered severely in the fight, and now, all told, numbered about 400 men.[57]

By now, Negley's view of the battle must have been panoramic. He could see part of the repulse of Breckinridge and the struggle near the McDonald house. The battle smoke rising above the trees to his front indicated heavy fighting along the length of Thomas's line around Kelly field. On the road directly below, General Wood was heading north in response to Rosecrans's soon-to-be infamous order that created a gap at Brotherton field: In passing, Wood noted the presence of the guns and a brigade of infantry atop Snodgrass Hill.[58] Shortly after Wood marched past, however, the scene worsened dramatically. The first precursor was the flight of stragglers and wounded men pouring out of the woods to the southeast, from the direction where first his own and later Wood's divisions had been deployed around Brotherton field. Major Lowrie described the situation, writing that "it became evident that some disaster had happened to portions of General McCook's and General Crittenden's corps. A large number of fugitives came up through the ravines and over the ridge. Batteries were dragged up with all the haste that horses and men could exert. Some of these did not stop on the ridge; others sought positions and prepared again for action. One corps battle-flag went past without an officer or escort. Division and brigade battle-flags and regimental colors were hastily carried to the rear."[59]

Negley's response was to try and cover as much of the ridge as possible. His initial location had been in the open fields running northeast from the Snodgrass house, typically described as Snodgrass Hill. South of the Snodgrass house was a higher, wooded ridge complex, divided into separate rises—

labeled Hills One, Two, and Three—and typically described as Horseshoe Ridge. These hills formed a curving line facing mostly south, and beyond them the ridge extended west to the main part of Missionary Ridge, perhaps a mile farther west. This high ground would become a powerful natural fortress for the Federals in the wake of the disaster of the late morning, and it was imperative to keep the Rebels from capturing it.

Initially, Negley had posted his batteries in various commanding points along the ridge complex and detailed the 74th Ohio to support them.[60] Now the remnant of Bridges's battery came up, also fleeing the disaster in McDonald field, where Bridges lost half his guns. Negley posted Bridges alongside Smith's Battery 1, 4th U.S., directly in front of the Snodgrass cabin.[61] A little later, the rest of Beatty's brigade arrived; the 15th Kentucky and 104th Illinois, dragging the three guns Bridges had lost earlier. Beatty was not with them. Led by Colonel Taylor of the 15th Kentucky, these two commands also had a rough morning. After his initial defeat, Beatty had attached Colonel Taylor's half of the brigade to Stanley's brigade, who, as noted earlier, Negley had sent forward to help Beatty. Leaving Taylor with Stanley, Beatty had tried to scrape up other troops to restore the line shattered by Breckinridge. He spent most of the morning engaged in the fighting around Kelly field and lost track of the 15th and 104th during that action. Taylor's two regiments eventually fell in among the gathering force on Snodgrass Hill, which was becoming a general rallying point for the fragments of other commands.[62] Among these were some of the regiments of Brannan's division, who, having been outflanked from the south, had conducted a tenacious but disorganized fighting retreat back to the high ground.

Around 11:30, Brannan's defense crumbled, outflanked and attacked from the rear.[63] His division fell back in disorder. Colonel John M. Connell's brigade, which occupied the now-exposed flank closest to the breakthrough, was the worst handled. After a desperate fight, they fell back to Negley's position, where Connell and some of the regimental officers attempted to rally fragments of the 17th Ohio, 31st Ohio, and 82nd Indiana Regiments.[64] Just a couple hundred yards to the south, unknown to Connell, Colonel Moses Walker was doing the same with other elements from several brigades: Walker noted that "the troops I succeeded in forming consisted first of Smith's Battery 'I' 4th Art. four guns, about fifty men from the 17th Ky Inf headed by the brave Col. Stout, the 21st Ohio Inf commanded by Lt. Col. Stoughton, a part of the 17th Ohio Inf commanded by Col. Ward, a part of the 82nd Ind. commanded by Col. Hunter, a part of the 10th Ky Inf. Comd. by Col. Hays, a part of the 31st Ohio commanded by it's line officers."[65] The scene atop Snodgrass Hill was becoming chaotic.

It was probably at this moment that Brannan first asked for help. As Walker noted, the 21st Ohio was already incorporated into his line on Hill One, and Walker also claimed control of Smith's battery. The 21st Ohio had been placed there before the fighting started; southeast of the Snodgrass house and to the right of the artillery, Negley was massing atop Snodgrass Hill.[66] In the course of forming the new line, Sirwell reported that Brannan asked him for a regiment to support some other artillery, and he obliged with the 21st.[67] Eben Sturges, in Schultz's battery, noted that his command had also been loaned to "some officer" who, he later discovered, was General Brannan.[68]

What was left of Brannan's artillery also washed up against Negley. Captain J. W. Church, commanding the 4th Michigan Battery, reported a harrowing tale: with his infantry support gone, firing double canister at point-blank range, he ordered his men to retreat when they were flanked, dragging five of his six guns back by hand about fifty yards, but could only limber three of them. Those three pieces reached the "hill occupied by the reserve artillery," but losses in horses and equipment were so heavy that ultimately, only one gun could be gotten completely away.[69] Similarly, Battery C of the 1st Ohio Light also engaged Rebels on both the front and flank, losing a cannon in its own retreat to Negley's line.[70]

Into this confusion, still more troops arrived. Parts of General Wood's division were broken up in the disaster, but his lead brigade under Colonel Charles G. Harker was intact and ready to fight. Wood led Harker's men back south along the Glenn-Kelly Road and into line to attack toward the Rebels now moving east to west through the Dyer field.[71] Initially, Harker checked the Confederate advance, but enemy reinforcements counterattacked. Falling back, Harker's regiments formed a line along the north end of Dyer field between the road and the hill where Negley had sent Schultz's battery earlier. Here Harker, supervised by both Wood and Thomas, made a stubborn stand against Brigadier General Joseph B. Kershaw's South Carolina brigade.[72] Kershaw's troops pressed home the attack, however, and Harker's men withdrew slowly up the slope of Horseshoe Ridge to the open fields just northeast of the Snodgrass farm, where just a short while before Negley had been standing. The time was 1:30, and Harker's men had been fighting for nearly two hours.[73] Negley was gone.

Sometime around 12:30, Negley witnessed a new threat: "a strong column of the enemy, who pressed forward rapidly between me and the troops on my left."[74] Worse yet, one group of stragglers from Beatty's brigade reported that "they had counted 7 stands of [enemy] colors across the road in that direction."[75] This meant that at least a brigade of Rebels was working its way around Negley's left flank and might already be between him and Thomas's main line at Kelly field. If that were true, Negley's whole command might be on the verge of being surrounded. It is impossible to be certain who these Rebels were, but there are some intriguing clues. After Breckinridge's division had been repulsed by the Federal counterattack in Kelly field, Brigadier General St. John R. Liddell's two brigades had replaced Breckinridge's battered Rebels. Liddell's westernmost brigade, under Colonel Daniel C. Govan, crossed the La Fayette Road and then swung south to attack in that direction, seeking the Union flank.[76] Govan's brigade had become spread out during this advance and found itself outflanked in turn by Union troops near the Kelly field line. Instead of trying to cut their way back to Rebel lines by going back the way they came, elements of three of Govan's regiments, led by Lieutenant Colonel John E. Murray of the 5th Arkansas, moved west and then north to circle back out of danger that way.[77] While this force was a far cry from seven-regiments strong, it was a considerable command, moving west and potentially behind Negley's left, at a time when the right and center had already been routed. To further compound matters, "reliable information," according to Negley, reached him that "the enemy's cavalry was moving from our right to our rear."[78] He was beginning to feel isolated.

In response, he sent two aides, ordered to take different routes, to Rosecrans to appeal for help.[79] He did not try to reach Thomas. Negley reported that he was "unable to communicate" with Thomas, and at least two other aides also had problems reaching the 14th Corps commander, having to take roundabout routes via Rossville to reach him later that afternoon.[80] However, it is a bit of a mystery as to why, exactly, Thomas was unreachable. During this critical half hour or so, Thomas was only a few hundred yards away, with Wood and Harker. As Harker withdrew, Thomas went with him back to the Snodgrass cabin, establishing 14th Corps headquarters there. Thomas likely reached the spot between 12:30 and 1:30 P.M., when he told Harker, "this hill must be held and I trust you to do it."[81] Negley was at the same spot until sometime after noon and should have been able to observe a good portion of Harker's advance, engagement, and subsequent retreat during that time. For a while, the right flank of Harker's brigade rested on the same hill where Schultz was so heavily engaged with his battery. Moreover, Negley's last orders to assemble the reserve artillery had come from Thomas. Presumably, Thomas would want that artillery at some point.

Shortly after noon, Negley started back toward the right and the wooded ridges west of Hill Three. On the way, he met John Brannan, who was still building up a battle line any way he could. Brannan and Negley had a quick conversation: too quick, apparently, since each came away from the discussion with a different understanding of what the other had promised. Brannan understood that Negley was going to give him the 21st Ohio to extend his own line on Hill One, and, with the rest of Sirwell's brigade, "pledged himself," in Brannan's words, "to hold my right and rear."[82] Negley, however, only understood that Brannan was asking for a regiment to strengthen his line on Hill One—the already discussed 21st Ohio—and later dismissed the idea of the pledge as "incredible."[83]

This was apparently the moment that Negley decided he could no longer remain on the field: "All was agonizing doubt and irresistible confusion. It was now, in my judgment, time to retire."[84] One of the messengers from Rosecrans had just returned with the information that no help was forthcoming. Instead, the commanding general, along with corps commanders McCook and Crittenden, were all leaving the field. Negley was on his own, apparently, with his command now reduced to three regiments and nearly fifty cannon, which he felt the urgent need to safeguard.[85]

However carefully considered his decision to exit the battlefield had been, the actual execution betrayed signs of sloppiness, even panic. None of the brigade commanders were informed of the retreat. Sirwell, who was only momentarily absent posting the 74th Ohio, returned to discover his other regiments gone, and when he went back to the 74th, found them gone as well.[86] Eben Sturges noted that he first heard an order to "get that battery out of here," but was ordered back into position by Brannan himself, only to hear the order repeated a few minutes later.[87] Schultz's guns soon joined Negley in marching off the field.

Colonel Ward, leading the 37th Indiana, also received conflicting orders. Ward watched regiment after regiment move off, hither and yon, until he felt that his was the only command left in the division. He then received an order from "some one to halt and charge the enemy over the hill," but just as he was about to execute this apparently suicidal order, another aide rode up and ordered Ward to instead move to the right and follow Negley, ultimately back to Rossville.[88]

Lieutenant Colonel Archibald Blakely, commanding the 78th Pennsylvania, had an even more confused experience. While supporting Bridges's three cannon near the Snodgrass house, Blakely watched the gunners limber and leave without informing him of their changed orders. Dutifully, Blakely rode back to where he had last seen the rest of the brigade, only to find them gone as well. Not knowing what else to do, Blakely took the regiment and started west. They moved about 1,000 yards when, suddenly, they found Negley, all alone. The general posted them to guard a brush-covered ravine and cover the retreat and promptly forgot about them again. Riding forward, Blakely observed a large column of Rebels in the open fields to the south and quickly overruled the regiment's overly aggressive Major Bonnaffon when that officer suggested a charge. Returning to the regiment, Blakely freely confessed that he "did not know what to do" until one of Thomas's staff officers rode up and ordered Blakely to head for the Dry Valley Road and Rossville, where he might find a way back to the rest of the army.[89]

Negley also apparently carried with him that portion of Brannan's 1st Brigade that had rallied with Colonel Connell. Negley later denied this, but Connell's own report makes it clear that he accompanied the general off the field.[90] So too did both halves of John Beatty's brigade, but without Beatty, who came looking for them shortly after Negley had gone and found only Brannan and Wood. Beatty pitched in to help build up a scratch line around the Snodgrass farm and support Harker, but he could not find any men of his own command. In fact, he would not discover that they had left with Negley until hours later.[91]

Colonel Stanley had a similar experience, but managed to keep his brigade. The last of Negley's troops to disengage from the Kelly field actions, Stanley and his command arrived to find no sign of Negley, but did locate Beatty and General Thomas, who placed them on the ridge.[92] Colonel Stanley was wounded about this time, and Colonel William L. Stoughton of the 11th Michigan assumed command of the brigade, playing a critical role in the defense of Hill One for the rest of the afternoon.[93]

It is also difficult to determine exactly how much artillery Negley took with him. Negley claimed that he took fifty cannon to Rossville, but it is unclear if that figure represents the number he ordered off the field or the number he had under his ad-hoc command by the time he halted.[94] Initially, Negley had charge of sixteen guns: six each in Marshall's and Schultz's batteries, and four from Smith's. Bridges's battery brought three more guns to the fight later on, increasing the total to nineteen. Smith never got the order to retreat, so of these nineteen, fifteen cannon departed.[95] In addition, when Colonel Taylor of the 15th Kentucky came up with the other half of Beatty's wayward brigade, he brought with him four guns; the three of Bridges's battery and one extra, recovered along the La Fayette Road near McDonald field. Negley also ordered off the remnants of two of Brannan's batteries. Church's Battery D, 1st Michigan, left three guns in Rebel hands at the Poe house and two more atop the ridge for lack of horses, leaving only one gun to escape to Rossville.[96] Lieutenant Marco B. Gary, commanding Battery C, 1st Ohio Light, also retreated with Negley, bringing off five of his six pieces.[97] Next, Captain Cullen Bradley's 6th Ohio Light Battery, Wood's division, was caught up in the initial panic of the breakthrough, and his six guns ended up with Negley.[98] Thus, of the approximately 37 guns that came under Negley's control while still on the ridge (Marshall, 6; Schultz, 6; Smith, 4; Bridges, 3; Taylor's infantry, 4; Church, 3; Gary, 5; and Bradley, 6) he took off 31, since Smith stayed and Church had to abandon 2 damaged guns on the ridge.

In addition, parts of 4 more batteries may have joined him in the course of the retreat. A thousand yards southwest of Negley's position at the Snodgrass house, Major John Mendenhall of Crittenden's staff formed another gun line. This line was completely independent of Negley's mission, and it was ultimately overwhelmed by Rebel infantry, who captured 15 cannon there, but at least some of the survivors of this fight ended up joining Negley's retreat.[99] This line included 5 more batteries and 26 cannon, of which 11 pieces ultimately escaped. Captain George R. Swallow, commanding the 7th Indiana Battery, reported that his 5 surviving guns joined Negley's column as it passed to his rear.[100] If the other batteries followed Swallow, Negley took off between 36 and 42 cannon.

A substantial number of infantry also left the fight. Sirwell's brigade, less the 21st Ohio, numbered 1,100 men. Beatty's brigade went, and, after deducting losses, they numbered about 900, minus an unknown number of stragglers. Connell later reported that by the time he got to Rossville and sorted out the fragments of his command, he had 350 men with him.[101] Pieces of other commands, unrecorded and uncounted, also went along. Thus, Negley took with him somewhere between 2,000 and 2,500 men, or more than the double the scratch force Brannan was able to initially rally for the defense of Hill One. Clearly, those troops could have made a significant contribution to the defense had they stayed.

Negley's demeanor during this time seems to have been for the most part calm and collected. A number of officers testified at his court of inquiry, and all of them gave substantially the same answer as Lieutenant William H. Moody, when asked what Negley's military deportment was at this time: "Cool, deliberate, and comprehensive," he replied.[102] However, there are some hints that there were moments when he was less so. Eben Sturges, who recorded the actions of Schultz's battery in such detail, saw Negley at Rossville and wrote, "Negley was here gathering his division which (through his own bad general-ship according to my idea) was badly scattered."[103] Writing home on October 2, nearly two weeks after the battle, Sturges echoed the same sentiment, informing his family "that I think Negley managed miserably."[104] A staff officer, Lieutenant Ambrose Bierce, encountered Negley at some point in this retreat and was much more scathing: "I met General Negley, and as my duties as topographical engineer having given me some knowledge of the lay of the land, offered to pilot him back to glory or the grave. I am sorry to say my good offices were rejected a little uncivilly, which I charitably attributed to the general's obvious absence of mind. His mind, I think, was in Nashville behind a breastwork."[105] Describing the day, Colonel Ward wrote:

Why we received so many conflicting orders and were moved so frequently from one position to another without any severe fighting was then and now is a mystery to me. I can only account for it on the theory that the leading officers on that part of the line . . . were unable to keep cool enough under the trying circumstances to comprehend what was best to do and to do what the emergency demanded. Of all the Gen'ls I saw on our part of the field Gen'l Jeff C Davis was the only one who seemed to know what to do, and cool enough to try to do what the necessities of the case required.[106]

This contempt was not limited to a few junior officers. Brannan, naturally enough, was furious at being abandoned. He pulled few punches in his report, noting that Negley had agreed to support his right and then departed without telling him. He wrote, "so far from holding my right as he had promised, [Negley] retired, with extraordinary deliberation, to Rossville at an early period of the day."[107] Wood put no condemnation in his report, but was extremely vocal about Negley's negligence around headquarters in Chattanooga after the army retreated to that place. At one point, Wood expressed a great deal of bitterness toward Negley and threatened to "damage General Negley's reputation."[108] Years later, Wood, still as angry as ever, wrote a letter to Emerson Opdyke (one of Wood's subordinates and commander of the 125th Ohio regiment), which expressed his sentiments. Discussing the events of September 20, he wrote of *"cowards and drunkards, and men who lost their heads in the time of danger and trial abandoned the battlefield and fled miles to the rear."*[109]

Questions concerning Negley's conduct were being asked at army headquarters as well. On October 17, 1863, Assistant Secretary of War Charles A. Dana, who had been with the army since before the battle, wrote to Washington suggesting that Rosecrans thought Negley "should be shot," and Dana added his personal opinion that the reports of Wood, Brannan, and Harker "leave no doubt of his guilt."[110] Rosecrans wrote that Negley "left the battlefield without orders" and suggested that since the rest of the army had already judged him on that fact, he should take thirty days' leave and ask for a court of inquiry into the matter.[111]

Negley, by this time, was not with the army. Once the Federals settled into Chattanooga, Negley finally took sick leave and went home to Pittsburgh. While there, he discovered that his division had been broken up and parceled out to other commands.[112] Initially, he tried to avoid the onus of a formal court, but after Major General Ulysses S. Grant, the new departmental commander, ordered him out of the department, he had no choice.[113] That court convened in January 1864, and after twenty-one days of testimony exonerated him, even going so far as to rebuke Wood for relying on hearsay as the basis for his own comments. In the end, it mattered little to Negley's career.[114] He was not assigned to another command, and after a year's inactivity, finally resigned in January 1865.[115]

Negley blamed his woes on the bias of West Pointers against nonprofessionals in the army. After the war, he served several terms in Congress, and after his first election in 1868, one of his first official acts was to introduce a bill calling for the reduction in the number of officers for the army, which his only biographer described as indicative of "his attitude towards the army."[116]

In reality, Negley had made a major mistake at Chickamauga. Whether his judgment was affected more by extreme sickness and fatigue or by a momentary panic on the battlefield can never be determined beyond speculation, but the fact that he abandoned the field with so many troops and cannon left an indelible stain on his career, which until then had been admirable. The nature of his departure also clearly shows a lack of sound reasoning. He made no effort to locate any of his three brigade commanders and inform them of the departure. His efforts to inform Thomas, who was his direct superior at this time and who had given him the order to hold Snodgrass Hill just an hour or so earlier, were ineffectual at best. His claim that it was impossible to get through to Thomas can easily be refuted by the fact that Thomas had no trouble reaching the ridge Negley had just vacated. When Negley departed, he pulled troops out of line haphazardly, with no rhyme or reason. Bridges's battery was ordered away, but neither Smith's battery nor the 78th Pennsylvania was ordered to follow. Schultz's battery was ordered out of line, then back in by Brannan, and then out again to join the retreat. Sirwell, discovering the 78th Pennsylvania gone, next went back to find Marshall's guns and the 74th Ohio, whom he had just posted, only to find them also ordered away. Nor was Brannan informed, despite a face-to-face discussion just a short time before. Since Negley was taking troops away that were currently holding both of Brannan's flanks (Bridges and the 78th Pennsylvania were on Brannan's left, while Marshall and the 74th Ohio were on his right) this failure was especially significant. Negley also failed to note the efforts Brannan was making to build a new line on Hill One, or, more importantly, the temporarily successful counterattack Harker launched directly in front of his position that bought time for Brannan to assemble that line, under the supervision of both Wood and Thomas. At a critical, even desperate, moment in the battle, Negley disappeared from the field when others were counting on him.

Notes

1. U.S. War Department, *The War of the Rebellion: A Compilation of the Official Records of the Union and Confederate Armies*, 70 vols. in 128 pts. (Washington, D.C.: U.S. Government Printing Office, 1880–1901), ser. 1, vol. 30, pt. 1: 343 (hereafter cited as *O.R.*; all citations are to series 1).

2. Today, the University of Pittsburgh.

3. David S. and Jeanne T. Heidler, "Negley, James Scott: Union General" *Encyclopedia of the American Civil War* (Santa Barbara, Calif.: ABC-CLIO, 2000), 3:1403–4.

4. *O.R.*, vol. 30, pt. 1: 336–37. Negley first reached Hazen around 5 P.M., and Lowrie reported that he did not find Thomas and Palmer at Rosecrans's headquarters until 10:30 P.M. It was after midnight before the division settled in.

5. William D. Ward, Recollections, 137, DePauw University, Greencastle, Ind.

6. J. Henry Haynie, *The Nineteenth Illinois: A Memoir of a Regiment of Volunteer Infantry Famous in the Civil War of Fifty Years Ago for Its Drill, Bravery, and Distinguished Services* (Chicago: M. A. Donahue, 1912), 219.

7. Francis Carlisle Reminiscences, 42nd Indiana File, Chickamauga-Chattanooga National Military Park (hereafter cited as CCNMP).

8. *O.R.*, vol. 30, pt. 2: 140.

9. Ibid., 214.

10. Joseph E. Charlaron, "Memories of Major Rice E. Graves, C.S.A.," *Daviess County Historical Quarterly* 3, no. 1 (January 1985): 11. Originally printed in the *New Orleans Messenger*, May 27, 1900.

11. John Beatty, *The Citizen-Soldier; or, Memoirs of a Volunteer* (1879; repr., Lincoln: University of Nebraska Press, 1998), 332–33.

12. Fred Joyce, "Kentucky's Orphan Brigade at the Battle of Chickamauga," *Kentucky Explorer*, April 1994, 28. Reprint of 1885 reminiscences.

13. William Wirt Calkins, *The History of the One Hundred and Fourth Regiment of Illinois Volunteer Infantry: War of the Great Rebellion, 1862–1865* (Chicago: Donohue and Hennenberry, 1895.), 129–30.

14. J. T. Gibson, *History of the Seventy-eighth Pennsylvania Volunteer Infantry* (Pittsburgh: Pittsburgh Printing, 1905), 97.

15. Charles E. Belknap, *History of the Michigan Organizations at Chickamauga, Chattanooga, and Missionary Ridge, 1863* (Lansing, Mich.: Robert Smith , 1897), 113.

16. James Martin to "Dear Parents," October 24, 1863, James A. Martin Letters, Bentley Historical Collection, University of Michigan, Ann Arbor.

17. George H. Puntenney, *History of the Thirty-seventh Regiment of Indiana Infantry Volunteers* (Rushville, Ind.: n.p., 1896), 54.

18. Entry for September 19, 1863, Eben Sturges Diary, U.S. Army Military History Institute, Carlisle, Pa. (hereafter cited as AMHI).

19. *O.R.*, vol. 30, pt. 1: 347.

20. David A. Powell, "Numbers and Losses Study," CCNMP.

21. Gibson, *History of the Seventy-eighth Pennsylvania*, 97–98.

22. Ward Recollections, 138.

23. Haynie, *Nineteenth Illinois*, 238–39.

24. Belknap, *History of the Michigan Organizations*, 113.

25. Entry for September 19, 1863, James Fenton Diary, Lincoln Library, Springfield, Ill.

26. *O.R.*, vol. 30, pt. 1: 329.

27. Ibid, 367.

28. Peter Cozzens, *This Terrible Sound* (Urbana: University of Illinois Press, 1992), 294–95. Cozzens paints a vivid picture of the scene in Rosecrans's headquarters that night.

29. Ibid., 297. The lyrics are reproduced in full, and the final line is "bitter tears I shed for thee." Given the horrific casualties suffered on the nineteenth, the song must have seemed dirgelike to the men gathered in that close, cramped room.

30. *O.R.*, vol. 30, pt. 1: 337–38.

31. Ibid, 360.

32. Ibid., 348.

33. Ibid., 251 and 277. Thomas notes the time he received the note from Baird as 2 A.M., September 20, while Baird reported that he did not post his troops in their new position until 3 A.M.

34. Ibid., 251.

35. Ibid., 69–70.

36. Sharp Letter, 15th Kentucky File, CCNMP.

37. *O.R.*, vol. 30, pt. 1: 357.

38. Ibid., 355.

39. Ibid., 342.

40. Ibid., 348.

41. Ibid., 1014.

42. Ibid., 357.

43. Barker claims that he did not leave Thomas on this mission until 9:30. This seems a little too late, because if so, he would have been present when Beatty arrived and would have known about the lack of relief, from Willard. Barker had to have left Thomas before Willard arrived. See *O.R.*, vol. 30, pt. 1: 350.

44. Ibid., 360.

45. *O.R.*, vol. 30, pt. 1: 355. Wood's previous orders apparently placed his command in reserve. Captain Hough, from Negley's staff, also attempted to induce Wood to come forward, but he refused both Hough's and Willard's entreaties.

46. Ibid., 355–56, and 350.

47. This meeting is one of the more controversial of the war, because of a famous and much-debated dispute over subsequent orders Rosecrans sent to Wood later that morning, after Negley had gone. This incident, of course, opened the famous gap through which the Rebels attacked and drove nearly one third of the Union army from the field. According to Rosecrans's partisans, Wood was severely upbraided by Rosecrans at this time for all the delay in relieving Negley. Wood, by contrast, denies that Rosecrans scolded him at all. The entirety of that disagreement is far beyond the scope of this article, and it is discussed only in passing, as it relates to Negley's actions throughout the day.

48. *O.R.*, vol. 30, pt. 1: 360.

49. Ibid, 348.

50. Puntenney, *History of the Thirty-seventh Regiment*, 56; Ward Recollections, 139.

51. *O.R.*, vol. 30, pt. 1: 609.

52. Ibid., 368.

53. Ibid., 383 and 397.

54. Ibid., 338 and 438.

55. Silas S. Canfield, *History of the 21st Regiment Ohio Volunteer Infantry, in the War of the Rebellion* (Toledo, Ohio: Vrooman, Anderson, & Bateman, 1893), 135.

56. *O.R.*, vol. 30, pt. 1: 369.

57. David A. Powell, "Strengths and Losses at Chickamauga" (unpublished manuscript), 65–66, CCNMP.

58. *O.R.*, vol. 30, pt. 1: 1020; Wood's testimony at Negley's court-martial.

59. *O.R.*, vol. 30, pt. 1: 339.

60. Ibid., 383; entry for September 20, 1863, Sturges Diary, AMHI; *O.R.*, vol. 30, pt. 1: 397; Theodore W. Blackburn, *Letters from the Front: A Union "Preacher" Regiment (74th Ohio) in the Civil War* (Dayton, Ohio: Press of Morningside Bookshop, 1981), 151.

61. *O.R.*, vol. 30, pt. 1: 354.

62. Kirk C. Jenkins, *The Battle Rages Higher* (Lexington: University Press of Kentucky, 2003), 181–85.

63. *O.R.*, vol. 30, pt. 1: 1040–41.

64. Ibid., 409–10.

65. Report of Col. Moses Walker, George H. Thomas Papers, RG 94, NARA. Walker commanded the brigade before being placed under arrest for a minor infraction, so Connell was in charge of the brigade until that matter was resolved. Walker was acting as a staff officer for Brannan, and, when he discovered his old brigade in such confusion, he jumped in to rally the men. His report illustrates the confused nature of that moment on Snodgrass Hill.

66. Undated letter fragment, McMahan Papers, Bowling Green State University, Bowling Green, Ohio.

67. *O.R.*, vol. 30, pt. 1: 385

68. Entry for September 20, 1863, Sturges Diary, AMHI.

69. *O.R.*, vol. 30, pt. 1: 414.

70. Rev. S. Hendrick, "Chickamauga: The Part Taken in the Great Battle by Battery C, 1st Ohio L. A.," *National Tribune*, November 5, 1891.

71. Entry for September 20, 1863, E. G. Whiteside Diary, Civil War Times Illustrated Collection, AMHI.

72. Charles T. Clark, *Opdyke Tigers: 125th O.V.I.; A History of the Regiment and of the Campaigns and Battles of the Army of the Cumberland* (Columbus, Ohio: Spahr and Glenn, 1895), 105–10.

73. Ibid., 110.

74. *O.R.*, vol. 30, pt. 1: 330.

75. Ibid., 343.

76. Park Tablet, west side of La Fayette Road, 400 yards south of the Kentucky Monument, CCNMP

77. *O.R.*, vol. 30, pt. 2: 265.

78. Ibid., 331.

79. Ibid., 349.

80. Ibid., 331, 1022, and 1028.

81. Wilbur F. Hinman, *The Story of the Sherman Brigade* (Alliance, Ohio: Press of the Daily Review, 1897), 429.

82. *O.R.*, vol. 30, pt. 1: 402–3, 1041.

83. Ibid., 1045.

84. Ibid., 1048.

85. The three regiments were the 37th Indiana, 74th Ohio, and 78th Pennsylvania. In his reports, Negley ignored the four regiments of Beatty's brigade, but they were also present.

86. *O.R.*, vol. 30, pt. 1: 385.

87. Entry for September 20, 1863, Sturges Diary, AMHI.

88. Ward Recollections, 140.

89. *O.R.*, vol. 30, pt. 1: 1066–67.

90. Ibid., 1046.

91. John Beatty, *Citizen Soldier* (1879; repr., Lincoln: University of Nebraska Press, 1998), 337–40.

92. Launcelot C. Scott, "On Snodgrass Ridge," *National Tribune*, July 14, 1910.

93. Haynie, *Nineteenth Illinois*, 229.

94. *O.R.*, vol. 30, pt. 1: 1049.

95. Smith noted that "General Negley had moved off with all his artillery but my battery, leaving no orders." *O.R.*, vol. 30, pt. 1: 438.

96. Battery D, 1st Michigan Light Artillery Monument, Poe Field, CCNMP.

97. *O.R.*, vol. 30, pt. 1: 426–27.

98. Joseph C. McElroy, *Chickamauga: Record of the Ohio, Chickamauga and Chattanooga National Park Commission* (Cincinnati: Earhart and Richardson, 1896), 129.

99. Cozzens, *This Terrible Sound*, 397–402, has a good description of this action. Signs in the park state that fourteen Union cannon were captured here, but Union reports total fifteen losses.

100. *O.R.*, vol. 30, pt. 1: 836.

101. Ibid., 410.

102. Ibid., 1013.

103. Entry for September 20, 1863, Sturges Diary, AMHI.

104. Letter to "Dear Folks," October 2, 1863, Sturges Papers, AMHI.

105. Ambrose Bierce, "A Little of Chickamauga," *Ambrose Bierce's Civil War* (Chicago: Gateway, 1956), 35.

106. Ward Recollections, 142.

107. *O.R.*, vol. 30, pt. 1: 403.

108. Ibid., 1016.

109. Letter from T. J. Wood to "My dear Opdyke," May 18, 1872, Emerson Opdyke Papers, Ohio Historical Society, Columbus (emphasis in original).

110. *O.R.*, vol. 30, pt. 1: 206–7, 220.

111. Ibid., 333.

112. Ibid., 362.

113. *O.R.*, vol. 52, pt. 1: 506.

114. *O.R.*, vol. 30, pt. 1: 1043–44.

115. Alfred P. James, "General James Scott Negley," *Western Pennsylvania Historical Magazine* 14, no. 2 (April 1931): 81–82.

116. Ibid., 82.

8

HENRY VAN NESS BOYNTON AND CHICKAMAUGA
THE PILLARS OF THE MODERN
MILITARY PARK MOVEMENT

Timothy B. Smith

The two veterans were obviously moved at the sight on that beautiful summer Sunday in 1888. Having fought at the Civil War battlefield of Chickamauga some twenty-five years earlier, these two ageing men were here remembering, reflecting, and rejoicing. The trees had just put on their newly grown leaves and the landscape almost sang with peace and tranquility. Then, the two old soldiers passed a small church, from which they heard "the voice of solemn song." Yet even amid the serenity, the veterans could not help but remember their horrific ordeal of nearly three decades earlier. One of them remembered, "The last music which had fallen on our ears, as we left that field a quarter of a century before, was the screech, the rattle, the roar, the thunder of that hell of battle which had loaded the air with horror through all that earlier and well-remembered Sabbath."[1]

If Union veterans Henry Van Ness Boynton and Ferdinand Van Derveer were at Chickamauga that summer of 1888 to remember and reflect, they had little thought of the reconciliation then beginning to sweep the nation. Indeed, as the two followed their own Union lines, the idea hit them that "this field should be a western Gettysburg—a Chickamauga memorial." At Gettysburg, Pennsylvania, a private association had bought land and marked, with state cooperation, the Union lines on the battlefield. Impressed with the serenity at Chickamauga, Boynton and Van Derveer wanted their battlefield to be preserved as a Union memorial just like the one at Gettysburg.[2]

As the diminutive but heavily bearded Boynton stood silently on the battlefield, however, he had "a flash forward in thought." Why preserve only the Union side, as had occurred at Gettysburg? "Aye, it should be more than Gettysburg, with its monuments along one side alone; the lines of both armies should be equally marked," Boynton thought. The two old soldiers, becoming increasingly excited, traced the lines, as best they could, of the Confederate army as well. The results were spectacular. "Born in the mind" that day was not only the novel idea of one small but all-inclusive park at Chickamauga, but also the entire military park system as we know it today.[3]

Henry Van Ness Boynton was born in the small mountain community of West Stockbridge, Massachusetts, on July 22, 1835. There, on the extreme western side of the Bay State, almost on the line with New York, young Henry spent his first eleven years with his parents, notable Presbyterian minister Rev. Charles B. Boynton and Maria Van Buskirk Boynton. In 1846, the Boyntons moved westward to Ohio, settling in Cincinnati, where young Henry earned a degree from Woodward College in 1855. Wanting a technical education, Henry secured an appointment to the United States Military Academy at West Point, New York. He visited the school before making his final decision and "looked the institution over with that care and precision that characterized his entire life work," one newspaper reported. Desiring the education but not wanting a military career, Boynton turned down the nomination and instead matriculated at the nearby Kentucky Military Institute. He graduated at the top of his class from that well-known institution in 1858 and was retained at the institute as a professor of mechanics and astronomy from 1859 to 1860. While teaching at the school, Boynton was also learning, gaining a master of arts degree in 1859 and a civil engineering degree in 1860.[4]

The young man was obviously talented and looked forward to a successful career, but war intervened. He quickly found himself caught up in the preparations for war. Because of President Abraham Lincoln's call for seventy-five thousand volunteers, officers were sorely needed. Henry Boynton became a training instructor for the new recruits forming into regiments at Cincinnati. He drilled hundreds of troops in those early days of the war.[5]

By midsummer of 1861, officers were now needed to lead those trained troops to the field. Boynton helped recruit and organize the 35th Ohio Volunteer Infantry at Hamilton, Ohio, and he was commissioned its major, mustering into Federal service on September 20, 1861. Boynton signed on for three years and served his entire time in the army with the 35th. The regiment was first employed in guarding the Kentucky Central Railroad, but in November 1861 it was attached to the Army of the Ohio. Boynton and his men were present at Mill Springs in January 1862 but did not engage the enemy, and then took part in the march under Don Carlos Buell to and beyond Nashville in February and March. The regiment arrived too late to participate in Shiloh's carnage, but it was involved in Henry W. Halleck's march on Corinth. Boynton and the Ohioans then pursued the Confederates into Kentucky and were at Perryville in October 1862, although they again did not get into the battle. The regiment was on guard duty during the Battle of Stones River in December. In 1863, Boynton took part in the Tullahoma campaign, moving through Hoover's Gap.[6]

Then, three major events were to alter Boynton's life in the middle to latter portion of 1863. First, he was promoted to lieutenant colonel of the 35th Ohio on July 19, 1863, and often commanded the regiment when its colonel, Ferdinand Van Derveer, was tasked with commanding the brigade to which it was assigned. Second, Boynton and the regiment took part in the fighting at Chickamauga in September, forever tying him to the history of that September 1863 battle. Third, Boynton took part in the battles around Chattanooga, where he was severely wounded, ending his Civil War military career.[7]

Boynton's efforts at Chickamauga were "highly credible," according to his brigade commander, as he struggled to keep his regiment in line when George Thomas made his famous stand on Snodgrass Hill. Boynton's men fought with emptying cartridge boxes, at one time even obtaining a new supply from a nearby regiment. Although overpowered and sent retreating back to Chattanooga, Boynton and his men were some of the last of Thomas's soldiers to leave Snodgrass Hill. Boynton summed up his personality and perspective in his Chickamauga report: "returning our heartfelt thanks to our Heavenly Father, the God of Battles, that we were able thus to discharge our whole duty, and sorrowing as soldiers only can over the deaths and wounds of our noble comrades fallen, we pray that the future may find us ever ready to combat treason both on Southern battle-fields and, when the war is over, among the vile traitors of the North."[8]

After enduring weeks of horrible siege conditions at Chattanooga, Boynton led the regiment in the Army of the Cumberland's legendary attack on Missionary Ridge in November 1863. George H. Thomas's army assaulted the Confederate line and completely shattered the entrenched enemy, the 35th Ohio capturing three cannon. It was a glorious victory.[9]

Boynton would on March 13, 1865, be brevetted a brigadier general for "good conduct at Chickamauga and Missionary Ridge." Years later, he would receive the nation's highest military award, the Medal of Honor, for gallantry at Chattanooga. But all these awards were dimmed by the wound he received at Missionary Ridge and his subsequent resignation from the army. While leading his men up the ridge, Boynton was hit in the groin and leg and severely wounded, the bullet passing through the genitals and into the thigh. Sadly, one medical report noted, "the spermatic cords were involved;" Boynton would never father children. The wound incapacitated him for a year and ended his career with the 35th Ohio. The regiment fought in the Atlanta campaign, but Boynton did not lead them.[10]

Boynton was not out of the war entirely, however. After a year's convalescence in which he served on a commission screening board in Cincinnati, he embarked upon the profession that would dominate much of the rest of his life: newspaper correspondent. He had written letters to home front newspapers before, particularly concerning Shiloh and Perryville, but he did not officially become a war correspondent with the *Cincinnati Gazette* until December 1864. After a year of faithful service, Boynton landed the prestigious position he would hold for the next twenty-five years. He succeeded the famed reporter Whitelaw Reid, at the latter's request, as the Washington correspondent for the Cincinnati newspaper. Reid had broken the story of the Federals being surprised at Shiloh and faithfully defended the Army of the Ohio and its successor, the Army of the Cumberland, during the rest of the war. Boynton continued Reid's position in his columns, a stance that put him at odds with many other Union army veterans.[11]

During his quarter century in Washington, Boynton covered national politics, signing his columns with the well-known "H.V.B." and rubbing shoulders with the elite of Washington society. He was an intimate of presidents, cabinet secretaries, and congressmen and an avid Republican. By the latter part of his career, Boynton was characterized as the "Dean of the Press Gallery," holding court in his office in the center of "Newspaper Row" on Fourteenth Street. He pushed newspaper correspondents to reform themselves and their practices that caused them, in the public's mind, to be lumped together with lobbyists and other sorts of riffraff in the House and Senate galleries. Boynton led in the establishment of the reformist Standing Committee of Correspondents for the House in 1877, serving as the first president of the association. He also led in the establishment of the Gridiron Club in 1885, aiming to promote friendship between correspondents and politicians. He likewise served as that body's president, even after he left the correspondents' corps. In addition to his newspaper duties, Boynton was also heavily involved in veteran and political societies. He was a faithful member of the Society of the Army of the Cumberland as well as the Military Order of the Loyal Legion of Massachusetts. He later also served as District of Columbia School Board president and was on the commission governing Washington's Rock Creek Park, prompting some to complain that Boynton held three paid federal jobs at once.[12]

Most of all, Boynton worked hard at his job, "keeping his army habits of rising early, retiring late, and eating little." He also found time to begin a family. He married Helen Mason on June 1, 1871, and the couple lived on R Street in the district. Having no children of their own because of his war wound, the Boyntons adopted Henry's niece Marie, who was apparently orphaned and had been under Boynton's care since she was a child. Henry also had a brother in Washington, Charles, who was also a newspaperman, the manager of the Southern Associated Press. His parents later moved to Washington, Boynton's father serving as chaplain of the United States House of Representatives.[13]

During his reporting career, Boynton developed the tenaciousness of a bulldog in not only seeking out a political story, but also in arguing his beliefs to the point of personal animosity. He once wrote a colleague with whom he was feuding, "you say that you have not visited Washington for a long time, and I say, so far as I am concerned, I hope that you will not for a long time to come." He managed to become embroiled in controversies wherever he was, whether it be on the Washington, D.C., board of education or in politics. Likewise, Boynton's interest in the Civil War and its history caused conflicts with other veterans and veteran groups over how the history of the war should be remembered and presented.[14]

Boynton, a reporter for a Republican newspaper, seemed to revel in the idea of scorching corrupt politicians, even Republican ones, once saying that he was going to roast one politician "for the fun of the thing and to see him wiggle." He once even became embroiled in a fist fight with a Washington claims agent over a corruption story Boynton had broken. During his career, he saw nine presidents come and go, as well as numerous senators and representatives. He was an intimate of President Rutherford B. Hayes, who often fretted in his diary and letters about the powerful correspondent's repeated "estrangement" from him due to policy. Hayes remarked, "His nature makes it impossible for him to see fairly the character and merits of those he dislikes."[15]

The combative Boynton reported on some of the major Washington scandals. He investigated the Indian Pension fraud case that involved President Andrew Johnson's secretary of the interior, James Harlan, and the so-called Washington Safe Burglary Conspiracy, in 1874, which implicated President Ulysses S. Grant's private secretary, Orville E. Babcock. Boynton wrote a lengthy summary of the latter case and the trial in the *American Law Review*. He also penned a lengthy review of the more famous "Whiskey Ring" scandal in the *North American Review*. And he implicated Grant's vice president, Henry Wilson, as well as presidential candidate James G. Blaine, in other scandals, most notably the Credit Mobilier affair.[16]

Boynton particularly performed a major role in the "Delano Affair," in which he helped secure Secretary of the Interior Columbus Delano's resignation in 1875. Boynton broke the story that President Grant had asked for Delano's resignation in response to papers showing that Delano's son had received special treatment in several surveying contracts. Ultimately, Delano resigned, one newspaper commenting that "While General Boynton sometimes permits his animosities to warp his sense of justice, we have much confidence in his general accuracy." In another heated political controversy, Boynton in 1877–78 took on a government special agent, W. B. Moore, over embezzlement, false imprisonment of witnesses, and hindering an investigation. Moore responded that Boynton had conjured up statements about the charges through blackmail and suppression money. Headlines in the papers read: "Boynton Has His Say." Boynton ultimately not only saw Moore removed from office but then also sued him for conspiracy and libel.[17]

Perhaps the most remarkable of Boynton's scuffles involved Speaker of the House Joseph Warren Keifer, a longtime friend, in 1883. The ruckus began on the final day of the 47th Congress before a large crowd of family members who had gathered to watch the proceedings. A motion was made to let the overflow crowd into the press gallery, where there was space. The correspondents objected, and Speaker Keifer "profanely" dismissed the newspapermen's objection. As president of the Washington correspondents' association, Boynton called a special meeting, out of which came numerous anti-Keifer articles. The Speaker responded in anger, and so did Boynton. Keifer then stated on the floor of the House that Boynton had earlier met with him in private and had advised him to make an illegal deal concerning a California land grant claim of one William McGarrahan. Boynton denied the charges and demanded an investigation. A House committee hearing took place, and Boynton was acquitted of all wrongdoing. Needless to say, Boynton and Keifer were no longer friends, and Keifer was defeated in his next election.[18]

All of Boynton's controversies easily attest to his prickly and argumentative nature. It is interesting, however, that Boynton would work so diligently against Grant's Republican administration because he worked for Cincinnati's Republican newspaper. Boynton's attacks on the Grant administration were possibly borne out of something else, which leads to the other major topic of controversy for the newspaperman. Boynton's political fights paled in comparison to his veteran controversies, and these efforts included the top tier of veterans, most notably President Grant and his chief lieutenant, William T. Sherman, then General of the Army. Borne out of a desire to defend the Army of the Ohio/Cumberland veterans against the Army of the Tennessee veterans who, he thought, were distorting history, Boynton became involved in several high-profile controversies. His dogged search for scandals in the Grant terms, even though it was a Republican administration, was no surprise. To Boynton, Civil War memory was more important than even party politics.

When he took on Grant himself, he did so through Grant's chosen biographer, Adam Badeau. Boynton reviewed Badeau's work, insisting that Grant's defender "suppressed [the] most important documents." He also attacked books such as John Fiske's *The Mississippi Valley in the Civil War.* As chairman of the District of Columbia school board, Boynton discredited many books he did not deem accurate about the conflict.[19]

By far, the major controversy of Boynton's life came after William T. Sherman published his memoirs in 1875. Boynton took issue with a number of Sherman's claims, including his denial of having been taken by surprise at Shiloh, his criticism of the Army of the Cumberland at Chickamauga and Chattanooga, and his descriptions of the Atlanta campaign, the March to the Sea, and Ulysses S. Grant. "General Sherman labors ingeniously," Boynton wrote, "but inaccurately, as the official record will show, to shirk the responsibility for the surprise at Shiloh." He also railed against Sherman's actions in the closing days of the war, arguing that "hitherto unpublished documents from the Confederate archives" showed Sherman's peace "terms [were] drafted in the Rebel Cabinet." Boynton reached a wide audience when he collected all his writings on Sherman's memoirs and published them as *Sherman's Historical Raid: The Memoirs in Light of the Record: A Review Based upon Compilations from the Records of the War Office* (1875). This scalding attack on Sherman, "bound up in a volume as closely as possible resembling the 'Memoirs' in size, color of cover, lettering, &c., probably so as to suggest the propriety and convenience of putting his book side by side with the 'Memoirs' wherever the latter had gone," basically accused Sherman of incompetence. In another volume borne out of the Sherman controversy, *Was General Thomas Slow at Nashville?*, Boynton defended his old corps commander George Thomas at Nashville, whom Sherman had criticized in his memoirs. Boynton's lengthy and acidic attacks received high-level support from such notables as Don Carlos Buell, Whitelaw Reid, and the Comte de Paris.[20]

There were others who did not take so positive a view of Boynton, chief among them Sherman himself, who had never had much love for reporters anyway. "General Boynton is a profound ignoramus so far as military movements are concerned," Sherman wrote insultingly, labeling him "Brevet Liar Boynton," a dig at his lower and ceremonial brevet rank as compared with Sherman's position as General of the Army. The loose-tongued Sherman went on to write that "he is entirely without character; why, for a thousand dollars he would slander his own mother." In response, Boynton began court proceedings, suing Sherman for slander and libel and requesting a court martial for Sherman with the charge of "conduct unbecoming an officer and a gentleman." The request went all the way to Boynton's friend, President Rutherford B. Hayes, who denied the court martial, causing Boynton to be "deeply offended with me," Hayes remarked. Sherman challenged Boynton to take the case to the civil courts, but Boynton did not take the bait and the matter eventually faded away. Still, Boynton gained through the exchange. His Sherman writings, coupled with a plethora of other books and articles, made him one of the major, though hardly beloved by all, Civil War historians of his day.[21]

At the age of fifty-three, the argumentative but widely known Henry Boynton made a career move from being a newspaper correspondent to becoming a battlefield preservationist. While he still wrote for various newspapers with his customary signature H.V.B. and even used that medium to aid his new passion, from 1888 onward Boynton was consumed with the memory of the Civil War through the avenue of battlefield preservation. Up to that point, his newspaper career had produced a passionate, dogged, determined, and prolific writer and researcher, and those talents helped create America's first national military park. Likewise, his role in numerous controversies about the war and his voluminous writings about its commanders, battles, and operations had made him famous. The bitterness with which he wrote on some issues turned many disagreeing Americans away from him, yet Boynton became a leader of those who defended the Army of the Cumberland. His talents as a detail-oriented writer and researcher as well as his experiences in the very battles he argued about provided him with status in early Civil War historiography. There was perhaps no man better positioned to lead the effort of creating national parks out of battlefields than Henry Boynton. After his 1888 epiphany, Boynton used his major press outlets in "publicly suggesting the scheme" of a military park at Chickamauga. Upon his return home to Cincinnati, Boynton wrote a reconciliatory article which appeared in the *Cincinnati Commercial Gazette*. "The survivors of the Army of the Cumberland should awake to great pride in this noble field of Chickamauga," he implored. "Why should it not, as well as Eastern fields, be marked by monuments, and its lines be accurately preserved for history? There was no more magnificent fighting during the war than both armies did there. Both sides might well unite in preserving the field where both, in a military sense, won such renown." Boynton wrote many other articles on the idea, which he compiled into a book entitled *Chattanooga and Chickamauga: Reprint of Gen. H. V. Boynton's Letters to the Cincinnati Commercial Gazette, August, 1888.*[22]

Boynton and his fellow veteran Ferdinand Van Derveer later floated the idea of a Chickamauga park at the 1888 annual meeting of the Society of the

Army of the Cumberland in Chicago. The idea received hearty backing, the organization favorably approving a motion to organize a committee of five to look into the idea and report back at the following year's Chattanooga meeting. General William S. Rosecrans, president of the society, appointed several well-known officers such as Henry M. Cist, Charles F. Manderson, Absalom Baird, and future secretary of war Russell A. Alger to the committee. Boynton was also appointed and quickly became the major leader in the effort.[23]

Boynton and the committee met in Washington, D.C., on February 13, 1889, along with Rosecrans and War Department official Sanford Kellogg. Desiring Southern support, the group decided to meet the next day, February 14, after invitations had been sent to former Confederate veterans of Chickamauga. The next day, an inter-sectional group of the seven Union officers and eight Confederate officers met in the committee room of the Senate Committee on Military Affairs and discussed plans to memorialize and preserve the battlefield. Along with the Federal veterans, Confederates such as senators William Bate, Edward Walthall, John Morgan, and Alfred Colquitt, as well as Representative Joseph Wheeler and War Department Confederate agent Marcus Wright, met that day. In order to obtain a charter, the group quickly decided to form a memorial association organizational committee. Boynton and the formation committee met the next day, February 15, and finalized plans for creating the association. The first meeting was to take place at Chattanooga on the anniversary of the battle, September 19, 1889.[24]

This bi-sectional Chickamauga Memorial Association, along with "strong representations of both armies and leading citizens," held its first official meeting on September 19 during the Society of the Army of the Cumberland's annual reunion in Chattanooga. Meeting in a large tent set up for the reunion, the group of some 12,000 veterans heard speeches by such luminaries as Rosecrans and Boynton. The latter told the veterans of the association's plans: to ask Congress for an appropriation to make a park out of the Chickamauga and Chattanooga battlefields and to have the states place monuments there. The next day, September 20, the veterans met at Crawfish Spring for "one of the largest barbeques ever held in the South, tables being set for 12,000 people, and all of them filled." After the meal, the leaders met at "the Baptist Church on the battle field of Chickamauga" and formally organized the Chickamauga Memorial Association. The veterans elected "incorporators" from each state, the number being based on the representation of troops at the battle. They also elected from those a group of twenty-eight higher level "directors." Henry Boynton, the prime mover of the idea, was a member of both groups.[25]

By the time the association charter became effective in December 1889, efforts were already in full swing to secure federal government support for preserving the battlefield. The resources of the federal government, it had been decided, could do more than a struggling association of veterans, such as the one at Gettysburg, to establish such a historic site. Thus, after the success of setting up the association, emphasis soon turned to gaining congressional approval for the Chickamauga venture.

Boynton dove headlong into the world of federal government politics, a place he knew and was known in as the Washington correspondent for the *Cincinnati Commercial Gazette.* The timing was perfect for this "novel conception on a vast scale." The decade of the 1890s was the only real opportunity the nation had to preserve its battlefields. Such a unified movement was not possible before 1890, because of all the lingering animosity from the war and Reconstruction. Congressmen who in the 1870s and 1880s were drawn into vehement sectional debates were suddenly loosed from those differences in the 1890s as the nation backed away from racial issues that had split the sections for decades. They concentrated on sectional reconciliation instead. A more tangible reason large-scale preservation and monumentation was not possible at Chickamauga before the 1890s was the lack of historical sources: the federal government had been compiling official reports and correspondence for years but the Chickamauga volumes of *The War of the Rebellion: A Compilation of the Official Records of the Union and Confederate Armies* did not appear in published form until 1890. Then, too, the time was fast approaching when battlefield preservation, on the scale it was done in the 1890s by the veterans, would be an impossibility. Their impending departure from this life was very much on the veterans' minds. Unknown at the time, a wave of urbanization and industrialization (the second industrial revolution) was also looming on the horizon, and that phenomenon threatened many of the battlefields. By 1890, the window of opportunity for reconciliation and preservation had opened, but it would close in a matter of a few years. Boynton and the other veterans' efforts could not have come at a better time.[26]

In writing the bill to establish America's first federally preserved battlefield as a park, Boynton was on his own; he had no precedent to use for guidance. When later park bills such as those for Shiloh, Gettysburg, and Vicksburg emerged, those writers had Chickamauga's bill (and the others for later parks) to use as guides. Boynton had no such aide. What developed into the legislation that would ultimately create the first park was a creation of his fertile mind. What he developed in 1889 and early 1890 was entirely new, and it served as a guide for many new parks and indeed for today's battlefield preservation efforts. Boynton's initial development of the fundamental principles of the national military park was thus a watershed event with profound future impact.

First and foremost, Boynton had to devise a name befitting the subject. He coined the term "national military park," and the name remains a standard in today's preservation efforts. Today's most revered battlefield parks, such as those at Chickamauga, Shiloh, Gettysburg, and Vicksburg, are still national military parks, as well as several newer battlefields that have since been added to the system. The name was not thrown together haphazardly, though; Boynton intentionally used the word "national" to convey that this was not a Union effort or a Confederate cause. It was a joint effort between the two sides that were now one again. Unlike the work begun at Gettysburg, the park would commemorate both sides.[27]

Boynton made other necessary decisions in the process of writing the bill. What would the park look like? How big would it be? Would it contain the entire fighting area? That was a major consideration. Boynton forcefully argued for the preservation of the entire battlefield of Chickamauga. He envisioned a site of thousands of acres, enough to encompass every fighting locale. He wanted Chickamauga to be preserved in total.[28]

Boynton also came to the conclusion that much of the Chattanooga area should be included in the plan, although demographic factors precluded conservation of that entire battlefield. Chattanooga had grown through the years and by 1890 already sprawled over much of the battlefield. Boynton planned to preserve certain bits and pieces, most notably roadways to serve as "Approaches" to the main part of the park at Chickamauga. He desired to include the roadways "along Missionary Ridge, and thence over Lookout Mountain," proudly writing, "It was to be known as the Chickamauga and Chattanooga National Military Park."[29]

Then there was the question of which federal government entity would govern and build the park. The Department of the Interior was concerned with locales within the United States, but the park was also a battlefield, so the War Department was also a possibility. Who would oversee the park itself? Obviously there would be no stockholders, but would there be a large group of directors like the Chickamauga and Gettysburg associations had?

Boynton had definite ideas about who should run the park. First and foremost, he determined that this effort was a military as well as a commemorative venture, so it should be placed within the War Department. Boynton also began to think along the lines of using the park as a military reservation both for the study of the battle by professional officers as well as a quickly established military base if needed.[30]

Boynton thought that veterans of the battles would be the ideal choices to oversee the supervision of the park once it was established. The question was, how many? Boynton decided on three, also calling for other support positions such as historian and engineer. The use of three directors, whom Boynton called commissioners, was a major decision; all the national military parks established from the 1890s to 1933 would be placed within the War Department and governed by commissioners. Most important, Boynton made sure one of the commissioners was a Confederate representative, thus ensuring at least partial reconciliation. It was good thing Boynton put so much thought into his bill, for what he envisioned remained the face of battlefield preservation for decades to come.[31]

Congressman Charles Grosvenor, Republican from Ohio, took Boynton's bill and ushered it through Congress. It passed the House and Senate by August 1890. Immediately upon passage, Representative H. Clay Evans, a friend of the proposed park and a Union veteran who now represented Chattanooga in the House, took the bill to the White House. President Benjamin Harrison signed the measure into law on August 20, 1890.[32]

Secretary of War Redfield Proctor quickly made appointments to the commission, including Joseph S. Fullerton, Sanford Kellogg, and Alexander P. Stewart. Not surprisingly, Boynton became the park commission's historian, a position he no doubt preferred over a commissioner slot. For the next few years, these ageing veterans put all their effort into building the park. By the end of the 1894 fiscal year, the commission and its historian, Boynton, had the park nearing completion, both in its physical aspects and in the "official" story of the battle. Most of the land had been acquired, many of the states were nearing completion of their monuments, iron tablets marked corps and division unit positions, ten-foot-tall pyramids of cannon balls marked mortuary sites of general officers, and newly opened roadways offered access to visitors. Brigade tablets and the four hundred artillery tubes the commission obtained from the Ordnance Department still needed to be placed, but by and large the park, which Boynton called "a most complete object lesson in war," was almost ready. In all, the commission spent $581,056.05 in its first three years. The grand dedication ceremonies took place on the anniversary of the battle, September 18–20, 1895.[33]

In blazing the way for future preservation efforts in that same decade and beyond, when other parks were established, Boynton and the commission made several major decisions that are still affecting preservationists today. The park actually developed into two separate parks. The Chickamauga and Chattanooga portions were different entities, although sections of the same parent park. Chickamauga was intended to be a massive area of land that would encompass the entire battlefield. As such, much of its appropriated money went toward land acquisition. At Chattanooga, however, only a small percentage of the battlefield was intended to come into government hands. Rather than buying the entire area, which by that time had already become engulfed in the city's urbanization and industrialization and thus was unobtainable, Boynton envisioned buying roadways and establishing small "reservations" at which important events took place. The plan at Chattanooga, as opposed to Chickamauga where the tactical movements were to be traced in vivid detail, was to interpret the events from the main roads and points of high elevation, such as Lookout Mountain and Missionary Ridge, that offered a panoramic view.

The dual paradigm at Chickamauga and Chattanooga National Military Park was duplicated at the other parks established in the 1890s. By 1899, Congress had established parks not only at Chickamauga and Chattanooga, but also at Antietam, Shiloh, Gettysburg, and Vicksburg. With others doubtless to follow, the War Department recommended that Congress establish a "fixed policy" concerning the nature of the parks. Two methods of park development had been established by 1895: the Chickamauga method devised by Henry Boynton, in which the entire battlefield was bought and developed into a park; and the technique used at Chattanooga, but more famously known as the "Antietam Plan," with key parcels incorporating points of interest and historical markers along roads. The preservation community has alternated between these two methods since that first federally preserved battlefield emerged in 1890 and is still trying to achieve a balance between these two competing plans even in the twenty-first century.[34]

By 1897, much of the historical work had been done at Chickamauga and Chattanooga, and Boynton received a deserved promotion, although through tragic circumstances. Commission chairman Joseph S. Fullerton died in a railroad accident in March 1897, and Secretary of War Russell Alger, who probably never considered anyone but Boynton to become the next chairman, appointed him on April 8. In applauding the decision, various newspapers praised Boynton as "a newspaper writer of high standing" and noting he was "perhaps the most active member of the commission for some years, and it was due largely to his efforts that the park was established."[35] Boynton's term as chairman of the commission lasted for several years During that time, he continued to oversee the park, even in the midst of the army's use of it during the Spanish-American War. Boynton even received a brigadier general's commission and was generally pleased with the army's use of the park, although there was a tremendous mess when it left. There were also rumors of the unhealthiness of the park, but this was due not to the park itself, but to the lack of sanitation among the troops.[36]

Perhaps Boynton's most important contribution to Chickamauga was his interpretation of what happened during the battle, which is largely still accepted today. He was, one historian has stated, "more responsible than any other one party" for the story of Chickamauga. In all fairness, we know more about Boynton's role than that of any other establishment participant simply because he left the most records. Boynton could be humble at times, but there is no doubt that he controlled the battlefields' history to make him, his regiment, and his friends look good in the light of history. As a result, he became involved in many historical quarrels through the years, and he won most of those quarrels. One antagonist was certainly right when he remarked, "General Boynton's influence at Washington is such we cannot hope while he lives to secure the desired location of our monument on the field of Chickamauga."[37]

Boynton's creation of a collective memory for Chickamauga and Chattanooga and the backlash against it can be seen in his quarrels with Archibald Gracie Jr., John B. Turchin, and David W. Reed, the commission historian at Shiloh. Much material on these debates still exists in books such as Gracie's *The Truth about Chickamauga* (1911) and contemporary letters. These sources and many others alleged Boynton "deliberately," according to Gracie, dominated the historiography and story of Chickamauga and Chattanooga. Even the tablets and monuments at the battlefields show his hand. One of the main assertions made by Gracie and other veterans was that Boynton moved many of the monuments and troop positions on Snodgrass Hill to place his own unit, the 35th Ohio, on the dominant spot. Although some members of the regiment defended Boynton, one veteran of the 21st Ohio went so far as to say: "There is a greater effort on the part of Gen. Boynton and others to get [their monument on] the top of Snod Grass Hill . . . if Gen. Boynton keeps on he will be on top of the hill." A reading of the tablet text at the park, written by Boynton, similarly betrays his enthusiasm for his own unit. On a tablet for Dibrell's Confederate brigade, which Boynton's command fought against as a part of Van Derveer's brigade, there is more information on Van Derveer's actions than Dibrell's. To be sure, Snodgrass Hill, where Boynton fought and where he placed most of his emphasis, is still the most popular and most focal point of Chickamauga visitation and interpretation today.[38]

Boynton's chief non-Chickamauga influence, not surprisingly, was also in the area of battlefield preservation. By 1900, he was one of the two major preservation advisers to Secretary of War Elihu Root. Brigadier General George B. Davis, soon to be the army's judge advocate general, served as an adviser on policy while Boynton handled more of the procedural issues. Together, these two men made up the most important duo of battlefield preservationists in the veteran generation. They also represented the dichotomy in War Department theory about preservation: Davis favored small parks along the Antietam/Chattanooga Plan, while Boynton favored preserving entire battlefields.[39]

Boynton helped push military park efforts at other places than Chickamauga, aiding the writing of a bill for an Atlanta National Military Park and assisting the newly formed Shiloh commission in its fight against Eliel T. Lee, who had taken options òn the lands needed for the park in order to blackmail the government into making him a commissioner. Boynton was also a frequent correspondent with other commissioners creating other battlefields, men such as George B. Davis at Antietam and John P. Nicholson at Gettysburg. Boynton's most important role, however, and most controversial, as it would turn out, would be with the commissioners at Shiloh and Vicksburg.[40]

Secretary of War Root sent Boynton to Vicksburg to aid that commission early in its work. The Vicksburg commission seemed to be somewhat in awe of the legendary Boynton. The Vicksburg veterans realized that they needed to make friends with powerful men in the preservation community, most notably Boynton, so when the Chickamauga chairman proposed a visit to Vicksburg in 1899, Vicksburg commission chairman Stephen D. Lee recommended to his commission that no expense be spared, even if they had to split some of the costs among themselves.[41]

Secretary Root also sent Chickamauga's "careful and economical" engineer Edward E. Betts to redo the Vicksburg commission engineer's work. Trouble soon began. The Vicksburg commission took exception to what the members viewed as the secretary of war's unwanted tampering in its business. More ominously, the secretary asked Boynton to get involved. Chairman Lee betrayed his gloomy thoughts on the problem, telling Vicksburg commissioner William T. Rigby, "the actions of Gen. B. and Betts with the secretary, destroys our individuality as Park Commissioners." Lee also complained that because of so much Chickamauga influence, Vicksburg National Military Park would not be unique. "So it looks now to me," Lee complained, "we are to follow in almost every detail, in [the] steps of Chickamauga Park, regardless of physical and other conditions surrounding our park."[42] The commission complained of the "Scofield-Betts-Boynton" trio running Vicksburg National Military Park.[43]

The dispute revolved around Betts's topographical maps and his sighting of the park roads, and this soon led to an even larger controversy. The Vicksburg commissioners complained bitterly to the secretary of war about

Betts's survey and his use of maps as sources, but the secretary again sided with his veteran engineer and Betts's ultimate boss, Henry Boynton. Lee railed against the Chickamauga chairman, writing Rigby that "it would not be wise for us to lay down our self respect, and willingly accept Gen. Boynton as our mentor and advisor . . . He is not our friend but Mr. Betts' friend." Lee even got the commission into some trouble by going over the secretary's head and appealing to friends in Congress. Realizing the serious position in which the commission found itself, Lee counseled, "we owe it to ourselves to try and get right with the secretary, but not through Gen. B." Vicksburg Commissioner James G. Everest and others counseled caution: "The Secretary of War depends largely upon General Boynton for every thing connected with Military Parks in general and . . . his word and his judgment goes a long way with the Secretary." The Vicksburg historian John S. Kountz went so far as to write that they did not want to "arouse the animosity of Gen. Boynton and Mr. Scofield, who are his [the secretary of war's] friends, which would be unfortunate."[44]

The following year, in April 1904, Acting Secretary of War Robert Shaw Oliver again sent Boynton to Vicksburg "for the purpose of advising you in regard to certain park matters under your jurisdiction." No doubt, Lee, Rigby, and Everest were in no mood to hear Oliver's glowing letter telling of Boynton's "wide experience in this line of work and particularly in view of his exact information of the conditions which surround your park appropriations." Nevertheless, the event is illustrative of Boynton's stature in and use to the War Department.[45]

Boynton also quarreled with the Shiloh commission in what he termed a "Shiloh Inquiry." As there was no veterans' society for the Army of the Ohio, the Society of the Army of the Cumberland, in which Boynton was heavily involved, became the de facto defender of the Ohio army's legacy. "[It] has devolved upon the Army of the Cumberland the duty of protecting its fame under the name of the Army of the Ohio," Shiloh commissioner Don Carlos Buell advised Boynton, and Boynton took the lead against the Shiloh commission's perceived effort to "influence public opinion in the interest of the Army of the Tennessee."[46]

In 1905, now chairman of the Society of the Army of the Cumberland, Boynton took issue with Shiloh commission historian David W. Reed's official history of the battle, stating that gross inaccuracies existed in regard to the Army of the Ohio. Notable among Reed's errors, Boynton said, were the allegations that the Army of the Tennessee had not been surprised on the morning of April 6. Boynton also railed against Reed's failure to recognize the positive effect of Buell's arrival on the evening of April 6, his failure to state truthfully when the Army of the Ohio engaged the enemy on April 7, and even Reed's small stylistic lapses. Boynton also complained that the Army of the Tennessee veterans had ignored the Army of the Ohio representative, his friend Don Carlos Buell, whom he had actually talked into taking the commissioner position back in 1895. Finally, Boynton also alleged that the Shiloh commission underrepresented the Army of the Ohio in placing tablets. He stated that Reed erected almost 200 tablets for the Army of the Tennessee and more than 160 for the Confederate army. By contrast, the Army of the Ohio had only forty-one.[47]

Finally tiring of the dispute, Assistant Secretary of War Robert Shaw Oliver submitted the entire case to a "specially constituted Committee of the War College for consideration and report." The special committee made no formal report but did recommend that "the changes suggested by the [Shiloh] National Military Park Commission be adopted." Reed had won, a major event in and of itself. Not many people fought the legendary Boynton and prevailed.[48]

Boynton enjoyed excellent health until March 1905, when he suffered stomach and heart ailments. He recovered enough to continue his duties with the park, but soon had a relapse. In May, he traveled to Atlantic City to recuperate. "He stood the trip from Washington to the sea shore fairly well," one newspaper reported, but he could not seem to shake the illness. He never gave up, however, telling a friend, "I think this is the first time I ever was real sick. . . . It is pretty bad, but as I have been such a healthy man all my life, I guess I will survive it." Unfortunately, he did not. He died on June 3, 1905, at the age of seventy.[49]

Newspapers printed glowing comments about him. "He was popular and able as a soldier and officer; able and fearless as a journalist; loyal and true as a citizen; and upright and noble as a man," reported the *Washington Post*. The *New York Times* editorialized that "The death of Gen. Henry Van Ness Boynton recalls a public service at once unique and worthy of fitting commemoration." The Chickamauga commission itself stated that Boynton's death "was a distinct loss to the public service, and particularly to the park, to the development of which he had given unremitting study and constant work." It suspended all work at the park on June 7, the day of his funeral.[50]

Boynton's funeral services were completely in accord with his wishes expressed immediately before his death. Held at the New York Avenue Presbyterian Church and officiated by the Rev. Dr. Wallace Radcliffe, the ceremony mixed a healthy portion of religious observances with honors allowed to a brigadier general. A portion of the 13th United States Cavalry escorted the casket, which was borne to Arlington National Cemetery on a black hearse.

A riderless horse followed. As the casket passed Fort Myer, an eleven-gun salute was fired, that being the salute for a brigadier general. At the grave itself, a brief prayer was said and two songs sung, with a final salute and taps.[51]

Many realized with gratitude the significance of Boynton's lifework. "The temporary fame of ambitious men may be sweet, but the long, honest, thorough life work of Gen. Henry Boynton is an influence that will never perish," one newspaper eulogized. With Boynton's death, the idea surfaced to place a monument to him at Chattanooga or Chickamauga. This monument would not be a regular commemoration of his life specifically, however; it was to be a monument to what he believed: a "Peace Memorial" that would "symbolize permanent peace founded upon mutual love and respect re-established between geographical divisions once politically divided and at war." The monument never came to be, however, perhaps because the originators of the idea realized that there was already such a monument and memorial in existence: the Chickamauga and Chattanooga National Military Park.[52]

The work at Chickamauga and Chattanooga was the first effort of its kind in United States history. Never before had the federal government become involved in preserving a battlefield in its entirety. The private association at Gettysburg had managed to obtain some federal funds to map the battlefield and also to mark Regular Army positions at the site, but the work at Gettysburg had been thoroughly a private and a sectional effort. And, of course, there were limitations to what that association had done. Without the resources of the federal government, the association had bought only a small portion of the battlefield. Likewise, the association, made up exclusively of Northerners, memorialized only Northern states and units, with a few exceptions. It primarily marked only Union positions and did not even purchase the land on which the Confederate lines had rested.[53]

In comparison, what developed at Chickamauga and Chattanooga under Boynton's careful eye was entirely a federal government effort (with state cooperation in placing state monuments). Moreover, what happened at Chickamauga was groundbreaking in nature. As the park evolved, everything about it had to be developed from nothing. The inclusion of the Confederates, which offered a bi-sectional feel, the type of governing body, which became the three-man commission, the manner in which the park was monumented, which developed into the tablet/monument design, and the size of the park were all developed by Boynton and were carried on in future park efforts, some to this day. Even the name "national military park" was designed as the park emerged. Henry V. Boynton was right when he remarked that the work at Chickamauga was "a new thing under the sun."[54]

Henry Van Ness Boynton has been described as "the Father of the Chickamauga National Park Enterprise," but his effect went far beyond Chickamauga. His plan of preserving entire battlefields such as at Chickamauga and Shiloh dominated preservation efforts at first before yielding to Davis's more cost-effective "Antietam Plan" of preserving small areas of battlefields. Boynton was not against such a practice when necessary, as illustrated in his use of it at Chattanooga. But when battlefields were available for purchase, he preferred to save them in their entirety. Nevertheless, although the cheaper way of preserving portions of battlefields prevailed for some nine decades—into the 1990s—preservationists have once again begun thinking in terms of preserving not just a small portion of a battlefield here and there, but *entire* battlefields. The "Antietam Plan" has seemingly been thrown on the trash heap of history. Modern-day preservationists are busy trying to buy up as much land as possible. There is no more ironic illustration of this phenomenon than at the Antietam National Battlefield itself, after which the original "Antietam Plan" was named. In recent years, the National Park Service has bought hundreds of acres of the battlefield that were purposefully left in private hands in the 1890s. Henry Boynton's idea of preserving entire battlefields has won out.[55]

Today, few if any visitors who step onto a preserved Civil War battlefield think of Henry Boynton. And that is regrettable. Whether Boynton was right or wrong in his many quarrels, whether he was accurate in his creation of memory or in his conclusions, the fact remains that he was one of America's greatest preservationists. He literally invented the process by which the Chickamauga and Chattanooga battlefields, as well as those of Shiloh, Antietam, Gettysburg, and Vicksburg, were not only preserved but transformed into national military parks. They, in turn, formed the basis for the parks established since that time. Boynton's hand, as well as his forethought and wisdom, can be seen in the many hallowed battlefields of America If Boynton was brash, hardheaded, and forceful, he was also a visionary and an enabler. He was the "father of the Chickamauga and Chattanooga National Military Park," but perhaps a better title would be "father of the modern military park movement." Without Henry Boynton, the face of our preserved military parks would look much different today.

Notes

1. Henry V. Boynton, *The National Military Park: Chickamauga-Chattanooga; An Historical Guide, with Maps and Illustrations* (Cincinnati: Robert Clarke, 1895), 224.

2. Ibid.

3. Ibid., 224–25.

4. *Society of the Army of the Cumberland: Thirty-third Reunion, Chattanooga, Tennessee, 1905* (Cincinnati: Robert Clarke, 1906), 157–63; "Gen. Boynton Dead," *Washington Post*, June 4, 1905; Donald Ritchie, *Press Gallery: Congress and the Washington Correspondents* (Cambridge: Harvard University Press, 1991), 114.

5. *Society of the Army of the Cumberland*, 157; "Gen. Boynton Dead."

6. Frederick H. Dyer, *A Compendium of the War of the Rebellion*, 3 vols. (Des Moines: Dyer, 1908), 3:1513; *Society of the Army of the Cumberland*, 157; "Gen. Boynton Dead." See Henry Van Ness Boynton's Compiled Service Record, National Archives and Record Administration (hereafter cited as NARA), for more information on his Civil War career.

7. *War of the Rebellion: A Compilation of the Official Records of the Union and Confederate Armies* (Washington, D.C.: Government Printing Office, 1880–91), ser. 1, vol. 23, pt. 2: 575. (hereafter cited as *O.R.*; all citations are from series 1); *Society of the Army of the Cumberland*, 157; Boynton Compiled Service Record, NARA..

8. *O.R.*, vol. 30, pt. 1: 437; "Gen. Boynton Dead," *Washington Post*, June 4, 1905.

9. *O.R.*, vol. 30, pt. 1: 86, 405; vol. 31, pt. 2: 528; *Society of the Army of the Cumberland*, 157; "Gen. Boynton Dead."

10. *O.R.*, vol. 31, pt. 2: 538; Dyer, *Compendium of the War of the Rebellion*, 3:1513; *Society of the Army of the Cumberland*, 157; "Gen. Boynton Dead"; "An Honor Soldiers Prize," *New York Times*, November 10, 1893; Boynton Compiled Service Record, NARA.

11. Boynton to *Cincinnati Gazette*, November 19, 1862, Boynton to *Cincinnati Daily Commercial*, April 15, 1862, and "Indian Pension Fraud" Scrapbook, all in Henry Van Ness Boynton Papers, Massachusetts Historical Society (hereafter cited as MHS); *Society of the Army of the Cumberland*, 157; "Gen. Boynton Dead"; "Death of Gen. Boynton," undated obituary in unidentified newspaper clipping, box 4, folder 7, Ezra A. Carman Papers, New York Public Library (hereafter cited as NYPL); Boynton Compiled Service Record, NARA. Boynton resigned from the army on August 24, 1864.

12. "Dean of the Press Gallery," undated newspaper clipping in Folder: "Reminiscences of Chickamauga," Boynton Papers, MHS; "Gen. Boynton Dead"; Ritchie, *Press Gallery*, 109–10, 113–14, 121, 127, 130; "Gen. Boynton Not Worried," Miscellaneous Folder, Boynton Papers, Library of Congress, hereafter cited as LOC. Boynton first worked for the *Cincinnati Gazette* and then the *Cincinnati Commercial Gazette* when the *Gazette* combined with the *Cincinnati Commercial* in 1883.

13. "Gen. Boynton Dead"; Ritchie, *Press Gallery*, 114.

14. Boynton to S. S. Dunham, December 2, 1898 and "Western Press" Speech, June 4, 1868, both in Boynton Papers, MHS; Boynton to editor of *Washington Times*, undated, 1903 Folder, Boynton Papers, LOC.

15. Charles Richard Williams, ed., *The Diary and Letters of Rutherford B. Hayes, Nineteenth President of the United States*, 5 vols. (Columbus: Ohio State Archeological and Historical Society, 1922), 3: 445, 451, 594; Ritchie, *Press Gallery*, 113–14, 116.

16. Henry V. Boynton, "Washington Safe Burglary," April 1877, Boynton Papers, MHS; Henry V. Boynton, "The Washington 'Safe Burglary' Conspiracy," *American Law Review* 11, no. 3 (April 1877): 401–46; Henry V. Boynton, "The Whiskey Ring," *North American Review* 123 (October 1876): 280–327; "Indian Pension Fraud" Scrapbook, Boynton Papers, MHS; William S. McFeely, *Grant: A Biography* (New York: W. W. Norton, 1982), 406–15; Ritchie, *Press Gallery*, 105–6, 118–20, 140–41.

17. "Delano Affair" Scrapbook, "Boynton v. Moore" Scrapbook, and "Moore Conspiracy, 1877–1878," in Boynton Papers, MHS; Mcfeely, *Grant*, 430–32.

18. Harvey S. Ford, ed. "The Diary of John Beatty, January–June 1884, Part I," *Ohio Historical Quarterly* 58 (April 1949): 150–51; *Charges against H. V. Boynton: Hearings before the United States House Select Committee to Investigate Charges against Henry V. Boynton* (Washington: Government Printing Office, 1884); Ritchie, *Press Gallery*, 122–27.

19. Adam Badeau, *Military History of Ulysses S. Grant, from April 1861 to April 1865*, 3 vols. (New York: D. Appleton, 1868–81); Folder: "News Clippings," undated newspaper clippings in Boynton Papers, MHS; "Book Full of Errors," *Washington Post*, March 18, 1901; "Condemns Text Books," *Washington Post*, February 21, 1901; List of Badeau Errors, box 4, folder 5, Ezra A. Carman Papers, NYPL.

20. William T. Sherman, *Memoirs of General W. T. Sherman: Written By Himself*, 2 vols. (New York: D. Appleton, 1875); "Sherman vs. Boynton" Scrapbook, and Comte de Paris to Boynton, April 2, 1877, Boynton Papers, MHS; D. C. Buell to Boynton, April 18, 1881, and Whitelaw Reid to Boynton, April 21, 1881, both in box 4, folder 1, Carman Papers, NYPL; Henry Van Ness Boynton, *Sherman's Historical Raid: The Memoirs in Light of the Record; A Review Based upon Compilations from the Records of the War Office* (Cincinnati: Wilstach, Baldwin, 1875); "The Sherman-Boynton Case," *New York Times*, February 2, 1880; *Was General Thomas Slow at Nashville? With a Description of the Greatest Cavalry Movement of the War and General James H. Wilson's Cavalry Operations in Tennessee, Alabama, and Georgia* (New York: F. P. Harper, 1896); John F. Marszalek, *Sherman: A Soldier's Passion for Order* (New York: Free Press, 1993), 464–66.

21. "General Sherman on Boynton" and "Brevet Liar Boynton," undated newspaper clippings, and "Boynton vs. Sherman" Scrapbook, in Boynton Papers, MHS; "The Sherman-Boynton Case," *New York Times*, February 2, 1880; Marszalek, *Sherman*, 464–66; Williams, *Diary and Letters of Hayes*, 3:594.

22. *Cincinnati Commercial Gazette*, August 17, 1888; Henry V. Boynton, *Chattanooga and Chickamauga: Reprint of Gen. H. V. Boynton's Letters to the Cincinnati Commercial Gazette, August, 1888* (Washington, D.C.: Gray & Clarkson, 1888).

23. Boynton, *National Military Park*, 220.

24. "The Chickamauga Battle Field," *Washington Post*, February 15, 1889; Henry Van Ness Boynton, *Dedication of the Chickamauga and Chattanooga National Military Park* (Washington, D.C.: Government Printing Office, 1896), 318; H. V. Boynton, "The Chickamauga Memorial Association," *Southern Historical Society Papers*, 38 vols. (Richmond: Southern Historical Society, 1888), 16:348–49. Wright was the Confederate representative on the commission collecting war records for publication in the *O.R.*.

25. Boynton, *Dedication of Chickamauga and Chattanooga*, 319–21; John C. Paige and Jerome A. Greene, *Administrative History of Chickamauga and Chattanooga National Military Park* (Denver: National Park Service, 1983), 14–15, 22; Boynton, *National Military Park*, 243, 247, 250; *Chickamauga Memorial Association Proceedings* (Chattanooga Army of the Cumberland Reunion Entertainment Committee, n.d.), 27. See E. M. Holland to Sanford C. Kellogg, March 18, 1889, letters of acceptance and nonacceptance from incorporators, box 9, folder 5, Carman Papers, NYPL. For a list of the board of directors see Boynton, *Dedication of Chickamauga and Chattanooga*, 321.

26. "Our National Military Park," unidentified newspaper clipping in "Reminiscences of Chickamauga," Boynton Papers, MHS; *O.R.*, vol. 30, pts.1–4. For an overview of the reconciliation of the time, see David Blight, *Race and Reunion: The Civil War in American Memory* (Cambridge: Harvard University Press, 2001).

27. Boynton, *National Military Park*, 251.

28. Ibid.

29. Ibid.

30. *Congressional Record*, 51st Cong., 1st sess., 21, no. 6: 5393.

31. Boynton, *National Military Park*, 251.

32. *Congressional Record*, 51st Cong., 1st sess., 21, no. 8: 7335; ibid., no. 9: 8473, 8693, 8695, 8903; "The Chickamauga Bill Signed," *Washington Post*, August 20, 1890; Boynton, *Dedication of Chickamauga and Chattanooga*, 329; Boynton, *National Military Park*, 260; James W. Livingood, "Chickamauga and Chattanooga National Military Park," *Tennessee Historical Quarterly* 23, no. 1 (Mar. 1964): 15.

33. Boynton, *National Military Park*, 12, 273; *Annual Report of the Secretary of War—1894*, 28; Boynton, *Dedication of Chickamauga and Chattanooga*, 16; "Chickamauga Military Park," *New York Times*, December 1, 1894.

34. *Annual Report of the Secretary of War—1895*, 31–32.

35. Henry C. Conklin to Henry V. Boynton, March 26, 1897, Box 4, Folder 3, Ezra A. Carman Papers, NYPL; "To Succeed Gen. Fullerton," New York Times, March 29, 1897; "Commission Reorganized," Washington Post, April 9, 1897; "Boynton Succeeds Fullerton," New York Times, April 9, 1897.

36. *Annual Report of the Secretary of War—1899*, 321.

37. Archibald Gracie, *The Truth about Chickamauga* (Dayton: Morningside, 1997), 32, 409.

38. Ibid., 226; J. H. Bolton to A. W. McMahan, July 10, 1889, box 13, folder 3, Arnold McMahan Papers, Bowling Green State University (hereafter cited as BGSU; Wilson Vance to Arnold McMahan, August 13, 1889, box 13, folder 18, McMahan Papers, BGSU; James A. Kaser, "The Army of the Cumberland and the Battle of Chickamauga: An Exercise in Perspectivist Historical Research" (PhD diss., Bowling Green State University, 1991), and *At the Bivouac of Memory: History, Politics, and the Battle of Chickamauga* (New York: Peter Lang, 1996); Chickamauga Battlefield Tablet no. 1150.

39. Timothy B. Smith, *The Golden Age of Battlefield Preservation: The Decade of the 1890s and the Establishment of America's First Five Military Parks* (Knoxville: University of Tennessee Press, 2008), 6, 44.

40. "Roasting E. T. Lee," unidentified newspaper clipping in "Reminiscences of Chickamauga," and "National Park Matters to Come Up in Both Branches of Congress," unidentified newspaper clipping,, Boynton Papers, MHS; Henry V. Boynton to John P. Nicholson, January 31, 1905, Henry Van Ness Boynton Letter, United States Military Academy; George B. Davis to Boynton, Nov. 17, 1894, RG 92 (Records of the Office of the Quartermaster General), E 707, box 1, NARA.

41. Stephen D. Lee to William T. Rigby, Apr. 27, 1899, Frank G. Smith to William T. Rigby, Aug. 1, 1899, and Cornelius Cadle to William T. Rigby, Aug. 23, 1899, RG 79, Letters Received, Vicksburg National Military Park Commission, Box 1, NARA—Southeast.

42. Boynton to William T. Rigby, May 9, 1901, RG 79, Letters Received—Vicksburg National Military Park Commission, box 2, folder 1, NARA—Southeast; S. D. Lee

to William T. Rigby, July 29, 1901, July 31, 1901, and Oct. 31, 1901, William T. Rigby Series, box 1, folder 33, Vicksburg National Military Park (hereafter cited as VNMP).

43. *Annual Report of the Secretary of War—1901*, 391; *Annual Report of the Secretary of War—1905*, 250; James G. Everest to William T. Rigby, Feb. 28, 1902, RG 79, box 3, NARA—Southeast. John C. Scofield was an assistant secretary of war.

44. Elihu Root to William T. Rigby, Mar. 22, 1902, Administrative Series, box 1, folder 1, VNMP; S. D. Lee to William T. Rigby, Mar. 11, 1902, William T. Rigby Series, box 2, folder 34, VNMP; Herman Hattaway, *General Stephen D. Lee* (Jackson: University Press of Mississippi, 1976), 227, 229–30; James G. Everest to William T. Rigby, Mar. 7, 1902, RG 79, box 3, NARA–Southeast; Andrew Hickenlooper to D. B. Henderson, May 10, 1902, Administrative Series, box 1, folder 1, VNMP; John S. Kountz to William T. Rigby, Mar. 13, 1902, William T. Rigby Series, box 2, folder 34, VNMP; D. B. Henderson to Elihu Root, May 20, 1902, and John P. Nicholson to Secretary of War, May 15, 1902, RG 92, E 715, box 1, NARA.

45. W. T. Bell to Secretary of War, May 14, 1911, Administrative Series, box 1, folder 10, VNMP; Robert Shaw Oliver to William T. Rigby, Jan. 8, 1904, ibid., folder 3; John C. Scofield to William T. Rigby, June 4, 1903, ibid., folder 2; Robert Shaw Oliver to William T. Rigby, Apr. 30, 1904, ibid., folder 3; Hattaway, *General Stephen D. Lee*, 226.

46. Henry V. Boynton to James Barrett, January 16, 1905, box 3, folder 3, ; Don Carlos Buell to Boynton, October 29, 1898, box 4, folder 3; and Buell to Boynton, January 9, 1895, box 4, folder 2, Carman Papers, NYPL.

47. D. W. Reed to Cornelius Cadle, April 1, 1905, series 1, box 12, folder 94, Shiloh National Military Park (hereafter cited as SNMP); H. V. Boynton to Assistant Secretary of War, April 27, 1905, ibid,, folder 95; Whitelaw Reid to Henry V. Boynton, March 10, 1905, box 4, folder 4, Carman Papers, NYPL; D. W. Reed to Cornelius Cadle, February 20, 1905, series 1, box 11, folder 91, SNMP; D. C. Buell to Henry V. Boynton, March 11, 1895, box 4, folder 2, Carman Papers, NYPL.

48. Robert Shaw Oliver to Cornelius Cadle, May 5, 1905, series 1, box 12, folder 95, SNMP; W. W. Wotherspoone Memo, September 2, 1909, series 1, box 39, folder 630, SNMP.

49. "Gen. H. V. Boynton Dies in Atlantic City," *New York Times*, June 4, 1905; "Gen. Boynton Dead," *Washington Post*, June 4, 1905.

50. E. E. Betts to W. M. Stillwell, June 6, 1905, Boynton File, Chickamauga and Chattanooga National Military Park (hereafter cited as CHCH); "Gen. H. V. Boynton," *Washington Post*, June 7, 1905; "A Boynton Peace Memorial," *New York Times*, June 6, 1905; *Annual Report of the Secretary of War—1905*, 132.

51. "His Funeral Plans," *Washington Post*, June 6, 1905; "Gen. Boynton at Rest," *Washington Post*, June 8, 1905.

52. "Gen. Henry V. Boynton," *Washington Post*, June 4, 1905; "A Boynton Peace Memorial," *New York Times*, June 6, 1905.

53. Smith, *Golden Age*, 27, 36.

54. "Chickamauga-Chattanooga National Military Park," *Chattanooga Times*, July 1, 1903.

55. "The Father of the Chickamauga National Park Enterprise," unidentified newspaper clipping in Boynton Papers, MHS.

CONTRIBUTORS

INDEX

CONTRIBUTORS

John R. Lundberg received his PhD from Texas Christian University in 2007. He is the author of *The Finishing Stroke: Texans in the 1864 Tennessee Campaign* and is currently working on a history of Granbury's Texas Brigade and a study of Unionism during the secession crisis in Texas.

Alexander Mendoza received his PhD from Texas Tech University in 2001 and is currently an assistant professor of history at the University of Texas at Tyler. He is the author of *Confederate Struggle for Command: General James Longstreet and the First Corps in the West* (2008).

David Powell attended the Virginia Military Institute, graduating in 1983 with a BA in history. His work has appeared in the *Gettysburg Magazine* and in *North and South* magazine. He has focused his research on the Battle of Chickamauga, has led numerous tours to the battlefield, and has written an atlas of the battle, titled *The Maps of Chickamauga* (2009).

Ethan S. Rafuse received his PhD at the University of Missouri–Kansas City and is an associate professor of military history at the U.S. Army Command and General Staff College at Fort Leavenworth. He has published over two hundred articles, essays, and reviews, and is the author, editor, or coeditor of seven books, including *McClellan's War: The Failure of Moderation in the Struggle for the Union* (2005) and *Robert E. Lee and the Fall of the Confederacy, 1863–1865* (2008).

William G. Robertson received his PhD from the University of Virginia in 1975. He is the author of *Back Door to Richmond: The Bermuda Campaign, April–June 1864* and *The Petersburg Campaign: The Battle of Old Men and Young Boys, June 9, 1864*, as well as numerous articles and book chapters on American Civil War subjects. He is currently the director of the Combat Studies Institute and a Command Historian, U.S. Army Combined Arms Center, Fort Leavenworth, Kansas.

Timothy B. Smith received his PhD from Mississippi State University in 2001. He is a veteran of the National Park Service at the Shiloh National Military Park and now teaches history at the University of Tennessee at Martin. Among his books are *This Great Battlefield of Shiloh: History, Memory, and the Establishment of a Civil War National Military Park* (2004), *The Untold Story of Shiloh: The Battle and the Battlefield* (2006), and *The Golden Age of Battlefield Preservation: The Establishment of*

America's First Five Civil War Military Parks (2008). He is currently working on a history of Chickamauga and Chattanooga National Military Park and a study of the Civil War home front in Mississippi.

Lee White works as a historian and a park ranger at the Chickamauga and Chattanooga National Military Park. He graduated from the University of Tennessee at Chattanooga with a BA in history in 1996. He is currently researching the actions of the Army of Tennessee between the fall of Atlanta and the beginning of the 1864 Tennessee Campaign. He is the editor of *Great Things Are Expected of Us: The Letters of Colonel C. Irvine Walker* (2009).

Steven E. Woodworth received his PhD from Rice University in 1987 and is a professor of history at Texas Christian University. He is the author, coauthor, or editor of twenty-six books; a two-time winner of the Fletcher Pratt Award of the New York Civil War Round Table (for *Jefferson Davis and His Generals* [1990] and *Davis and Lee at War* [1995]); a two-time finalist for the Peter Seaborg Award of the George Tyler Moore Center for the Study of the Civil War (for *While God Is Marching On* [2001] and *Nothing but Victory* [2005]); and a winner of the Grady McWhiney Award of the Dallas Civil War Round Table for lifetime contribution to the study of Civil War history.

INDEX

Adams, Samuel, 107
Alabama Troops: First Infantry Regiment, 85; Fourth Infantry Regiment, 96; Ninth Infantry Battalion, 86; Sixteenth Infantry Regiment, 106, 107; Eighteenth Infantry Regiment, 85, 90, 93, 98, 106; Thirty-third Infantry Regiment, 106, 107; Thirty-sixth Infantry Regiment, 85; Thirty-eighth Infantry Regiment, 85, 92–93; Thirty-ninth Infantry Regiment, 85; Forty-fourth Infantry Regiment, 96, 97; Forty-fifth Infantry Regiment, 107; Fifty-eighth Infantry Regiment, 86, 96; Eufaula Light Artillery Battery, 86, 90–91; Semple's Artillery Battery, 104, 107
Alexander's Bridge, 21, 25, 88–89, 121
Alexander's Bridge Road, 125
Alexander's Mill, 25
Alpine, Georgia, 13–17, 71
American Law Review, 169
Anderson, Patton, 61, 64, 124
Anderson, Robert, 7
Antietam, Battle of, 69
Antietam National Military Park, 177, 179, 183
Appalachian Mountains, 1, 201
Arkansas, 57–59, 66
Arkansas Post, Battle of, 104
Arkansas Troops: Calvert's Artillery Battery, 104, 106–7; First Artillery Battery, 85; First Infantry Regiment, 85; Fifth Infantry Regiment, 155; Seventh Infantry Regiment, 57
Army of the Cumberland, 1, 5–6, 8–10, 12, 20, 23–24, 30, 34–35, 38, 40–42, 50–51, 60, 70, 84, 87, 102–4, 112–13, 120–21, 124, 132–33, 140, 167–68, 171–73, 180
Army of the Mississippi (Confederate), 57
Army of Tennessee (Confederate), 1, 2, 3, 11, 50, 52, 60, 65–66, 68–72, 75–81, 84, 90, 98, 99, 103–4, 111, 117–20, 133–34

Army of the Tennessee (Union), 2, 170, 180–81
Atlanta, Georgia, 14, 52, 77, 122, 168, 171, 179

Babcock, Orville E., 169
Bailey's Crossroads, 142
Baird, Absalom, 61–62, 64–65, 105–6, 108, 141, 147, 149, 151, 173
Baldwin, Philemon, 106, 108
Barbour County, Alabama, 85
Barker, J. D., 149–50
Barnes, Sidney, 28
Bate, William Brimage, 85–87, 89–90, 95–99, 125–26, 173
Baton Rouge, Louisiana, 85
Battle Creek, 13, 51
Beatty, John, 143, 145–46, 148–58
Beauregard, Pierre G. T., 57
Beech Grove, Tennessee, 87
Benning, Henry, 120, 128, 131
Betts, Edward E., 179–80
Blue Bird Gap, 20
Blunt, James G., 58–59
Bogue, R. G., 140, 142
Boynton, Henry Van Ness, 4, 165–83
Bragg, Braxton, 1–3, 11, 13, 15–17, 20–27, 29–30, 32, 50–55, 57, 59–66, 68–81, 84–85, 87–97, 99, 102–4, 111–13, 118–23, 126, 128–30, 132–34, 141
Brannan, John M., 51, 127, 154–60
Breckinridge, John C., 69–70, 113, 121, 143, 152–53
Bridgeport, Alabama, 11–13, 51, 71
Bridges, Hal, 75
Bridges, Lyman, 143, 153, 156–57, 160
Broomtown Valley, 14
Brotherton, Thomas, 122
Brotherton Cabin, 122, 127, 129, 131
Brotherton Farm, 29, 31–32, 36, 103–4, 120, 140, 145, 152
Brotherton Field. *See* Brotherton Farm
Brotherton Ridge, 94

Johnston, Joseph E., 69–70, 78, 87, 99, 118
Jones, Edgar W., 93
Joyner, W. H., 95

Kellogg, Sanford, 173, 176
Kelly Farm, 24, 91, 99, 105, 109, 112, 124, 129–30, 140, 147–48, 151–55, 157
Kelly Field. *See* Kelly Farm
Kelly, John H., 104
Kentucky Central Railroad, 166
Kentucky Military Institute, 166
Kentucky Troops (Confederate): Cobb's Artillery Battery, 143
Kentucky Troops (Union): Fifth Infantry Regiment, 106–8; Fifteenth Infantry Regiment, 148, 153, 157
Kershaw, Joseph B., 121, 123, 125–32, 134, 154
Killer Angels, The (Shaara), 116
Knoxville, Tennessee, 11, 50, 55, 70, 119, 133
Kountz, John S., 180

La Fayette, Georgia, 14–17, 52, 54–55, 60–61, 63–65, 71, 75, 87, 120, 141
La Fayette Road, 20, 24, 27–29, 52, 54, 94–96, 103–6, 112, 124, 126–29, 151, 157
Laiboldt, Bernard, 37, 39
Latrobe, Osmun, 120
Law, Evander, 92, 120–21, 123, 125, 126
Lawrenceville, New Jersey, 56
Lawrenceville Classical Institute, 55–56
Lee, Eliel T., 179
Lee, Pollock B., 91, 126
Lee, Robert E., 2, 60, 66, 69, 87, 116–19
Lee, Stephen, D., 179–80
Lee and Gordon's Mill, 15, 17–22, 24, 26–29, 52, 54–55, 59, 61, 63, 72–73, 75, 87–88, 91, 121, 142–43
Lee-Gordon Mansion. *See* Gordon-Lee Mansion
Liddell, St. John, 104–6, 113
Lillard, John M., 95, 98
Lilly, Eli, 89
Lincoln, Abraham, 6, 166
Longstreet, James, 70, 75, 77–78, 80–81, 87, 111–13, 116–35
Lookout Mountain, 13, 17–19, 51–54, 62, 65, 71, 73–74, 141, 175, 177

Lookout Valley, 12–13, 18, 71
Louisville, Kentucky, 7, 41
Lowe, Gideon, 95
Lowrie, James A., 142, 146, 152
Lytle, William, 37

Manassas. *See* Bull Run
Manning, Peyton T., 120, 129
Martin, C. C., 110
Martin, James, 144
McCook, Alexander, 3, 5–20, 22–27, 29–34, 36–42, 53, 71, 146–49, 152, 156
McLemore's Cove, 3, 15, 17–20, 50, 53, 55, 60–66, 71–75, 80, 141
McNair, Evander, 90, 124, 127
Mendenhall, John, 35–36, 158
Mexican War, 9, 56, 68–69, 78, 117, 140
Michigan Troops: Battery D, First Artillery Regiment, 157; Fourth Artillery Battery, 154; Ninth Infantry Regiment, 36; Eleventh Infantry Regiment, 144–145, 157
Middle Tennessee, 6, 70, 85, 87, 133
Military Order of the Loyal Legion, 168
Minty, Robert, 21–22
Missionary Ridge, 18, 31, 36, 54, 71, 77, 153, 167, 175, 177
Mississippi, State of, 1, 57, 68, 69, 87
Mississippi River, 1, 2, 201
Mississippi Troops: Second Infantry Regiment, 56; Fifteenth Infantry Regiment, 106; Forty-fifth and Thirty-second Infantry Regiment, 106; Fifteenth Sharpshooter Battalion, 104
Mississippi Valley in the Civil War, The (Fiske), 171
Mobile, Alabama, 85
Moody, William H. H., 147, 149–50, 158
Moore, W. B., 170
Morgan's Farm, 55, 59, 73
Morgan's House. *See* Morgan's Farm
Murfreesboro, Battle of. *See* Stones River, Battle of

Nashville, Battle of, 171
Nashville, Tennessee, 6, 14, 141, 159, 166
Nashville and Tennessee Railroad, 71

Wartrace, Tennessee, 87
Was General Thomas Slow at Nashville?
   (Boynton), 171
Washington, D.C., 7, 11, 14, 30, 40, 68, 159,
   168–70, 173–74, 178, 181
Welsh, William R., 93
Wert, Jeffrey, 118, 133–34
West Point. *See* U.S. Military Academy
Western University of Pennsylvania, 140
Wheeler, Joseph, 121, 132, 173
Widow Glenn. *See* Glenn, Eliza
Wigfall, Louis, 117–18
Wilder, John, 15–16, 21–22, 24, 28–29, 31,
   33, 37, 39, 87, 89

Wilkes, Frank, 110
Willard, J. P., 148–50
Willich, August, 106
Winchester, Tennessee, 11, 50
Winfrey Farm, 25, 106–9, 146
Winfrey Field. *See* Winfrey Farm
Winston's Gap, 12–14, 17–18, 51
Withers, Jones M., 70
Wood, S. A. M., 103, 106, 126
Wood, Thomas, 15–24, 26–28, 33–35,
   38–39, 127, 148–50, 152, 154–55, 157,
   159–60
Woodward College, 166
Woodworth, Steven E., 29, 70

199

CIVIL WAR CAMPAIGNS IN THE HEARTLAND

The area west of the Appalachian Mountains, known in Civil War parlance as "the West," has always stood in the shadow of the more famous events on the other side of the mountains, the eastern theater, where even today hundreds of thousands visit the storied Virginia battlefields. Nevertheless, a growing number of Civil War historians believe that the outcome of the war was actually decided in the region east of the Mississippi River and west of the watershed between the Atlantic and the Gulf of Mexico.

Modern historians began to rediscover the decisive western theater in the 1960s through the work of the late Thomas Lawrence Connelly, particularly his 1969 book *Army of the Heartland*, in which he analyzed the early years of the Confederacy's largest army in the West. Many able scholars have subsequently contributed to a growing historiography of the war in the West. Despite recent attention to the western theater, less is understood about the truly decisive campaigns of the war than is the case with the dramatic but ultimately indecisive clashes on the east coast.

Several years ago, three of my graduate students pointed out that the western theater possessed no series of detailed multiauthor campaign studies comparable to the excellent and highly acclaimed series Gary W. Gallagher has edited on the campaigns of the eastern theater. Charles D. Grear, Jason M. Frawley, and David Slay joined together in suggesting that I ought to take the lead in filling the gap. The result is this series, its title a nod of appreciation to Professor Connelly. The series' goals are to shed more light on the western campaigns and to spark new scholarship on the western theater.